EFFECTIVE

SELF-DEVELOPMENT

Effective Management
Series Editor: Alan H. Anderson

Effective Personnel Management
Alan H. Anderson

Effective Business Policy
Alan H. Anderson and Dennis Barker

Effective General Management
Alan H. Anderson

Effective Organizational Behaviour
Alan H. Anderson and Anna Kyprianou

Effective Labour Relations
Alan H. Anderson

Effective Marketing
Alan H. Anderson and Thelma Dobson

Effective International Marketing
Alan H. Anderson, Thelma Dobson and James Patterson

Effective Marketing Communications
Alan H. Anderson and David Kleiner

Effective Entrepreneurship
Alan H. Anderson and Peter Woodcock

Effective Enterprise and Change Management
Alan H. Anderson and Dennis Barker

Effective Accounting Management
Alan H. Anderson and Eileen Nix

Effective Financial Management
Alan H. Anderson and Richard Ciechan

Effective Market Research
Alan H. Anderson and Bal Chansarkar

Effective Information Management
Alan H. Anderson and Margaret Thompson

Effective Self-development
Alan H. Anderson, Dennis Barker and Peter Critten

EFFECTIVE SELF-DEVELOPMENT

a skills and activity-based approach

ALAN H. ANDERSON
DENNIS BARKER
and
PETER CRITTEN

This book is dedicated to our respective partners. Alan Anderson would like to dedicate it also to Alexander Sharp.

First published 1996

Blackwell Publishers Ltd
108 Cowley Road
Oxford OX4 1JF
UK

Blackwell Publishers Inc.
238 Main Street
Cambridge, Massachusetts 02142
USA

British Library Cataloguing in Publication Data
A CIP catalogue record for this book is available from the British Library.

Library of Congress Cataloging-in-Publication Data
Anderson, Alan H., 1950–
Effective Self-development (Effective management)
Includes bibliographical references and index.
ISBN 0-631-20015-0 (pbk.)

Designed and typeset in Plantin
by Archetype, Stow-on-the-Wold
Printed in Great Britain by TJ Press Ltd., Padstow, Cornwall.

This book is printed on acid-free paper

Contents

Figures

Boxes

Activities

Introduction to the Series

> " He that has done nothing has known nothing. "
>
> *Carlyle*

The Concept

In this series 'effective' means getting results. By taking an action approach to management, or the stewardship of an organization, the whole series allows people to create and develop their skills of effectiveness. This interrelated series gives the underpinning knowledge base and the application of functional and generic skills of the effective manager who gets results.

Key qualities of the effective manager include:

- **functional expertise** in the various disciplines of management;
- an understanding of the **organizational context**;
- an appreciation of the **external environment**; and
- **self-awareness** and the power of **self-development**.

These qualities must fuse in a climate of **enterprise**.

Management is results-oriented so action is at a premium. The basis of this activity is **skills** underpinned by our qualities. In turn these skills can be based on a discipline or a function, and be universal or generic.

The Approach of the Series

These key qualities of effective management are the core of the current sixteen books of the series. The areas covered by the series at present are:

People Management	*Effective Personnel Management*
	Effective Labour Relations
	Effective Organizational Behaviour
	Effective Self-development
Finance	*Effective Financial Management*
	Effective Accounting Management
	Effective Information Management

Marketing and sales	*Effective Marketing*
	Effective International Marketing
	Effective Marketing Communications
	Effective Market Research
Enterprise Management	*Effective General Management*
	Effective Business Policy
	Effective Enterprise and Change Management
	Effective Entrepreneurship

The key attributes of the effective manager are all dealt with in the series, and we will pinpoint where they are emphasized:

- *Functional expertise* The four main disciplines of management – finance, marketing, enterprise/operations and personnel management – make up sixteen books. These meet the needs of specialist disciplines and allow a wider appreciation of other functions.

- *Organizational context* All the 'people' books – the specialist one on *Effective Organizational Behaviour*, and also *Effective Personnel Management* and *Effective Labour Relations* – cover this area. The resourcing/control issues are met in the 'finance' texts, *Effective Financial Management*, *Effective Information Management* and *Effective Accounting Management*. Every case activity is given some organizational context.

- *External environment* One book, *Effective Business Policy*, is dedicated to this subject. Environmental contexts apply in every book of the series, especially in *Effective Entrepreneuship*, *Effective General Management*, and in all of the 'marketing' texts – *Effective Marketing*, *Effective International Marketing*, *Effective Marketing Communications* and *Effective Market Research*.

- *Self-awareness/self-development* To a great extent management development is manager development, so we have one generic skill (see later) devoted to this topic running through each book. The subject is examined in detail in *Effective General Management*, and *Effective Self-Development* is devoted to the topic.

- *Enterprise* The *Effective Entrepreneurship* text is allied to *Effective Enterprise and Change Management* to give insights into this whole area through all the developing phases of the firm. The marketing and policy books also revolve around this theme.

Skills

The functional skills are inherent within the discipline-based texts. In addition, running through the series are the following generic skills:

- self-development
- teamwork
- communications
- numeracy/IT
- decisions.

These generic skills are universal managerial skills which occur to some degree in every manager's job.

Format/Structure of Each Book

Each book is subdivided into six units. These are self-contained, in order to facilitate learning, but interrelated, in order to give an effective holistic view. Each book also has an introduction with an outline of the book's particular theme.

Each unit has *learning objectives* with an overview/summary of the unit.

Boxes appear in every unit of every book. They allow a different perspective from the main narrative and analysis. Research points, examples, controversy and theory are all expanded upon in these boxes. They are numbered by unit in each book, e.g. 'Box PM1.1' for the first box in Unit One of *Effective Personnel Management*.

Activities, numbered in the same way, permeate the series. These action-oriented forms of learning cover cases, questionnaires, survey results, financial data, market research information, etc. The skills which can be assessed in each one are noted in the code at the top right of the activity by having the square next to them ticked. That is, if we are assuming numeracy then the square beside Numeracy is ticked (✓), and so on. The weighting given to these skills will depend on the activity, the tutors'/learners' needs, and the overall weighting of the skills as noted in the section below on 'The Series: Learning, Activities, Skills and Compatibility', with problem solving dominating in most cases.

Common cases run through the series. Functional approaches are added to these core cases to show the same organization from different perspectives. This simulates the complexity of reality.

Instructor's manual

For each book in the series, there is an *instructor's manual*. This is not quite the 'answers' to the activities, but it does contain some indicative ideas for them (coded accordingly), which will help to stimulate discussion and thought.

The Audience

The series is for all those who wish to be effective managers. As such, it is a series for management development on an international scale, and embraces both management education and management training. In management education, the emphasis still tends to be on cognitive or knowledge inputs; in management training, it still tends to be on skills and techniques. We need both theory and practice, with the facility to try out these functions and skills through a range of scenarios in a 'safe' learning environment. This series is unique in encompassing these perspectives and bridging the gulf between the academic and vocational sides of business management.

Academically the series is pitched at the DMS/DBA types of qualification, which lead on to an MA/MBA after the second year. Undergraduates following business degrees or management studies will benefit from the series in their final years. Distance learners will also find the series useful, as will those studying managerial subjects for professional examinations. The competency approach and the movement towards Accredited Prior Learning and National Vocational Qualifications are underpinned by the knowledge inputs, while the activities will provide useful simulations for these approaches to management learning.

This developmental series gives an opportunity for self-improvement. Individuals may wish to enhance their managerial potential by developing themselves without institutional backing by working through the whole series. It can also be used to underpin corporate training programmes, and acts as a useful design vehicle for specialist inputs from organizations. We are happy to pursue these various options with institutions or corporations.

The approach throughout the series combines skills, knowledge and application to create and develop the effective manager. Any comments or thoughts from participants in this interactive process will be welcomed.

Alan H. Anderson
Melbourn, Cambridge

The Series: Learning, Activities, Skills and Compatibility

The emphasis on skills and activities as vehicles of learning makes this series unique. Behavioural change, or learning, is developed through a two-pronged approach.

First, there is the **knowledge-based (cognitive)** approach to learning. This is found in the main text and in the boxes. These cognitive inputs form the traditional method of learning based on the principle of receiving and understanding information. In this series, there are four main knowledge inputs covering the four main managerial funtions: marketing/sales, operations/enterprise, people, and accounting/finance. In addition, these disciplines are augmented by a strategic overview covering policy making and general management. An example of this first approach may be illustrative. In the case of marketing, the learner is confronted with a model of the internal and external environments. Thereafter the learner must digest, reflect, and understand the importance of this model to the whole of the subject.

Second, there is the **activity-based** approach to learning, which emphasizes the application of knowledge and skill through techniques. This approach is vital in developing effectiveness. It is seen from two levels of learning:

1 The use and application of *specific skills*. This is the utilization of cognitive knowledge in a practical manner. These skills emanate from the cognitive aspect of learning, so they are functional skills, specific to the discipline.

   For example, the learner needs to understand the concept of job analysis before he or she tackles an activity that requires the drawing up of a specific job evaluation programme. So knowledge is not seen for its own sake, but is applied and becomes a specific functional skill.

2 The use and application of *generic skills*. These are universal skills which every manager uses irrespective of the wider external environment, the organization, the function and the job. This is seen, for example, in the ability to make clear decisions on the merits of a case. This skill of decision making is found in most of the activities.

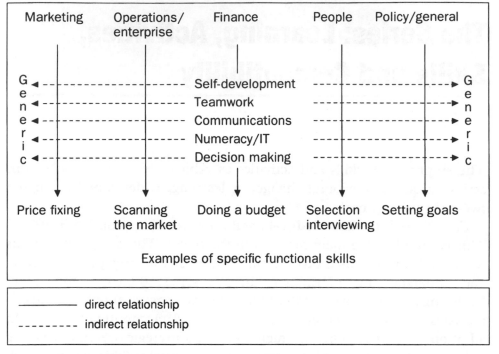

Figure SK.1   Series skills matrix: functional and generic skills

There is a relationship between the specific functional skills and the generic skills. The specific functional skills stand alone, but the generic skills cut across them. See figure SK.1.

In this series we use activities to cover both the specific functional and the generic skills. There are five generic skills. We shall examine each of them in turn.

Self-development

The learner must take responsibility for his or her learning as well as 'learning how to learn'. Time management, work scheduling and organizing the work are involved in the procedural sense. From a learning perspective, sound aspects of learning, from motivation to reward, need to be clarified and understood. The physical process of learning, including changing knowledge, skills and attitudes, may be involved. Individual goals and aspirations need to be recognized alongside the task goals. The ultimate aim of this skill is to facilitate learning transfer to new situations and environments.

Examples of this skill include:

- establishing and clarifying work goals;
- developing procedures and methods of work;
- building key learning characteristics into the process;
- using procedural learning;
- applying insightful learning;
- creating personal developmental plans;
- integrating these personal developmental plans with work goals.

Teamwork

Much of our working lives is concerned with groups. Effective teamwork is thus at a premium. This involves meeting both the task objectives and the socio-emotional processes within the group. This skill can be used for groups in a training or educational context. It can be a bridge between decision making and an awareness of self-development.

Examples of this skill include:

- clarifying the task need of the group;
- receiving, collating, ordering and rendering information;
- discussing, chairing and teamwork within the group;
- identifying the socio-emotional needs and group processes;
- linking these needs and processes to the task goals of the group.

Communications

This covers information and attitude processing within and between individuals. Oral and written communications are important because of the gamut of 'information and attitudinal' processing within the individual. At one level communication may mean writing a report, at another it could involve complex interpersonal relationships.

Examples of this skill include:

- understanding the media, aids, the message and methods;
- overcoming blockages;
- listening;
- presenting a case or commenting on the views of others;
- writing;
- designing material and systems for others to understand your communications.

Numeracy/IT

Managers need a core mastery of numbers and their application. This mastery is critical for planning, control, co-ordination, organization and, above all else, decision making. Numeracy/IT are not seen as skills for their own sake. Here, they are regarded as the means to an end. These skills enable information and data to be utilized by the effective manager. In particular these skills are seen as an adjunct to decision making.

Examples of this skill include:

- gathering information;
- processing and testing information;
- using measures of accuracy, reliability, probability etc.;
- applying appropriate software packages;
- extrapolating information and trends for problem solving.

Decision Making

Management is very much concerned with solving problems and making decisions. As group decisions are covered under teamwork, the emphasis in this decision-making skill is placed on the individual.

Decision making can involve a structured approach to problem solving with appropriate aims and methods. Apart from the 'scientific' approach, we can employ also an imaginative vision towards decision making. One is rational, the other is more like brainstorming.

Examples of this skill include:

- setting objectives and establishing criteria;
- seeking, gathering and processing information;
- deriving alternatives;
- using creative decision making;
- action planning and implementation.

This is *the* most important skill of management and is given primary importance in the generic skills within the activities as a reflection of everyday reality.

Before we go about learning how to develop into effective managers, it is important to understand the general principles of learning. Both the knowledge-based and the activity-based approaches are set within the environment of these principles. The series has been written to relate to Anderson's sound principles of learning which were developed in *Successful Training Practice*.

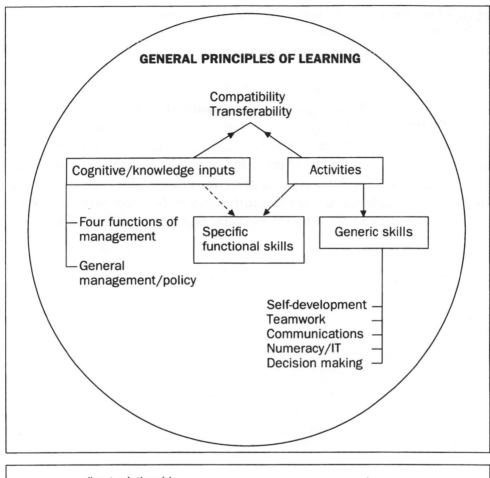

Figure SK.2   Series learning strategy

- *Motivation*   Intrinsic motivation is stimulated by the range and depth of the subject matter and assisted by an action orientation.

- *Knowledge of results*   Ongoing feedback is given through the instructor's manual for each book in the series.

- *Scale learning*   Each text is divided into six units, which facilitates part learning.

- *Self-pacing*   A map of the unit with objectives, content and an overview helps learners to pace their own progress.

- *Transfer*   Realism is enhanced through lifelike simulations which assist learning transfer.

- *Discovery learning*   The series is geared to the learner using self-insight to stimulate learning.

- *Self-development* Self-improvement and an awareness of how we go about learning underpin the series.

- *Active learning* Every activity is based upon this critical component of successful learning.

From what has been said so far, the learning strategy of the series can be outlined in diagrammatic form. (See figure SK.2.)

In figure SK.2, 'compatibility and transferability' are prominent because the learning approach of the series is extremely compatible with the learning approaches of current initiatives in management development. This series is related to a range of learning classification being used in education and training. Consequently it meets the needs of other leading training systems and learning taxonomies. See figures SK.3–SK.6.

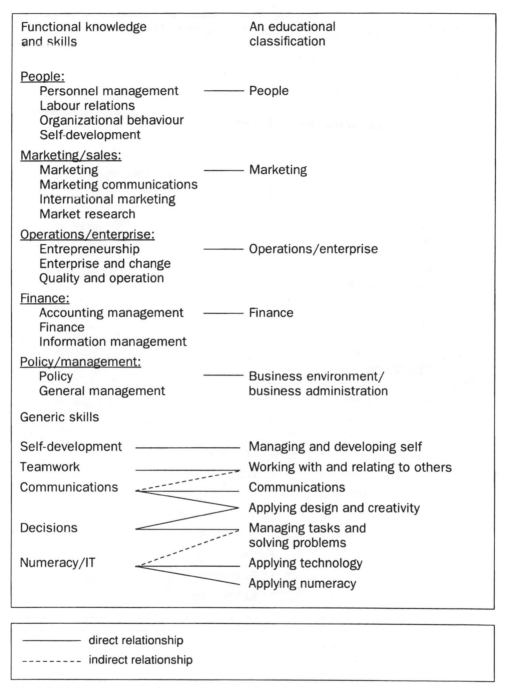

Figure SK.3   Series knowledge and skills related to an educational classification

Source: Adapted from Business Technician and Educational Council, *Common skills and experience of BTEC programmes.*

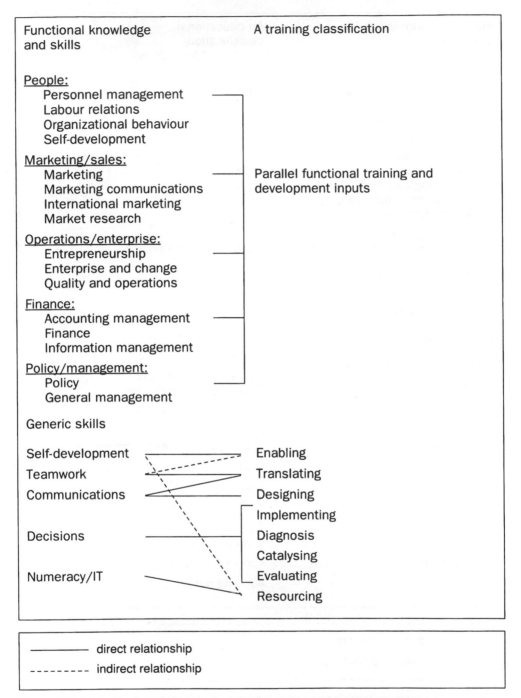

Figure SK.4   Series knowledge and skills related to a training classification

Source: Adapted from J. A. G. Jones, 'Training intervention strategies: making more effective
training interventions', *ITS Monograph no. 2* (Industrial Training Services Ltd,
London, 1983), and experience of development programmes.

Functional knowledge and skills	MCI competency
People:	Managing people
Personnel management	
Labour relations	
Organizational behaviour	
Self-development	
Marketing/sales:	
Marketing	Managing operations and
Marketing communications	managing information
International marketing	(plus new texts pending)
Market research	
Operations/enterprise:	
Entrepreneurship	
Enterprise and change	
Quality and operations	
Finance:	Managing finance
Accounting management	
Finance	
Information management	
Policy/management:	Managing context
Policy	
General management	
Generic skills	
Self-development	Managing oneself
Teamwork	Managing others
Communications	Using intellect
Decisions	Planning
Numeracy/IT	

——————— direct relationship

- - - - - - - - indirect relationship

Figure SK.5   Series knowledge and skills related to Management Charter Initiative (MCI) competencies

Source: Adapted from MCI, *Diploma Level Guidelines* (MCI, London, n.d.)

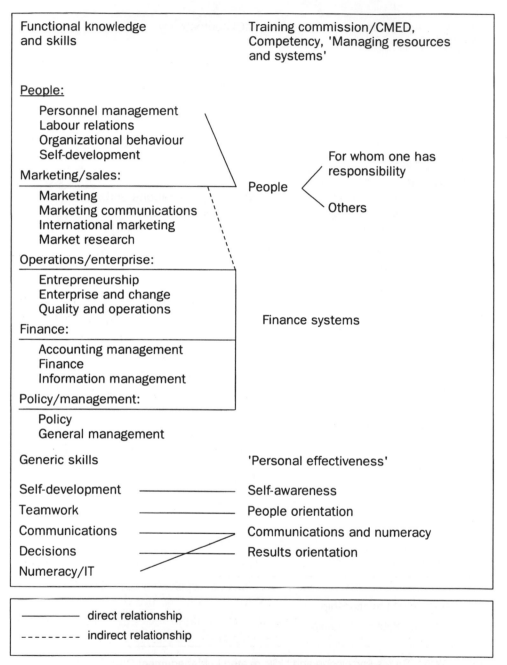

Figure SK.6   Series knowledge and skills related to Training Commission/Council for Management Education (CMED) competencies

Source: Adapted from Training Commission/CMED, *Classifying the components of management competencies* (Training Commission, London, 1988).

Preface

❝ Knowledge cannot be pumped into human beings . . .
the individual may learn; he is not taught. ❞

(McGregor, 1960)

Themes

To a great extent all development is self-development. The individual must be motivated and committed. It is the learner who internalizes the external support systems of organizations, who seeks out opportunities for development and who can seek self-fulfilment through the process of taking responsibility for his or her learning at the place of work.

This does not mean some *laissez faire* approach to development by the organization. It is not learning on the cheap – or it ought not to be. It should be a learning partnership between the individual and the organization, between the process and the structures of learning, between self-developmental practices and the development plans of the organization.

It does mean less forced feeding from the organization and hopefully less developmental programmes for their own sake or training being seen as rations for all irrespective of need.

In some cases self-development may mean some form of 'empowerment'. The concept has its critics but taking control of one's learning opportunities and maximizing personal strengths can only mean that the individual is taking some power or control over his/her destiny.

Self-development is not some drug-induced state of euphoria where we can chant 'all we need is love' reminiscent of the music of the late 1960s. Self-development must be linked into organizational need to make it meaningful both to the individual and to the firm.

The organization should not abandon its self-developers. Needs analysis, the design and development of initiatives, putting action plans into effect and evaluating these initiatives can be down to the individual and the learner. Self-development ultimately is about creating effectiveness.

Learning Aims

Specifically *Effective Self-development* aims to:

- outline the importance of the concept of self-development;
- link self-development to ideas of effectiveness in general and within the series;
- help conduct a self-analysis;
- construct personal competencies;
- analyse the value of the idea of capability;
- construct task competencies;
- review current trends such as NVQs and the MCI movement;
- understand that learning is the basis of self-development and be able to review a range of applicable theories;
- carry out in-house and external audits of resources and opportunities available for self-development;
- relate self-development to changing organizational and environmental scenarios;
- examine the implications of these changes for self-development;
- apply the generic skills of the series and to relate self-development to the concepts of management development within the series.

Format and Content

The book follows the common format of the whole series with its learner orientation and interactive mechanisms (see series introduction).

On content, Unit One sets the scene for self-development, putting it in context and linking it to effectiveness. It also gives an indicative overview of the book.

Self-development has a focus on the individual and personal effectiveness and this is illustrated through competencies (Unit Two). Equally though, task effectiveness must be met and the medium of competence is a useful way forward (Unit Three).

The oil of the whole machinery is of course learning (Unit Four). The learner is clearly centre stage here as is the application of experiential learning theory. However the system of learning, the context in which the learners find themselves and other learning theories must have weight in the equation as well.

Resources (Unit Five) must be mobilized to give the self-developer an opportunity to move on from his/her current base of knowledge, skill, attitudes and competence. Organizational learning may provide a useful backcloth to resources and commitment to the concept of self-development.

The last unit (Unit Six) pulls the strands together and also moves the debate on further arguing that change is inevitable and that higher order competencies may be needed as a baseline to gauge both competence and capability. We conclude by examining the series view of management development and place self-development into this context.

The diagrammatic outline is below:

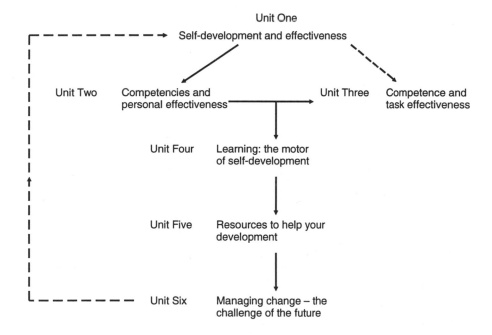

So there is an overwhelming need for self-development. We must constantly develop our knowledge, skills, competence, attitudes and behaviour to meet turbulence in the organization and in the external environment. It can mean greater 'employability', adaptability, more independence and taking an adult-like responsibility for yourself. It can stimulate your whole career and career pattern. It is not anti-institution-alized learning but it is against an overtly bureaucratic conformist approach to learning. It can build your expertise as well as your levels of confidence. It does need resources and it does need organizational assistance, resources and co-operation. Perhaps above all it focuses on you and how you learn.

We set out to develop this capacity of learning to learn; so let us start by going deeper into the ideas behind self-development and effectiveness.

The authors would like to thank Paul Stringer and First Class for their work on this book. In addition, thanks are due to Maureen Anderson for her assistance in the co-ordination of this project.

Reference

McGregor, D., *The Human Side of Enterprise* (McGraw-Hill, New York, 1960).

ESD Unit One

Self-development and Effectiveness

Learning Objectives

After completing this unit you should be able to:

- be aware of the importance of the idea of self-development both to the individual and the organization;

- note the context of self-development and its link to organization, management and employee development;

- link self-development to the aims of effectiveness;

- examine a range of approaches to effectiveness;

- be aware of the approach of the text and of the series towards self-development; and

- apply the generic skills.

Contents

A. Overview

B. Self-development
▶ Concept

▶ Influences

– A changed philosophy?

– Power devolution?

– Humanism

– Environmental turbulence and change

– Learning

▶ The process – an example

C. Developmental Contexts
▶ Personnel development

▶ Management development

▶ Organizational development (OD)

D. Effectiveness
▶ Nature – general

▶ The MCI approach

▶ A case study

▶ Organizational effectiveness – the approach of the series

▶ Managerial effectiveness – the approach of the series

E. Effectiveness and Self-development – the approach of the book

ESD Unit One

A. Overview

This unit sets the scene by looking at the idea of self-development, its philosophical origins and its value. Self-development is seen as a key element of any form of development within the organization. This includes employee, management, team and organization development. The limits of self-development are also outlined in this range of interventions from the individual to the group and then to the organization.

Self-development is linked to the idea of effectiveness. We trace some views on what constitutes effectiveness and extrapolate these ideas to show their influence on self-development.

Hence we fuse self-development and effectiveness and then begin to outline the rest of the text covering personal and task effectiveness, learning the dynamo of self-development and the need for organizational support. Finally we look to changing scenarios and put the case for self-development as a mechanism and as a facilitator of change.

Throughout this work we see self-development operating at the level of individual managers and at the level of their subordinates as managers have a key role in using self-development methods and techniques to cultivate their staff. So the onus may lie on individual initiative but there should be a 'cascade' effect from the top down as well as adequate support mechanisms to facilitate self-development.

B. Self-development

Concept

Self-development can be seen as a form of rampant individualism and as a part of a self-help philosophy. The individualism may be a counter to collectivism; self-help may be a reaction to 'a culture of dependency'.

Self-development can also be seen as an anti-institutional movement, a progression away from the classroom and away from learning systems and processes. There can be an anti-bureaucratic vision here which is supportive of the self-help/individualistic viewpoint.

It may also be linked to trends in learning. Structural inputs and systematic principles of learning have been eroded – if not replaced in many circles – by an onus being placed on the learner. Experiential learning and learner-oriented methods of analysis, design, delivery and assessment have crept in to both education and training particularly over the last 20 years or so. Self-development fits well into this 'cult of the learner'.

It does mean individuals taking responsibility for themselves and may be linked to some vision of 'empowerment'. Cynics argue that such a devolution of power exists only to fill the vacuum created by the wholesale removal of middle managers, known euphemistically in many organizations as 'delayering'.

This emphasis on the individual developing him/herself may also be linked to cheapness since corporations can quickly abandon sophisticated and costly development schemes by placing the onus on the individual.

Power to individuals at the workplace may be the clarion call and self-development meets both the philosophy of post-modernism as well as that of humanistic learning. Let us now develop some of these ideas.

Influences

A changed philosophy?

Taylor (1911) writing in the early part of this century consolidated the traditional mind-set dividing management from the workers. His first of five 'scientific' principles of management advocates organizations to 'shift all responsibility for the organization of work from the worker to the manager; managers should do all the thinking relating to the planning and design of work, leaving the workers with the task of implementation'.

Taylor's advice may seem archaic – from a different age of master and servant. We are sure that it is easy to identify many organizations where the manager/worker divide is as wide as ever – with Taylorite principles being vigorously applied by managers in the context of the critique postulated by Braverman (1974).

However a more liberal vision of work is seen in Box ESD1.1.

BOX ESD1.1

A new philosophy

In the last 20 years, there has been a philosophical shift away from seeing the world as something 'out there' subject to human control and reason. (This kind of mind-set has been termed 'Modernism'.)

In contrast there is a 'post-modernist' viewpoint which holds that humans 'construct the world around them'; that there is nothing absolute 'out there' but that the language we use to describe our world holds the key. In this 'brave new world', 'society is actually in transformation, new forms of social being are emerging that have little relation to the capitalist or industrialist systems that have constituted us throughout the last century. Connecting these currents is an assumption that new times need new methodologies, and novel ways of looking at social processes'.[1]

Three titles of books on management over the last six years give a flavour of the approach the so-called 'Post-Modernists' are taking – *Thriving on Chaos – handbook for a management revolution* (Peters, 1987)[2], *The Age of Unreason* (Handy, 1989)[3] and *Liberation Management – Necessary Disorganisation for the Nanosecond Nineties* (Peters, 1992)[4].

The manager can no longer rely on having a management role within an organization that is structured in a hierarchical way. Traditionally a manager has had what is called 'positional' power by virtue of the position s/he holds in the hierarchical structure.

> When organizations operate in a managerial culture the only claim for attention is the value of the role one performs: absent the role – gone the identity.[5]

Whereas the manager of old needed a hierarchy and support system to legitimatize his authority, the manager of today has to work out a very different role with staff who are increasingly taking 'ownership' of their own development. As Kanter tells us,

> Once high performance is established, once the standards are clear and clearly achieved, the subordinate no longer needs the goodwill of his/her boss quite so much.[6]

The same message comes from Megatrends' authors, Naisbitt and Aburdine:

> The shift from hierarchies to networking means that it matters less who your boss is (or how well the boss manages you) more how well you make the right connections with a supportive mentor or a sponsor to champion your ideas and contributions.

Self-development would seem to be part of this new world order. Certainly if we accept this viewpoint we would see organizations, work and management from a new perspective. Whether we accept this 'new world order' is debatable – but presumably some do and it may be an important philosophical change underpinning self-development.

Sources:
[1] Parker, M., 'Post modern organisations or post modern organisation theory', *Organisation Studies*, 13, 1, (1992).
[2] Peters, T., *Thriving on Chaos – handbook for a management revolution*, (Macmillan, London, 1987).
[3] Handy, C., *The Age of Unreason*, (Hutchinson, London, 1989).
[4] Peters, T., *Liberation Management – Necessary Disorganisation for the Nanosecond Nineties*, (Macmillan, London, 1992).
[5] Zalenzik, A., *The Managerial Mystique*, (Harper and Row, New York, 1989).
[6] Kanter, R.M., *The Change Masters: Corporate Entrepreneurs at Work*, (Allen & Unwin, London, 1984).
[7] Naisbitt, J. and Aburdine, P., *Reinventing the Corporation*, (Macdonald, 1986).

Power devolution?

If we accept the logic of the Post-Modernists (and to some of the authors – it is a big 'if'), in the organizations of the future everyone would have some form of managerial function. Handy (1989) summarizes the viewpoint:

> Everyone will increasingly be expected not only to be good at something, to have their own professional or technical expertise but will also very rapidly acquire responsibility for money, people or property, or all three – a managerial task in fact.

In these circumstances, managers would certainly have to review their roles and their attitudes towards management and have to come to terms with the absence of a supporting hierarchy. Without positional power – personal power would be at a premium. Self-development could be utilized to enhance this move to personal (not institutionalized) power.

Humanism

There is a strong humanistic influence on the concept and application of self-development. This ties into an humanistic approach to learning. Please refer to Box ESD1.2.

BOX ESD1.2

Sources of self-development: humanism

A humanistic vision of learning which permeates self-development includes the following.[1]

■ The potential for curiosity and learning must be encouraged.
■ The learning must be relevant to individual needs.
■ External 'threats' must be minimized.
■ Attempts to change people 'in themselves' is threatening and may be resisted.
■ Activity is important for significant learning.
■ Knowledge of 'how to learn' is important to individuals for coping with change.
■ Self-initiated learning is longer lasting and all pervasive.
■ Self-evaluation can stimulate independence, creativity and self-reliance.
■ The trainer/manager's role is that of a facilitator to provide an environment in which the learners can set their own goals.

Source:
[1] Adapted from Rogers, C., *Freedom to Learn* (Merril, Columbus, Ohio, 1969) and *Freedom for the 80's* (Merril, Columbus, Ohio, 1983).

Environmental turbulence and change

Real pressures to encourage self-development exist not only from within the individual but from outside of the individual and his/her organization. We pursue this issue in depth in ESD Unit Six: hence a brief example should suffice. Increasing 'environmental turbulence' is a fact of life for most of us. For example, the Balkanization, or severe fragmentation of the labour markets, particularly in the UK, during the 1980s and early 1990s gives us one pressure where self-development may be one of the few escape routes for people. Please refer to Box ESD1.3.

BOX ESD1.3

Flexible labour markets

Increasingly in the UK we are faced with the theme of flexible labour markets.[1] **Numerical flexibility** refers to the number of hours or employees which can be adjusted in line with business need. Part-timers, temporaries and the self-employed can fuse with shorter time working and annual contracts of hours for the 'core' labour force.

Multiskilling, the removal of traditional occupational and skill boundaries, can be seen as **functional flexibility**.

This flexibility can spread into the location of work which can cover teleworking, traditional home working and the 'normal' place of work, from office, shop or factory.

Pay flexibility relates remuneration to productivity, performance and the state of the product and labour markets.

Labour mobility can also be seen as part of this flexibility. Different jobs, occupations and geographical areas have always been behind such migration – but economic pressures may further stimulate such change.

So far as self-development is concerned, it may be a weapon to counter such changes in the labour market – or at least a tool to give the person a greater chance of survival in these turbulent times. In particular, the multiskilling form of flexibility can be accommodated through self-development. The ability to take responsibility for oneself and to update knowledge and skills constantly must be linked to a frame of mind or attitude that allows the individual to create some degree of independence, skill transferability (if necessary outside of the organization) and an ability to cope with change. Self-development is not the only answer to the 'Balkanization' of the labour markets but it does give the individual some weapons against the almost inevitable push for even more flexibility in the labour market.

Sources:
[1] For a useful analysis of the processes behind flexibility and the 'core' and 'peripheral' debate on labour markets please see:
- Atkinson, J. and Meager, J., 'Is flexibility just a flash in the pan?' *Personnel Management*, September (1986)
- Pollert, A., *Farewell to Flexibility*, (Blackwell, Oxford, 1991)
- Watson, G., 'The flexible workforce and patterns of working hours in the UK', *Employment Gazette*, July, (1994).

Learning

One of the key influences in self-development is that of a learner orientation to work and to behavioural change. The learner becomes centre stage in this view and his/her style or approach to the whole of learning takes on an importance out of all proportion to other aspects of learning systems.

In particular, experiential learning seems to be one of the bedrocks of the self-developmental movement. As we develop this more fully later, we shall be brief. A cycle of learning comes to the fore with ever increasing spirals based on the work of Kolb (1982) and Kolb *et al.* (1984).

Please tackle Activity ESD1.1 and then consult Boxes ESD1.4 Experiential Learning and ESD1.5 A learning system: self-development in context.

ACTIVITY ESD1.1

SELF-DEVELOPMENT – CONTEXTS

Activity code

✓ Self-development
✓ Teamwork
☐ Communications
☐ Numeracy/IT
✓ Decisions

Task

Putting the onus on the individual for development may not be adequate in terms of learning. Your (group) role is to determine which other factors need to be taken into account in developing a learning system within an organization to facilitate both training and development.

BOX ESD1.4

Experiential learning

Problems

- The learners may not be aware of what they have learned.
- They may avoid the conceptualization stage.
- Some people (young adults for example) may not have the experience to build on in the first place.
- It may give too many 'hard knocks'.
- It may be quite wasteful in time/resources, etc. with too much trial and error.
- Experiential learning requires reflection and an action-oriented management may not be able/willing to take the time to reflect.
- While we have different styles of learning, individuals are clearly not the same and some individuals may prefer more didactic approaches.
- People may need or prefer different types of learning inputs/experiences at different stages of their career.
- It assumes some degree of maturity and accurate analysis of experiences.

BOX ESD1.5

A learning system: self-development in context

This follows on from the Activity ESD1.1, 'Self-development – contexts'. You will find an example of a training system which can easily be extrapolated to our needs of self-development in figure ESD1.1.[1]

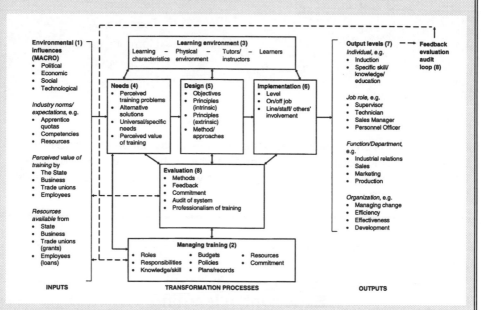

Figure ESD1.1   The training system

The inputs or environmental influences on training/development look to be transferable (Note 1). The transformation processes (Notes 4, 5, 6 and 8) involve the core learning cycle of needs, design, implementation and evaluation. Again they are relevant to self-development – the debate occurs when one questions who would actually conduct this analysis – the individual, the manager, the developer or some combination of these parties.

The management of training/development (Note 2) takes the onus away from the individual as resources, policies and commitment at organizational level are required.

The learning environment (Note 3) sees self-development as important with the learner not only as a key player – but also as part of a team.

The output levels (Note 7) illustrate the various levels, including individual levels, where learning can take place.

The feedback/audit (Note 8) continues the loop and emphasizes the need for continuous evaluation.

Source:
[1] Anderson, A.H., *Successful Training Practice* (Blackwell, Oxford, 1993).

The process – an example

One of the authors was working for a national industry training board at the time Burgoyne *et al.*'s *Self Development: Theory and application for practitioners* emerged in 1978. He vividly remembers the impact this book had on him as the training board, like most other institutions, struggled to encourage organizations to consider management development. Hitherto that had involved signing up for outside courses and it usually was restricted to senior managers. But Pedler *et al.* (1993) demonstrated that any manager could benefit from reflecting on his/her own experience and that they rather than the training department should be responsible both for identifying what their needs were and for choosing the most appropriate methods for achieving them.

The method was deceptively simple. The manager was first asked to compare his/her level of skill with those identified in research carried out by Burgoyne and Stuart (1976) into what skills successful managers demonstrate. (Please see Box ESD1.6.) Depending on what skills they wanted to develop, a number of activities and exercises were provided which the manager could carry out by themselves and/or with others.

BOX ESD1.6

Developing skills[1]

Basic knowledge and information

1 Command of basic facts
2 Relevant professional understanding

Skills and attributes

3 Continuing sensitivity to events
4 Analytical, problem-solving and decision/judgement making skills
5 Social skills and abilities
6 Emotional resilience
7 Proactivity – inclination to respond purposefully to events

'Meta-qualities'

8 Creativity
9 Mental agility

---

10 Balanced learning habits and skills
11 Self-knowledge.

Source:
[1] Burgoyne, J.G. and Stuart, R., 'The nature, use and acquisition of managerial skills and other attributes', *Personnel Review*, 5, (1976).

Thus, if 'proactivity' was a key skill identified, there were a range of activities that were appropriate, viz:

■ Making contacts
■ Choosing solutions with a chance
■ Planning change
■ Catastrophic contingencies
■ Asserting yourself
■ Practising group behaviours
■ Looking after yourself
■ Who's the boss?
■ Practising change
■ Action planning
■ Imaging.

Pedler and Boydell (1985) opened up these kinds of activities to anyone who was managing and produced a useful framework within which one's own self-development could be planned. There were two sets of dimensions which they suggested managers might want to consider when planning their self-development.

Consult Box ESD1.7 and then tackle Activity ESD1.2. Thereafter read Box ESD1.8 'Your development – an example'.

BOX ESD1.7

A self-developmental programme

Four aspects of self that need to be maintained and developed are:

■ Health – a sound mind in a sound body
■ Skills – mental, technical, social, artistic
■ Action – getting things done in the world
■ Identity – knowing who you are and having a personal agenda as to who you want to become.

Three inner processes that have an impact on behaviour are:

- Thinking – ideas, thoughts, perceptions, concepts, theories
- Feeling – emotions, moods, feelings
- Willing/Doing – intentions, motives, drives.

ACTIVITY ESD1.2

DEVELOPING YOURSELF

Activity code

✓	Self-development
	Teamwork
	Communications
	Numeracy/IT
	Decisions

Task

See if you can write some suggestions in the appropriate boxes to help you to maintain/develop yourself in each of the specified areas.

Inner processes that require managing

	Thinking	Feeling	Willing/Doing
Health			
Skills			
Actions			
Identity			

Aspects of self that need managing

BOX ESD1.8

Your development – an example

Inner processes that require managing

Aspects of self that need managing		Thinking	Feeling	Willing/Doing
	Health	Reading up on alternative medicines	Feeling good about your figure whatever others might say!	Planning to change diet/swim quarter mile every week
	Skills	Planning to improve solving skills	Planning to take up course on flower arranging	Planning to learn how to ski
	Actions	Keeping a diary to record and reflect on actions taken	Noting down feelings/emotions associated with actions	Going out of your way to get feedback from others as to consequences of actions taken
	Identity	Being clear about your personal values	Valuing yourself	Planning how to put your personal agenda into operation

---

This is a useful framework within which to plan your self-development. You might want to use it in connection with your learning contract (see ESD Unit One later) for example.

Reeves (1994) is particularly concerned with the dimension of personal identity:

A key element in a manager's development has to be to find an appropriate fit between his or her 'self' and what it is he or she has to do as a manager.

He suggests that very often new managers will try acting and imitating 'how a manager should behave' rather than being themselves and drawing out and developing their own management style. It is important to be your own manager.

Developing your 'self' is about fitting yourself to be able to manage all the different kinds of situations in your life and work. It involves:

■ knowing yourself and being aware of your behaviour and its effects;
■ seeing things differently and feeling differently;
■ learning to adapt to different roles and expectation;

- evolving your attitudes and your values in the light of your self-knowledge and experience; and
- being able to use your versatility and self-knowledge in practical accomplishments.

(Reeves, 1994)

So far, we have looked at self-development as a process by which the individual takes control of his/her own learning and development. This is a basic assumption on which later units in this book are based. However, we must also recognize that in so far as 'self-development makes the learner sovereign',

> that sovereignty creates problems for the managing of people in work organizations. Democratic rights have been slow to come to the workplace . . . Work organizations, on the whole, are predominantly authoritarian in tone. A libertarian idea such as self development creates all kinds of difficulties philosophical and practical, as well as all sorts of new freedoms.

(Reeves, 1994)

Attempt Activity ESD1.3 'Plus and Minus'. Thereafter consult Boxes ESD1.9 and ESD1.10.

ACTIVITY ESD1.3

PLUS AND MINUS

Activity code

✓ Self-development
✓ Teamwork
✓ Communications
☐ Numeracy/IT
✓ Decisions

Task

Your individual/group role is to outline the advantages and disadvantages of applying the principles of self-development for a manager.
    Comment critically on these advantages/disadvantages.

BOX ESD1.9

Self-development – disadvantages

- It can ignore all other relevant variables of the learning system.
- It puts too much emphasis on the individual learner.
- It may not impact on groups, functions/departments of management or at organizational level.
- It assumes that people are motivated to seize opportunities for self-advancement (this may not be the case and one could argue that expectancy of personal gain should follow).
- It assumes some accurate self-analysis of weaknesses and strengths but yet we know that individuals are over lenient in this analysis.
- Individual needs may be pursued through self-development which do not tally with organizational needs.
- As in other forms of training/development newly gained skills/knowledge/attitude will require opportunities if not reinforcement and reward from the organization – and this may not be evident.
- It may be too oriented towards experiential learning with few support systems and little consideration of other theories of learning.

BOX ESD1.10

Self-development – advantages

- It is learner-oriented so training and development are not some diktats from the training department, but are based on real individual needs.
- Past experiences can be built upon.
- Self-effectiveness can be stimulated through the acceptance of responsibility for one's own direction.
- It can cause behavioural change at the level of the individual.

A number of these constraints and objections disappear if we recognize that self-development, far from being a rather selfish, essentially self-centred way of bettering ourselves and 'doing our own thing' can be achieved only in relation to other 'selves'. As Heron (1977) notes 'Persons can only be persons in relation'. They can realize their authentic personal needs only in 'corporate systems of interdependence' but he also recognizes that such corporate systems are likely to be conservative and 'that tension and conflict will arise on the interface between individual need and corporate purpose'.

That tension can be resolved only by a joint recognition on the part of individual and organization that the effectiveness of their respective development depends on each other.

> Following the path of self-development is not simply to take an inward turning, it is to go in and to go out. The clear implication is that organization will not be responsive, innovatory and self-renewing on the outside unless we are able to nurture and release the energy of those on the inside. This is the vision of the learning organisation.
>
> (Heron, 1977)

In order to examine the kind of conflicts that can occur, Adlam and Plumridge (1990) divided into two a group attending a conference on self-development: one sub-group was encouraged to focus on issues of self-development while the other was to consider themselves as the parent organization charged with accommodating the needs of what was called the 'self-development' group. This group devised strategies by which it would aim to support the development process by all kinds of support mechanisms – debriefing meetings, access to resources, allocation of time, etc. but, despite having all these strategies, nothing prepared them for the reality of coming to terms with the very personal nature of the experiences emerging from the self-development group. Though it was only a simulated exercise, Adlam and Plumridge drew some conclusions which might help to resolve tension between self-development and organization needs:

1   Unless those responsible for supporting the growth and development of others in the organisation are themselves actively engaged in their own self-development they cannot actually attune to the quality of the experiences of self-developing others.

2   Despite the fact that participants at this conference were experienced developers and facilitators even they had difficulty connecting with the personal experiences of the designated self-development group. The kind of skills that managers are going to have to develop to help

facilitate integration between self and organisation development are: listening, empathising, reflecting, skilful confrontation and questioning techniques.

3   On the other hand the self-developer also has some responsibility for integrating his/her own experience within the context of the organisation.

4   In the final analysis, though, it is up to the organisation to invest in an infrastructure which recognises and supports self-development but also find ways to embed it within the organisation's culture. Again, this is the vision of the learning organisation.

(Adlam and Plumridge, 1990)

An overall conclusion they came to was that 'turning inwards' is not sufficient of itself:

> It is in the very act of trying to help others that we are likely to be allowed a sense of their inner selves – of their thoughts, values and feelings; and that process unlocks for us many insights into our own selves . . . This opening of others to self and self to others is a prerequisite for reciprocal behaviour and therefore the foundation stone of our own growth and development. Opportunities for such behaviour are constantly with us if we choose to take them.

(Adlam and Plumridge, 1990)

Before we link self-development to concepts of effectiveness, we need a wider angle on ideas of development.

C.   Developmental Contexts

In a related book of this series (Anderson, 1994), development is examined in depth from the perspectives of:

- self
- personnel and management development
- organizational development.

Consequently we shall be brief and touch upon the personnel, management and organizational themes.

Personnel development

So much time is spent on developing managers but the principles of self-development can be applied to a great extent to non-managerial staffs as well.

More and more companies are discovering that management develop-ment is not just about the development of a top elite as Ashridge Management College found when it undertook a survey of 150 organiza-tions to discover what was best practice. In particular, the researchers wanted to explore the closeness of the relationship between management development policy and business policy to see if it could improve business performance (see Jacobs, 1989). What the Ashridge survey found from companies like Nissan, United Biscuits, ICI, NFC, Thorn EMI and Rothmans was that it was all about creating conditions for 'total employee growth'.

Summarizing the findings of the survey, Willie (1990) notes:

This emphasis on joint responsibility and team building redefines management development as a collective activity rather than just an individual one and takes it beyond the top echelon into the total company.

Similar findings are publicized in Smythe, Dorward, Lambvert's 1991 report 'The Power of the Open Company' which compared the manage-ment style in top companies with varying levels of performance. The conclusion was that the better performers were more 'open' in their management style; this meant they delegated more responsibility, fostered employee involvement and personal initiatives and provided more effective internal communications.

To Zuboff, writing in 1988, information technology redresses the power imbalance consolidated by management particularly using Taylorite principles. Whether we accept this new equilibrium is debatable but certainly information and its control is no longer the monopoly of management.

Every worker, as Handy (1987) has indicated, is not just a potential manager he is a manager of his own work output. This is what the 'workers' Zuboff (1988) spoke to were discovering as they realized through the agency of information technology that they knew as much as management and therefore they could 'manage' equally well. But to succeed they needed to develop 'intellective skills'.

Learning goes to the heart of those skills and as such can form part of a new 'higher order of labour'. To Garratt (1991) the outcomes of learning become 'intellectual property' which is the basis of future wealth. Self-development forms the core of this 'wealth'.

This new liberalism may not spread to every office or factory but self-developmental concepts and techniques can unleash tremendous employee potential. Such learning can enhance labour mobility and job transferability as a minimum position, while enriching the work of many as a middle part of the spectrum or perhaps replacing some managerial aspects of work as a maximum viewpoint. The great thing about self-development is that it can include everyone at the place of work.

Management development

This has tended to be the preserve of an élite group of employees. Again self-development dovetails into this process. Like personnel development it does need organizational support systems – or perhaps team group support mechanisms.

Livy (1988) sees management development as:

> a series of processes and events both within and/or outside the organization designed to improve performance, both of the organiza-tion as a whole and of the individuals within it.

The prerequisites of successful management development include self-development but initial selection, succession planning, appraisal and assessment, career development and management training and education are all important facets of the 'processes or events'.

If we look at the main approaches to management development, we see a 'top down' or a 'bottom up' approach. The former is performance-based and starts with plans and goals at the top of the organization; the latter has a more self-developmental 'feel' to it as it starts with a developmental vision of the individual manager.

The level of intervention may impact on self-development. Some approaches look to the individual job and the managers derive specific performance and developmental needs. Clearly there may be some knock on to self-development in this instance. Other approaches focus on the team. Group roles and interpersonal skills may have some self-develop-mental implication. The common skills and competency approaches tend to be geared to core/generic skills – almost irrespective of individual need. The self-developmental aspects seem to be less obvious in these circum-stances unless specific competencies and competences are utilized (see ESD Units Two and Three). Another level of intervention concerns the manager and change (see ESD Unit Six). A new attitude, flexibility and interpersonal skills have a self-developmental aspect but the issue of developing the organization is wider than self-development.

Organizational development (OD)

The term OD covers planned efforts to improve the effectiveness of the organization using the techniques of the behavioural sciences.

The focus tends to be on the integration of people into the operation of the organization. Consequently organizational processes are emphasized in:

- the relationship between the external environment and the institution
- the communication processes between the firm and its environment and within the organization
- the integrative mechanisms to unify the organizational efforts, such as co-ordinated teams
- the style of management
- decision making and planning, etc.

These organizational processes need to be integrated with individual and group needs, particularly in the context of change.

Such improved collaboration within the firm and the dynamics of change to make the most effective use of people in changing scenarios clearly impacts on learning – at various levels. Hence there is a case for self-developmental concepts and techniques to be part of the OD initiative. Clearly it is not the whole story but self-development has a role to play in the management of change. We return to this topic in ESD Unit Six. Now we must integrate effectiveness with the ideas of self-development as one feeds off the other and both are important in meeting people and task needs. (See ESD Units Two and Three for a fuller discussion).

D. Effectiveness

Nature – general

According to the Oxford English Dictionary an 'effect' means 'something caused or produced, a result, a consequence, something attained or acquired by action, an accomplishment'.

The concept of 'effectiveness' in the context of management derives from the work of Drucker in the 1950s. Drucker (1954) popularized the distinction between 'doing things right' (efficiency) and 'doing the right things' (effectiveness).

He emphasized that success in business was not determined by production: it was not what the managers did within the firm but what they did for the customer.

This market-led insight redressed some of the production vision of business but in reality we need both a marketing and operations view of the enterprise in order for it to function properly – albeit the onus should be on the market place.

Drucker (1954) popularized the performance orientation of 'management by objectives' to stimulate the effective manager. Boss and subordinate agreed results which an employee would achieve over a given period. This was popular in the 1960s and the 1970s but then fell from favour as it was found that targets could either be unrealistic or, at the other extreme, not very challenging. Perhaps what was missing was linking targets for individual managers with targets for the organization as a whole. But in recent years the popular book, *The One Minute Manager* (Blanchard and Johnson, 1983) and the follow up book, *Leadership and the One Minute Manager* (Blanchard and Zigarmi, 1987) revived interest in the concept with the notion of setting SMART objectives. These objectives are

S   specific
M   measurable
A   achievable
R   relevant
T   timely

Please complete Activity ESD1.4.

ACTIVITY ESD1.4

A SMART PERFORMANCE?

Activity code

✓   Self-development
☐   Teamwork
✓   Communications
✓   Numeracy/IT
☐   Decisions

Below are contrasted characteristics of satisfactory and less than satisfactory objectives.

Satisfactory objectives	Unsatisfactory objectives
Measurable	Non-measurable
Quantitative	Qualitative
Specific	General
Results-oriented	Activity-centred
Individual	Shared
Realistic	Optimistic/pessimistic
Time bounded	Time extended

Task

Write down up to six objectives for yourself which can meet the above criteria

■

■

■

■

■

■

Examples of unsatisfactory objectives would be:

To improve morale in Department X

To improve the company's business image.

These could become satisfactory by taking account of SMART criteria as follows:

To reduce turnover amongst sales managers in Department X by 10 per cent by 1st January 1997 and

To increase the rating on popularity rating form (circulated to random sample of managers in region) by 7 per cent by end of September 1997.

However, you should not measure your effectiveness totally by achieving such objectives, however SMART they may be. For one thing they may bear little or no relationship to the goals by which the organization's effectiveness is to be assessed. Over the last decade there has been an increasing awareness of importance of linking individual development to that of the organization as a whole. Though it might seem obvious now, for a long time managers have tended to be trained in a vacuum, according to the latest management flavour of the month – with little thought as to how their performance and that of their staff could be linked to the strategic objectives of the organization as a whole. For this reason it has been very difficult to evaluate the effectiveness of training in the absence of criteria for organizational effectiveness. Indeed the concept of organization effectiveness is comparatively recent. It requires the capacity to view an organisation's goals in a much wider context. Cameron (1980) provides a framework for analysing organization effectiveness into four categories.

1 **Goal directed** Definitions focus on the output of the organization and how close it comes to meeting its goals.
   Examples include units produced, defects, backlogs, output per person per hour, running costs and the amount of overtime.
2 **Resource acquiring** Definitions judge effectiveness by the extent to which the organization acquires much needed resources from its external environment.
   Examples include new markets entered and skills developed.
3 **Constituencies** These are groups of individuals who have some stake in the organization – resource providers, customers, etc. – and effectiveness is judged in terms of how well the organization responds to the demands and expectations of these groups.
   Examples include customer complaints, company surveys and incorrect goods received.

4   **Internal process**   Definitions focus attention on flows of information, absence of strain and levels of trust as measures of effectiveness. Examples include turnover of employees and surveys of employee satisfaction.

Please refer now to Box ESD1.11 which provides a very useful approach to organizational effectiveness which may be transferable over to individual effectiveness.

BOX ESD1.11

Effectiveness - organizational context

Robbins usefully categorizes four main approaches to the concept of organizational effectiveness:

- goal attainment
- systems
- strategic constituencies
- competing values.[1]

The focus of the *goal attainment* approach involves the ends of the organization. It is a goal-oriented vision. Problems exist though as goals may have different timescales; they may not be agreed; management may have its own agenda; behavioural reality may differ from the Chairman's statements; and goals may alter over time.

A *systems approach* widens the debate. In simple terms, 'inputs' from the environment are 'transformed' into 'outputs' in a systems view of the business. Rather than focus on 'outputs', the whole process of getting there from acquiring resources, maintenance and interaction needs to be examined.

Really this emphasizes both means and ends. Are the means important if we meet our ends? If not, we could end up with some Machiavellian nightmare.

This *strategic constituencies* viewpoint starts from the premise – whose goals are we trying to meet? Many demands can be made from owners, managers, employees, customers, suppliers, creditors, trade unions, government, local authorities, charitable institutions and possibly other competitors.

Apart from bringing an ethical dimension into the debate, this stakeholder vision can be used by management to ward off potential threats – both from within and from outside.

The *competing values* approach takes the view further. The goals of the stakeholders may differ: the customer may want quality but management insist on cheap goods and high volume to keep down the price, etc. The competing value systems can rip managerial effectiveness apart.

Source:
[1] Adapted from Robbins, S.P., *Organization Theory, Structure Design and Applications* (Prentice Hall, Englewood Cliffs, NJ, 1987).

Another key writer on effectiveness was Reddin (1970) who developed what he called a 3-D approach to management effectiveness based on how well a manager integrated his/her approach to managing tasks and relationships. Following on from Drucker (1954), Reddin distinguishes 'efficient' managers from 'effective' managers in the areas outlined in Box ESD1.12.

BOX ESD1.12

Efficiency versus effectiveness[1]

Efficiency		Effectiveness
Do things right	rather than	Do the right things
Solve problems	rather than	Produce creative alternatives
Safeguard resources	rather than	Optimize resource utilization
Follow duties	rather than	Obtain results
Lower costs	rather than	Increase profit

Source:
[1] Adapted from Reddin, W., *Managerial Effectiveness* (McGraw Hill, London, 1970).

Reddin also warned that true managerial effectiveness (achievement of results) should be distinguished from apparent effectiveness and personal effectiveness. An example of what he considered 'apparent' effectiveness might be a manager who has a tidy desk – this does not necessarily mean he is going to be effective in terms of achieving results. He also warned against 'personal' effectiveness – 'satisfying personal objectives rather than the objectives of the organization'. This reflects the predominant view of the 1970s and to some extent the 1980s – where effectiveness was synonymous with achieving results for the business and had nothing to do with one's own personal agenda. We develop task effectiveness in ESD Unit Three.

An alternative role analysis, rather than a functional analysis, by Mintzberg (1989), demonstrated that results were not necessarily achieved in a cold rational and planned manner. The individual manager contributed to the concept of effectiveness as well. We develop some of these personal effectiveness ideas in ESD Unit Two. In the interim, please tackle Activity ESD1.5.

ACTIVITY ESD1.5

ORGANIZATIONAL AND MANAGERIAL EFFECTIVENESS

Activity code

✓ Self-development

✓ Teamwork

✓ Communications

☐ Numeracy/IT

✓ Decisions

Task

From an organization of your (or your group's) choice, outline some characteristics both of organization and of management which could be used to audit the effectiveness of the firm. This should include a goal orientation taking into account the needs of stakeholders, the organization and of management.

The MCI approach

The Management Charter Initiative (MCI) drew up UK standards of managerial performance. Measurable task competences and personal competencies are inherent in the MCI scheme.

We develop task effectiveness and competence in great detail in ESD Unit Three, and so we shall stay with personal effectiveness at this stage.

To the MCI there are four clusters of 'personal effectiveness':

■ Planning to achieve results

■ Managing others

- Managing oneself
- Using one's intellect.

Subsequently, the Department of Employment has simplified the dimensions so that they form a generic model of personal effectiveness which anyone can use. We have adapted their model and shown how it (and the MCI model) can be used by an individual to plan how they make most effective use of their own capacity. Consider Box ESD1.13 and complete Activity ESD1.16. We then turn to a real case study example.

BOX ESD1.13

Personal effectiveness within an organization

Context
Making the most of what is done

- Making things better
- Deciding what needs to be done
- Matching outcome with plan

Interpersonal
Involving other people

- Identifying and responding to the needs of others
- Getting on with others
- Getting people to work together
- Getting other people to see you in a positive way

Self

Matching awareness of self and own capabilities with opportunities for development within the particular context within which learning is taking place

Personal qualities
Managing yourself to get best results

- Showing sense of purpose
- Dealing with emotions/pressures
- Being responsible for own development

Knowledge/Competence
Using knowledge, skills and abilities to make the most of what is done

- Getting information and making sense of IT
- Choosing ideas and finding ways of using them
- Using situations
- Deciding on values and working within them

ACTIVITY ESD1.6

PLAN FOR YOUR OWN SELF-DEVELOPMENT

Activity code

☑ Self-development
☐ Teamwork
☑ Communications
☐ Numeracy/IT
☑ Decisions

Tasks

External factors

- What do you want to accomplish, to achieve?
- Why is it important to you to achieve this?
- What are your objectives?
- What will be the end result?
- How will you know when you have achieved it?
- How will you assess its success?
- How will your manager assess its success?
- How will the organization assess its success?
- What resources are you going to need to achieve your goal?
- How will you obtain them?
- Whose support do you need?
- How will you get it?
- When will project be accomplished?

Internal factors

Which qualities listed in Box ESD1.13 will you need to achieve your goal?

A case study

One of the authors was invited by a national catering company to design a development programme for selected senior managers who were to be the directors of the future. It was proposed that the most appropriate way to run the programme would be through individual self-development projects. The projects were to be agreed with each manager and their boss – but the programme had a strategic focus in that the organization as a whole also needed to approve and recognize the skills that were being developed.

We have used examples of forms and procedures that were used in the programme to illustrate how self-development can be facilitated within the context of one organization and the kind of management and organization commitment that is needed to make it a success.

The first stage was for the facilitator to meet with the Board to agree the shape of the programme and the kind of commitment and support that would be needed. Right from the outset the facilitator suggested that the programme should be determined by the kind of competences directors of the future needed in order to be effective in the future. It was further suggested that the candidates selected for the programme should work together to find out for themselves the key competences for effective, future directors; then, with outside guidance, each manager should agree on an individual development programme to enable him/her to demonstrate evidence of these competences. It was further suggested that the managers should be encouraged to compare these competences with those required by MCI to obtain an NVQ in management (Level II).

All this was agreed and the outline of the four stages in the programme is summarized in Box ESD1.14.

BOX ESD1.14

Proposed sequence for senior manager development programme (SMDP)

Time required – one day

Stage 1   Establishing the framework

Group meeting of SMDP
participants

1 Introducing the group to the concept of job competences and their application to management (MCI)

2 Establishing their relevance to the role of Senior Manager in company

3 Arriving at an overall picture of the Senior Manager role (e.g. Operations Director) through functional analysis

4 Making arrangements to interview Senior Managers to amend the model arrived at in (3) against the managers' perception of their role now and in the future and personal competencies required to be effective

Interviews with individual Senior Managers	SMDP participants interview managers in pairs and write up findings
Group meeting	1 Comparing findings and agreeing a common framework that describes the occupational competences and individual competencies required to be effective as a Senior Manager in the company
	2 Arranging individual interviews with tutor

Stage 2   Identifying management development needs

Individual interviews with tutor	1 Prior to interview, SMDP participant assessing own strengths and development needs against the common framework of competencies/competences agreed at the end of Stage 1
	2 At interview confirming competencies/competences which can already be demonstrated plus those that still need to be practised to meet requirements of a future senior management role
	4 Agreeing the outline of practical project which will enable participant to demonstrate competencies/competences required
Follow-up interviews between tutor and participants' superiors	Enabling Senior Managers to comment on the development plan agreed with their staff and modify nature of projects to fit operational priorities

Stage 3   Integrating individual development programmes with company objectives

| Senior Manager Group meeting | MD and Senior Management Team endorse individual development projects and internal mentor support needed (after having modified projects as necessary in line with company priorities) |

Stage 4   Implementation of projects and recognition of outcome

Individual work on designated projects	Supported by internal and external mentors as appropriate
Presentation of findings	Outcome of project and evidence collected to be presented to Board and action agreed as appropriate
Recognition of competencies/ competences	Documentation to be accumulated for assessment against MCI competencies/competences to enable NVQ accreditation to take place if appropriate/required

At the initial meeting emphasis was placed on the need to integrate the individual project with company objectives and to report back the outcomes of the project not only to the individual manager's own superior but to the Board as a whole. In this way the company was endorsing the importance given to the projects and individual and organisation effectiveness became as one. To ensure this integration was achieved, a management learning contract was drawn up for each candidate on the programme which covered the areas noted in Box ESD1.15.

BOX ESD1.15

Management learning contract

Name: Mentor:
Commencement date: Planned completion date:

1 Goal   What is the project all about? What is it meant to achieve?

2 Personal objectives   What do you hope to get out of it? In particular, what specific knowledge, skills do you hope to gain?

3 Resources   What resources will you need to achieve your objectives (books, reports, people)?

4 Activities   How are you going to achieve your objectives? What tasks, exercises will be involved?

5 Assessment   What evidence will you show to demonstrate what you have learned through this project? What criteria will the company use to assess the outcome of the project?

6 Verification   How will the company/outside Awarding Body verify that evidence is satisfactory?

7 Company recognition   How will the company recognize and put a corporate value on the outcome, findings from this project (e.g. presence of MD at presentation, change of procedure, dissemination of results)?

Having secured the commitment of the MD and the company Board, a one day workshop was arranged for all the participants to attend at which they were introduced to the concept of competence, as defined by analysis (see ESD Unit Three) and competencies (see ESD Unit Two) which identified the kind of characteristics a manager needed to be effective (see Woodruffe, 1991). One way of achieving this is through a technique called 'repertory grid' which is based on the concept of 'personal constructs' (see Kelly, 1955). The idea is that each of us 'construes' the world in a unique way but we are usually not aware of it until forced in some way to articulate it. Kelly (1955) proposed a technique by which we each compare different events, situations, people and are forced to make connections.

The facilitator of the Senior Management Development programme used this approach to encourage the participants to clarify how they construed effectiveness in their company's directors (a position to which they aspired). They were asked to compare three directors and describe in what ways two of them were the same and in what ways they were significantly different from the third. For example two might be perceived as 'receptive to change' which makes them different from the third who is 'set in his ways'. They then compared a different group of three and so on until they derived a list of what are called 'bi-polar' characteristics – examples of which can be seen in Box ESD1.16. In this way they were able to build up a profile of an 'effective' director.

In Box ESD1.16, is an extract from the profile drawn up by the team of what they considered were the competences and competencies of an effective director. They begin with what is the purpose of a director in their company (which is where a functional analysis of any job begins). They then identify the key functions that a director needs to master to achieve this purpose and then break down what kind of evidence would need to be demonstrated to show that this function was being directed effectively. Finally there are examples of underpinning competencies expressed as poles on a scale.

BOX ESD1.16

Towards competence

Competence profile

1 Purpose of job:
   to manage resources effectively in order to achieve company and group strategic objectives by implementing and influencing company policy
2 Key functions:
   Finance   People   Quality
3 Breakdown of FUNCTIONS to identify what evidence would need to be collected to demonstrate that functions were being effectively achieved and what is it that a Director uniquely does to bring this about

Function	Evidence of success	Director's unique contribution to make this happen
Finance	■ Cost to income ratios	■ Makes decisions
	■ Actual operating costs	■ Controls
	■ Average contract value	■ Takes corrective action
	■ Loss values	■ Allocates resources
	■ Net gains	
	■ Merchandizing targets	
	■ Budgets achieved	

> 4 Examples of competencies, traits against which the effectiveness of a Director would be assessed – effectiveness would tend to be associated with one pole rather than another – are shown below:
>
> | | | |
> |---|---|---|
> | Friendly/approachable | _____ | Distant |
> | Dependable/Trustworthy | _____ | Less dependable |
> | Humorous | _____ | Serious |
> | Listener | _____ | Self-opinionated |
> | Responsive | _____ | Low reactor/Unreadable |
> | Receptive to change | _____ | Set in ways |
> | Influential/Persuasive | _____ | Less convincing |
> | Proactive/Risk-taker/Opportunist | _____ | Cautious |

Having arrived at a group view of what they think a director should be doing and how they should behave to demonstrate effectiveness, the next stage is for the group to test this out by interviewing current directors and reviewing their profile (which is done at a subsequent group meeting).

What has been achieved is a corporate view of effectiveness. The next stage is for each manager to assess themselves against this profile and agree an individual development plan which will identify the competencies/competences each needs to acquire and how this might be achieved. It was also used as an opportunity for each manager to match these competencies/competences against the national standards as laid down by MCI (1991). The plan was put together at individual sessions between each manager and the facilitator. An example of one such plan is given in Box ESD1.17.

BOX ESD1.17

John's plan

---

1 Present position: Quality Control Manager
2 Position to which aspires: Operations Director role which incorporates responsibility for quality/Senior manager position with specific responsibility for quality
3 Areas of strength:

   (i)   Adaptable
   (ii) Capable of reading/analysing situations

    (iii) Very thorough
    (iv) Plans effectively/sets objectives
    (v) Capacity for seeing opportunities for change/application of new ideas
    (vi) People-oriented

4 Areas for development:

    (i)   Ability to 'sell' an idea, not just 'present' it
    (ii) Gain 'authority' for ideas/credibility within company overall
    (iii) Sense of what is 'realizable' and 'manageable'

5 MCI (Level II) competences:
Capable of demonstrating many of competences on basis of records of achievement kept when an Area Manager. Competences still needing to be demonstrated (or difficult to demonstrate in context of current job):

    4.1   Justification of expenditure
    5.1–5.3   Recruiting and selecting personnel

6 John needs a project which will:

    (i)   draw on experience and strengths
    (ii)   cover areas for development (see para 4 above)
    (iii) provide opportunities to get accreditation against MCI competencies/competences
    (iv) be of benefit to the profit centre.

BS5750 is a key issue for the company at present; an equally important issue is how the company can use this initiative in a strategic and proactive way to add value to its operations. How can accountability for quality be built into Operations and what are the organizational and resource implications? Given John's background in both Operations and as a Quality Control Manager, it is suggested the project be a vehicle for answering these kind of questions and at the same time for providing him with the means of testing out these ideas with colleagues within his profit centre.
In order to do this he will need to:

    (i)   liaise with colleagues and sell his proposals
    (ii)   demonstrate how a range of initiatives that company is currently undertaking (BS5750, quality self-assessment, client expectations, meetings, competencies/competences for all levels of staff) can be integrated within an overall 'quality' strategy
    (iii) identify the kind of savings/benefits that the profit centre should expect from implementing a quality approach throughout all units.

Consequences of this project will be:

    (i)   tangible and demonstrable operational and financial benefits from following a quality strategy
    (ii)   the opportunity for John to demonstrate the viability of a role within the profit centre which can integrate the quality control and operational functions
    (iii) selling the idea to MD and other companies/getting project report widely debated (i.e. outside John's own department).

In preparing the project report for presentation (both verbal and written) it is suggested that John gets individual tuition/feedback on how to:

(i)   present the report verbally to best effect to maximize the benefits
(ii) write it in such a way as to focus on the key objectives and how they can best be achieved.

Once this has been agreed with each candidate this plan would be discussed with the person's manager as a result of which there might well be revisions and additions to bring it into line with corporate objectives and targets. Then a contract would be drawn up which would agree the resources that the company would provide to support the project and how the outcome would be recognized. In this way both personal and organizational needs can fuse. Please tackle Activity ESD1.7 before moving away from this case study.

ACTIVITY ESD1.7

YOUR PLAN

Activity code

✓ Self-development
  Teamwork
  Communications
  Numeracy/IT
  Decisions

Tasks

Identify a senior management position in an organization which you would like to attain in the future.

1 Produce an 'effective competence/competency profile by describing:
  (a) the purpose of this position (i.e. how it contributes to the organization's goals)
  (b) the key functions that need to be covered to achieve this purpose
  (c) evidence of what needs to be done to achieve these functions
  (d) underpinning traits that characterize effectiveness in this role (expressed as a point of a bi-polar scale).

2 Assess yourself against this profile and draw up a personal plan like the one in Box ESD1.17 as to what kind of project you might take on that will give you the opportunity to demonstrate competences/competencies required to be seen to be effective in this job.
3 Draw up a contract for yourself which addresses the questions as listed in the contract in Box ESD1.17.

Organizational effectiveness – the approach of the series

How do we view effectiveness in this book and in this series?

First of all a managerial perspective is taken. This does not mean that other stakeholders are ignored – quite the reverse actually – but the lynchpin is management.

Secondly, effectiveness means bringing things about, a results orientation perhaps more than a means orientation. Of course there is an interaction between ends and means and the 'means justifying the ends' argument has been used from Machiavelli to Stalin. We add an ethical dimension to the attainment of goals.

These goals tend to be financial or economic. Businesses are run primarily for the economic gain of the owners – they tend not to be social clubs run for the common weal.

Yet if we do not take account of the needs and aspirations of others with a stake in the business, we can quickly or slowly perish. Flouting government legislation, ignoring customer needs, making undue demands on suppliers and not paying them or creditors promptly, ignoring environmentalists by pumping rubbish and waste into the countryside, engaging in unnecessary price wars with competitors, derecognizing unions and treating the labour force as machines will all result in breakdown. Hence there are social goals as well. Whether we like it or not these social goals tend to be subordinate to economic ends for the organization. They ought to be on par with economic goals for without them or through some deliberate flouting of them or by ignoring them, the economic vision may not be met. This is apart from any arguments on social responsibility of business – which cannot be ignored. The business reality is that economic goals dominate – often at the expense of social goals. We need to blend these goals together.

What of the systems perspective? Is this merely efficiency for goal attainment? To some extent this is correct. How we get there – the structure and the processes of action – is important but the goal orientation is the key. It is nice to know that you played well but if you did not win, the game itself could loose some of its edge. So the efficiency or effectiveness of getting there is important but it is subordinate to the outcomes. Again it is not goal attainment at any price. Social/ethical considerations should be guiding our systems perspective as well as our view of goal attainment.

Managerial effectiveness – the approach of the series

The introduction to the book gives an overview of the aspect of effectiveness being used in the series. Some elaboration may be useful.

Manager effectiveness is seen to revolve around an action orientation, a capacity for learning and a self-awareness which lends itself to a self-developmental vision.

There are common or generic skills which must be mastered:

- self development

- teamwork

- communications

- numeracy

- problem solving.

The effective manager needs an awareness and understanding of the main functions of management linked to an appreciation of business policy. This impacts on the knowledge and skills base of:

- enterprise/operations

- people

- finance/accounting

- marketing/sales.

The actual job itself revolves around the implementation of policy, task, people and function. (This has been developed from Anderson Associates Personnel and Management Advisors (AAMPA), 7 Water Lane, Melbourn, Cambs, SG8 6AY, England.) An attitude based on enterprise and business awareness alongside a generalist perspective needs to pervade the skills and knowledge of management (see Anderson, 1995). Finally an awareness of opportunities and constraints from the organization and its environment complete the picture. We return to this idea in the last pages of ESD Unit Six.

E. Effectiveness and self-development – the approach of the book

In line with the views of the series there is seen to be task and people elements impacting on effectiveness.

- Unit Two looks at the personal aspects of competencies and individual effectiveness.

- Unit Three moves to the task or job aspects, competences and job competences.

- Unit Four considers various approaches to learning to harness these personal and task elements.

- Unit Five relates self-development both to organizational support systems and resources.

- Unit Six looks to the future and to change and fuses the work to date.

Bibliography

Adlam, R. and Plumridge, M., 'Organisational effectiveness and self development: the essential dimension' in Pedler, M., Burgoyne, J., Boydell, T. and Welshman, G., *Self Development in Organisations* (McGraw-Hill, London, 1990).

Anderson, A.H., *Successful Training Practice* (Blackwell, Oxford, 1993).

Anderson, A.H., *Effective Personnel Management* (Blackwell, Oxford, 1994).

Anderson, A.H., *Effective General Management* (Blackwell, Oxford, 1995).

Blanchard, K. and Johnson, S., *The One Minute Manager* (Fontana, London, 1983).

Blanchard, K. and Zigarmi, D., *Leadership and the One Minute Manager* (Fontana, London, 1987).

Braverman, H., *Labour and Monopoly Capital* (Monthly Review Press, New York, 1974).

Burgoyne, J.G. Boydell, T. and Pedler, M. *Self Development: Theory and application for practitioners* (Association of Teachers of Management, London, 1978).

Burgoyne, J.G. and Stuart, R., 'The nature, use and acquisition of managerial skills and other attributes', *Personnel Review*, **5**, (1976), pp. 19–29.

Cameron, K., 'Critical questions in assessing organisational effectiveness', *Organisational Dynamics* (Autumn, 1980), pp. 66–80.

Drucker, P.F., *The Practice of Management* (Harper & Row, New York, 1954).

Garratt, B., *Learning to Lead: Developing your organisation and yourself* (Fontana, London, 1991).

Handy, C., *The Making of Managers* (MSC/NEDO/BIM, London, 1987).

Handy, C., *The Age of Unreason* (Hutchinson, London, 1989).

Heron, J., *Catharsis in Human Development* (Human Potential Research Group, University of Surrey, 1977).

Jacobs, R., *Assessing Management Competences* (Ashridge Management Research Group, Berkhampstead, 1989).

Kelly, G.A., *The Psychology of Personal Constructs* (Norton, New York, 1955).

Kolb, D.A., *Experimental Learning* (Prentice Hall, New York, 1982).

Kolb, D.A., Rubin, J.M. and McIntyre, J.M., *Organisational Psychology*, 4th edn, (Prentice Hall, Englewood Cliffs, NJ, 1984).

Livy, B., *Corporate Personnel Management* (Pitman, London, 1988).

MCI, *Middle Management Dynamics* (MCI, London, 1991).

Mintzberg, H., 'The manager's job: folklore and fact', *Harvard Business Review*, (July/August, 1975). Reprinted in H. Mintzberg, *Mintzberg on Management* (The Free Press, New York, 1989).

Pedler, M. and Boydell, T., *Managing Yourself* (Fontana, London, 1985).

Pedler, M., Burgoyne, J. and Boydell, T., *A Manager's Guide to Self Development* (McGraw-Hill, London, 1993).

Reddin, W., *Managerial Effectiveness* (McGraw-Hill, London, 1970).

Reeves, T., *Managing Effectively – Developing yourself through experience* (Butterworth & Heinemann, London, 1994).

Taylor, F.W., *Principles of Scientific Management* (Harper & Row, New York, 1911).

Willie, E., 'Should management development be just for managers?' *Personnel Management* (August, 1990).

Woodruffe, C., 'Competent by any other name', *Personnel Management*, (September, 1991).

Zuboff, S., *In the Age of the Smart Machine: The Future of Work and Power* (Heinemann, Oxford, 1988).

ESD Unit Two

Competencies and Personal Effectiveness

Learning Objectives

After completing this unit you should be able to:

- determine the parameters of personal (non task) effectiveness;
- outline key traits or qualities of such effectiveness;
- note the importance of career anchors and of value systems for such effectiveness;
- conduct a self-analysis;
- classify and construct personal competencies;
- construct a personal development plan; and
- apply the generic skills of the series.

Contents

A. Overview

B. Individual Differences and Effectiveness: A Sociological Perspective

C. Individual Differences and Effectiveness: A Psychological Perspective

- ▶ Personality

- ▶ Qualities

- ▶ Psychological types

- ▶ Perception

- ▶ Attitudes, beliefs and values

- ▶ Motivation

- ▶ Self-efficacy

- ▶ Learning

D. Personal Effectiveness in a Group Setting

E. Personal Effectiveness in an Organizational Setting

- ▶ Communications

- ▶ Career anchors

- ▶ Ethical responsibilities

- ▶ A question of 'fit'

F. Personal Effectiveness and Competencies

G. Conclusion

ESD Unit Two

" Some years ago I watched an interview of a woman who described her success in life as being due to her mother having given her the confidence to be herself as a child. The phrase 'confidence to be herself' struck me then, and now, as being a gift from which we would all benefit. "

(Townsend, 1991)

A. Overview

This unit is concerned with personal effectiveness. So often, personal and task effectiveness are fused together. This can inhibit analysis – though in reality they should fuse of course. Here we are concerned with personal effectiveness although at the end of the unit we move towards competencies which are behaviours which include a personal element as well as degrees of skill and knowledge. Consistent with the approach of the series we have focused the skills and knowledge aspects on the task element of the job (ESD Unit Three).

Although we deal with personal attributes of effectiveness, a shopping list of super human qualities or traits must be avoided.

Instead, we need to examine features of individual differences which may impact on this effectiveness in the context of the group and of the organization as a whole.

Consequently we examine key attributes making for individual difference which we believe are important underpinnings of our goal and process orientation. Behaviours rather than personality traits are seen to be more important in our analysis – but perhaps these behaviours are linked to 'qualities' within the individual.

Certainly these behaviours emanate from the individual and the concept of self-efficacy is seen to be very important to our analysis.

Behaviour does not occur in vacuum and we need to relate such effective behaviour to interaction in groups and the organization. Effective personal behaviour must have a context and indeed the debate exists over universal effective behaviours which transmit over frontiers and context-related effectiveness which moves more towards a contingency perspective. We

43

consider personal effectiveness in both group and organizational settings by pursuing a number of themes.

The current debate on competencies is touched upon at the end of the unit and the series view is related to the main arguments in this discussion on competencies before we look forward to task effectiveness and competence.

B. Individual Differences and Effectiveness: A Sociological Perspective

Individual differences tend to be explained through some psychological analysis and we will touch briefly on some of these themes in the next section. (See Anderson and Kyprianou, 1994, for a fuller treatment of this topic.) At the same time we should not neglect sociological influences such as:

- gender
- social stratification
- power structures
- educational system
- leisure and work
- the family.

The sociological features impact on the personal or 'internal' psychological factors. These features form our past life experiences and add to our life script for the future. Some brief examples will suffice as the psychological factors may have a more direct impact on our working effectiveness – or at least the psychological factors may be easier for us to 'manage' compared to these wider sociological features.

Yet these sociological factors can prove to be constraints and opportunities for individual effectiveness. Some sociological examples of features which may impact on individual effectiveness in the context of the wider society could include the following.

- Gender can impact on career routes. Entrepreneurship can be cited. Proportionately there are far fewer women entering the entrepreneurs ranks than men (see Anderson and Woodcock, 1996).

- Social stratification can give us our 'world views' of work. Goldthorpe *et al.*, (1969) for instance, compare the 'them and us' traditional working class perspective and the various strata seen by a middle class view of the world.

- Power structures can make for self-perpetuating elites with some limited recruitment of new blood or a more pluralistic society can open opportunity for those of merit and ability. The work of Lupton and Wilson (1973) emphasizes the close kinship and marital ties of senior managers and high ranking officials in various organizations.

- The educational system according to Bourdieu and de Saint-Martin (1974), is very much tied into the prevailing culture. Indeed education can mean wealth and power and so is linked to some 'cultural capital'. Meaning comes from above and educational success has to replicate that imposed perspective – according to this school of thought.

- Leisure and work are also relevant. For example, Child and Macmillan (1973) sampled UK managers and the results showed a clear division in their minds between leisure and work: leisure was not seen as an extension of work by some 98 per cent of the 964 sample.

- The family may act as the stabilizer of society. To Talcott Parsons (1959), for example, the family forms the primary socialization agent of the child. The family can provide the security, the safety net and the mutual support network for the individual child and for the parent.

These examples have attempted to show that individual behaviour at work and hence individual effectiveness at work can be influenced by wider – perhaps more deeper – aspects of our life script which may be difficult to alter. The psychological features may give us more scope to change behaviour.

Now try Activity ESD2.1 to relate these ideas to your own experience.

ACTIVITY ESD2.1

A LESSON FROM THE PAST

Activity code

✓ Self-development

☐ Teamwork

✓ Communications

☐ Numeracy/IT

✓ Decisions

Task

Using some of these sociological headings in the text you may wish to reflect on your life script or experiences to date and to isolate the constraints and opportunities that you have encountered.

Feature	Example of the feature	Opportunity/Constraint

C. Individual Differences and Effectiveness: A Psychological Perspective

As in the sociological area, the psychological features impacting on personal effectiveness can be relevant both to the individual manager's self-development and to the process of how he/she manages staff. We shall focus on the self-developmental aspect in line with the theme of the book.

Some of these differences include:

- personality
- qualities
- psychological types
- perception
- attitudes, beliefs and values
- motivation
- self-efficacy
- learning

Personality

The problem with personality is akin to the act of peeling an onion: every time you remove one layer there is another layer underneath and it may end in tears. Personality can be seen as an individual's mental 'make up' allied to the processes of how they behave. In our case the behaviour may be easier to track and to change than the individual's unique adjustment to the outside world. It is an important concept to self-understanding and awareness and to interaction with others. (According to Bayne, 1989, there are two types of self-awareness: *inner* - awareness of one's own thoughts, feelings and reactions - and *external* - awareness of one's own behaviour and its impact on others.)

However the concept of personality is difficult to pin down. Much of the early work of psychologists focuses on 'abnormal' personalities with attempts to establish a comprehensive theory. We seem to have moved on to 'normal' personalities now and the ambitious comprehensiveness has given way to more of a piecemeal approach. The role of nature: nurture, biology versus experience, uniqueness versus universal learning processes, a holistic vision of the self versus traits and an unconscious drive versus a total awareness by the individual are all issues inherent in this complex idea of personality.

So far as our needs are concerned, trait theory seems to dominate much of the managerial application of personality theories. Clearly this ignores other approaches, from the Freudian psychodynamic theories (Freud, 1960) to the social learning themes of Dollard and Miller (1950) right back to the phenomenological visions of the likes of Allport (1937). Hence the trait approach can be criticized from the perspective of the other theories.

Yet the trait approach with its facility of breaking down personality into units as well as having a facility of being quantified and measured ensures its popularity in some circles.

Eysenck (1960) investigated a large number of people and identified two major dimensions on which personality can vary, producing the four personality types:

extroversion – introversion
neuroticism – stability.

His theory is based on genetics through our physiology. For example, stability is associated with those aspects of the human nervous system which control the heart, body temperature and digestion. Extroverts need high levels of stimulation to attract and maintain their interest and this may also be related to neurophysiology. Thus according to Eysenck, personality is determined by genetic and biological factors rather than by the environment and culture.

Consider Box ESD2.1.

BOX ESD2.1

Personality traits

Eysenck[1] uses the following trait classification.

Active	Expressive
Impulsive	Irresponsible
Practical	Risk taking
Social	Autonomous
Calm	Casual
Free from guilt	Happy
Healthy	High self-esteem

Source:
[1] Adapted from Eysenck, H.J., *The Structure of Human Personality* (Methuen, London, 1960).

Cattell (1965) used three sources for his personality data – life record data, self-rating questionnaires and test data. He then factor analysed the data and identified 16 personality factors (16PF). These can be used to describe a person and Cattell believes environmental factors are involved.

Please see Box ESD2.2 and then complete Activity ESD2.2.

BOX ESD2.2

Personality factors

Cattell[1] uses the following traits to analyse personality.

Outgoing	Intelligent
Emotionally stable	Dominant
Optimistic	Conscientious
Adventurous	Tender minded
Suspicious	Imaginative
Shrewd	Insecure
Radical	Self-sufficient
Controlled	Tense, Frustrated

Source:
[1] Adapted from Cattell, R.B., '*The Scientific Analysis of Personality*' (Penguin, Baltimore, 1965).

ACTIVITY ESD2.2

YOUR PERSONALITY PROFILE

Activity code

✓ Self-development
   Teamwork
✓ Communications
   Numeracy/IT
✓ Decisions

Task

Using the attached list of traits, draft your personality profile.

- friendly
- confident
- creative
- clean living
- intellectual
- unaccountable
- down-to-earth
- hopeful
- influential
- stable
- untrusting
- thoughtful
- relaxed
- caring
- independent
- calculating
- easily pleased

Qualities

The trait approach has been captured by some adherents of 'effective qualities' of managers. These supertraits or qualities can be seen in a host of appraisal systems. For example, one major US banking institution which will remain anonymous, has headings such as: 'industry', 'energy', 'self-reliance', 'ingenuity', 'willingness', 'courtesy', 'tact' and 'acceptability'.

The potential problem with these qualities is that they become like the leadership traits, akin to 'The Great Man' theory of leadership. The traits can become discredited from being associated with a Corporate Superman. Further the trait theory of leadership has become untenable – and so perhaps the traits/quality theory of management will follow (see Stodgill, 1948).

'Qualities' are dominant however in many circles and are often derived from assessment centres which use a range of psychometric tests and behavioural anchor scales. (See Stevens, 1985 who examines three live cases in seeking qualities.) Please see Box ESD2.3.

BOX ESD2.3

Personal qualities

Burgoyne *et al.*,[1] put forward the following personal qualities of an effective manager:

- sensitivity to events
- mental agility
- emotional resilience
- creativity
- proactivity
- self-knowledge.

Source:
[1] Adapted from Burgoyne, J.G., Boydell, T. and Pedler, M., *Self Development: Theory and Applications for Practitioners* (Association of Teachers of Management, London, 1978).

Psychological types

Jung (1968) saw psychological typing as a way of helping people understand themselves and others. It is very useful for self-developmental purposes.

The theory identifies 16 types of people with different combinations of strengths. The types are based on four pairs of personal preferences which may or may not be expressed in behaviour, namely:

introversion (I)   –   extroversion (E)
sensing (S)   –   intuition (I)
thinking (T)   –   feeling (F)
judging (J)   –   perceiving (P)

The theory implies that people are more comfortable with one of each pair of preferences and so a person can be described as ESFP or any one of the other 15 combinations. The descriptions of the types take the interactions between the preferences into account. For example, the T in one type ESTP plays a different role to the T in ESTJ even though they do have something in common.

Certain aspects of management will be easier for some types than others. Therefore, it will be an asset to know one's own type and that of colleagues. For instance, the stereotype of an extrovert or introvert may be getting in the way of a personal relationship with a colleague. Now tackle Activity ESD2.3.

ACTIVITY ESD2.3

TYPES

Activity code

✓ Self-development
☐ Teamwork
☐ Communications
☐ Numeracy/IT
✓ Decisions

Jung[1] identified two of the pairs of personal preferences which are associated with information gathering and evaluation. These are:

sensing – intuition
thinking – feeling

	Thinking	Thinking	Intuition
Information evaluation method		Thinking Sensing	Intuition Thinking
		— BALANCE —	
	Feeling	Sensing Feeling	Intuition Feeling
		Sensing	Intuition

Information gathering method

Managers usually prefer one way of gathering information and one way of evaluating information. Therefore if you can identify these preferences in yourself or in another person, you will have a useful tool.

Sensing – would rather work with facts than possibilities
Intuition – would rather look for possibilities than work with facts
Thinking – evaluation based on analysis and logic and not on personal values
Feeling – evaluation based on personal values and not on analysis and logic

Task

Identify your personal preferences for gathering and evaluating information.

Search the literature for descriptions of successful executives and try to identify their personal preferences for gathering and evaluating information.

In what ways do the personal preferences influence the way the executive runs the organization?

Identify the personal preferences of colleagues or other managers in your organization.

Source:
[1] Adapted from Jung, C.G., *Analytical Psychology: Its Theory and Practice* (Routledge Keagan and Paul, London, 1968).

Briggs-Myers (1987) developed this theory into a questionnaire which is often used as a management tool for career development and is useful for self-analysis and development. (See also Hirsch and Kummerow, 1990.)

The various types are shown Box ESD2.4.

BOX ESD2.4

Psychological types

There are four areas and eight dimensions.[1]

Area	Dimensions	
Where do you direct your judgement and perception?	**Extrovert** Outer world and things dominate	**Introvert** Inner world and ideas dominate
Which type of perception do you rely on?	**Sensing** Detail, facts, concrete things preferred	**Intuition** Ideas, more imaginative possibilities preferred
How do you go about making judgements?	**Thinking** Logical rational perspective is employed	**Feeling** More subjective non-rational method is used
What is your dominant judgemental process?	**Judging** Clarity order and conclusions preferred	**Perceiving** Open 'endedness' preferred and ambiguity tolerated

Source:
[1] Adapted from Briggs-Myers, I., *Introduction to Type* (Oxford Psychologist's Press, Oxford, 1987).

Certainly you need to know what causes behaviour. Such knowledge of ourselves and others can highlight our weaknesses and our strengths. It may allow us to realize our potential and it can certainly give us a feel for what can and cannot be changed. Perhaps it can even allow us to predict things! Yet this brief review of personality – whatever its importance in its own right – is not sufficient to explain our personal effectiveness. We need to turn to additional individual differences.

Perception

The 'types' used in the last section move from pure personality to levels of judgement and perception. We shall pursue perception at this stage and come back to judgements under person perception.

To Mitchell (1982), perception is concerned with 'those factors that shape and produce what we actually experience'.

Perception is the process of taking information from the environment, making sense of it and responding to it. Perception involves an awareness and interpretation of the world in which we live. As a result of this perception we respond in a particular way. Thus, perception underpins our attitudes, feelings, motivation and so directly influences our behaviour. See figure ESD2.1.

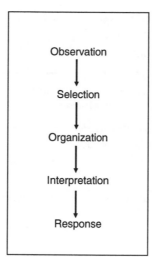

Figure ESD2.1   The perception process

Our observation of the world is based on our five senses:

■ Hearing

■ Sight

■ Smell

■ Taste

■ Touch

Then we select from the information available using external and internal filters to determine which will receive most attention.

External filters are:

- Size   The more intense (bright, loud, urgent) an external factor is, the more likely it is to be perceived.
- Contrast   Factors which stand out or are unexpected are more likely to be perceived.
- Motion   Moving factors are more likely to be perceived than stationary ones.
- Repetition   Repeated factors are more likely to be perceived than single ones.
- Novelty and familiarity   Familiar or novel factors in the environment are more easily perceived.

Any of these filters or any combination of them may effect perception at any time.

The more important of the internal filters which influence perception are:

- Learning
- Motivation
- Personality.

These are dealt with in more detail in other units.

Perceptual organization implies the grouping of environmental stimuli into recognizable patterns. Two principles influence our perceptual organization:

1   Figure ground principle – people tending to perceive those factors that stand out against the background; and
2   Perceptual grouping principle – the tendency to place stimuli into meaningful patterns using:
   - Continuity – the tendency to perceive continuous patterns in objects, behaviour, etc.;
   - Closure – the tendency to perceive a whole even though only a part of it can be seen;
   - Proximity – members of a group perceived as related because of their nearness to one another; and
   - Similarity – the more alike the objects, the greater the tendency to group them together.

The perception process we use for dealing with people also follows the above routine. For example, our perception of other people is determined largely by our own personality, values, attitudes, moods, past experiences, etc. At the same time we must also be aware of the situation or setting in which we perceive people. This is particularly important with regard to first impressions. Thus, our perceptions of people are more accurate when we:

- avoid generalizing from a single characteristic to a number of characteristics;
- do not assume that a particular behaviour will occur in all situations; and

- do not place too much reliance on physical appearance.

Our interpretation of the information we receive is subject to perceptual errors such as:

- a perceptual defence against ideas, objects or situations that are threatening;
- stereotyping by assigning attributes to a person solely on the basis of the category in which that person has been placed;
- a halo effect when we evaluate all aspects of a person on one impression either favourable or unfavourable (a blinding effect);
- projection where one's own traits tend to be seen in other people; and
- expectancy – the extent to which prior expectations bias the way in which events, objects and people are perceived.

Greater awareness of the factors which shape what you experience can only give greater insight into the organizational reality – or diverse organizational realities – around you.

In particular, person perception is very much a two-way process between the perceiver and the perceived. It may tell us more about the perceiver than the perceived. From first impressions through to an ongoing interaction and the selection of some cues from a vast array of information, people perception is fraught with difficulty. Yet as part of your self-development you need to be aware of how you go about perceiving external realities – including your own warts and all. This perception, as we have seen, can underpin your judgements based on your information gathering and analysis. As part of the process, how you go about perceiving things, events and people, is linked to your underlying attitudes, beliefs and values.

Attitudes, beliefs and values

Gahagan (1980) rightly distinguishes two approaches to the construct of an attitude – the 'latent process conception' whereby some variable operates within the individual to mediate observable behaviour, and 'a probability conception' whereby attitudes are based on external constraints based on consistencies of other people's behaviour. The former approach tends to dominate the literature and we apply it here.

Our attitudes grow out of our beliefs and develop as we live our lives. Some attitudes may turn into 'core attitudes' which are very resistant to change. Other attitudes, however, may change with our experience. Our beliefs tend to be based on 'what is' whereas our values are based on 'what should be'.

Gross (1987) believes that one can turn a belief into an attitude by adding a value statement about what is good, desirable, valuable or worthwhile. He says that a person can have thousands of beliefs, hundreds of attitudes but only a few dozen values.

Mullins (1993) believes that:

- Attitudes cannot be seen – they can only be inferred; and
- attitudes are often shared within organizations and as such are embodied in the culture of the organization.

The attitudes of managers can become part of the culture of an organization and this has implications for self-development. Core attitudes which are part of the organization culture may be very difficult to change and can be a barrier to development.

Tackle Activity ESD2.4 and then consult Box ESD2.5.

ACTIVITY ESD2.4

MANAGERIAL BELIEFS

Activity code

- ✓ Self-development
- ✓ Teamwork
- ☐ Communications
- ☐ Numeracy/IT
- ✓ Decisions

Task

From your experience to date, give a view on what sort of beliefs you would expect successful managers to hold.

Views

BOX ESD2.5

Beliefs and change

Real change or the possibility of even adapting to change, let alone anticipating environmental change, may well begin with changes in belief. Peters and Waterman identified seven beliefs held by successful managers:[1]

■ being the best

■ the importance of doing a job well

■ treating people as individuals

■ superior quality

■ people should be innovators and that, because of this, organizations should be willing to support failure

■ informality helps communication

■ the importance of growth and profits.

Peters and Waterman found that in successful companies managers focused on these beliefs and were able to get other people, down to the lowest levels, to share them. The strength of these beliefs and their validity, influence the success of the organization and individual managers.

Source:
[1] Adapted from Peters, T.J. and Waterman, R.H., *In Search of Excellence* (Harper & Row, New York, 1982).

Values are general, abstract ideas that guide our thinking and actions. They can be broadly classified as aesthetic, moral, religious and social. They are the basis of a set of attitudes about what is good or bad, desirable or undesirable. Values are behind the beliefs managers have about people and their organization. Managers' values are demonstrated by the actions they take, what they think, and how they allocate time, energy and skills. Starting about 1900, a manager's ethical and performance values have passed through several stages to reach those of the present day – profit maximizing, trusteeship, an emphasis on the quality of life and, perhaps, a more ethical approach. Waterman (1987) identified the following values/attitudes which he believed successful organizations require. They include the following:

- informed opportunism – keeping up to date to maintain strategic advantage;

- direction and 'empowerment' – identifying what needs to be done and allowing subordinates to find ways of doing it;

- friendly acts and congenial controls – using financial controls but giving managers freedom to be creative;

- a different mirror – gleaning ideas from a variety of sources – competitors, customers and employees;

- teamwork, trust, politics and power – accepting that fighting will occur but stressing teamwork and trust to get the work done;

- stability in motion – allowing rules to be broken when necessary;

- attitudes and attention – realizing that attention is more effective than exhortation and symbolic behaviour makes words come true; and

- causes and commitment – being aware of the grand cause so that it permeates the actions.

In successful organizations, effective managers may make values which become infectious. Values affect a person's thinking habits, the ways of relating to one another, the technology they use and the job descriptions, policies, procedures and rules they operate by.

Spranger (1928) identified six types of person based on the values they held.

- *Theoretical* Truth was dominant. The aim was to systematize knowledge – intellectuals, philosophers, scientists.

- *Aesthetic* Beauty and harmony in terms of fitness, grace and symmetry were important.

- *Social* Love, co-operation and humanism were reflected in kindness, sympathy and unselfishness.

- *Political* Power was dominant and this type is a characteristic of many leaders.

- *Religious* Unity was important together with belief, faith and the mystical.

- *Economic* Wealth, efficiency and practicality were important.

A manager does not necessarily behave as one type but has a profile of values which is characteristic for the manager. That is, certain value types are stronger than others for each manager. The strategies produced by managers tend to reflect their personal value profile. At the same time, the dominant value systems of an organization can be superimposed upon the personal value profile. Difficulties in reconciling both value systems can be quite stressful.

Please tackle Activity ESD2.5, then consult Box ESD2.6.

ACTIVITY ESD2.5

OPERATING VALUES

Activity code

✓ Self-development
✓ Teamwork
✓ Communications
☐ Numeracy/IT
✓ Decisions

There is a case for having operating values (rather than personal values) within a work organization.

Task

What sort of operating values would you expect a successful manager to have?

BOX ESD2.6

Values in operation

In contrast to these values which can be used to describe a person, Peters and Waterman[1] identified 8 operating values held and acted on by successful managers. They value:

- action – 'do it, try it, fix it' - with a view to gaining competitive advantage;
- customers, quality and service (customer needs and wants being seen as important);
- autonomy and innovation and being allowed a reasonable number of mistakes;
- people;
- actions which convey values to co-workers, customers and suppliers;
- underlying themes and a sense of direction;
- reducing bureaucracy and red tape; and
- flexibility, decentralization and an entrepreneurial spirit with sensible controls.

Source:
[1] Peters, T.J and Waterman, R.H., *In Search of Excellence* (Harper & Row, New York, 1982).

Peters and Waterman's (1982) operating values identify means rather than ends and can be used to satisfy Spranger's (1928) personal values.

Social values are an important part of an organization's external environment. For instance, the values associated with agrarian, industrial and post-industrial societies are different. Therefore managers should be aware of the values, both current and developing, in their society. Sometimes organizations deliberately incorporate the current social values into their strategies. For example, Volvo replaced their assembly lines by teams which built cars from start to finish in order to combat boredom.

All strategies are based on values and should be appropriate for the conditions, place and time in which the organization operates, i.e. values are not good or bad, but appropriate. Inappropriate values create products and services which customers will not pay for. However, more than one set of appropriate values can create a successful organization. Whether a strategy is successful or not depends on the values that underlie it and are part of an organization's culture. McDonald's core values are quality, service, cleanliness and value (QSCV) and these values are rewarded as part of its systems and procedures.

At this point it would be good to attempt Activity ESD2.6.

ACTIVITY ESD2.6

BELIEFS, VALUES AND ATTITUDES

Activity code

✓ Self-development
✓ Teamwork
☐ Communications
☐ Numeracy/IT
✓ Decisions

Task

1 Identify your own beliefs, attitudes and values.
2 Identify the beliefs, attitudes and values of your organization.
3 In what ways are they similar and in what ways are they different?
4 Explain why this is and, if necessary, what you can do about it.

Motivation

Organizations expect, if not demand, commitment. This commitment can often be one-sided though as labour, including management, can be sought after or discarded according to organizational whim.

Some degree of commitment to the flag is necessary but individuals also need some commitment to themselves. Self-motivation and the motivation of others are both linked to this degree of commitment.

We decided not to scan the many approaches to motivation preferring instead to utilize the interesting model of Huczynski and Buchanan (1991) in the first place and then to develop some ideas from McClelland's (1961) theories. Both approaches seem to emanate from personal effectiveness.

Huczynski and Buchanan look at motivation from three perspectives:

- personal goals
- mental processes
- social processes.

Most of us have reasons for the things that we do. Our personal goals such as achievement, friends, money, power and status are often given as the reasons for our behaviour. They motivate us. These needs can be divided into three groups:

- economic rewards – e.g. pay, fringe benefits, pensions, goods and security;
- intrinsic satisfaction – e.g. the nature of the work itself, interest in the job and personal growth and development; and
- social relationships – e.g. friendships, groupwork, desire for affiliation and status.

The dynamic relationship between these three sets of needs will determine our motivation, job satisfaction and performance.

Personal goals focus on what motivates us and these have been researched by:

- Maslow (1954) – hierarchy of needs model
- Alderfer (1972) – modified needs model
- Herzberg (1966) – two factor theory
- McClelland (1961) – achievement motivation theory.

Mental processes emphasize the process of motivation and major research has been done by:

- Vroom (1964) and Porter and Lawler (1968) – expectancy based models
- Adams (1963) – equity theory
- Locke (1967) – goal theory
- Heider (1958) and Kelly (1955) – attribution theory.

Social processes emphasize learning through our behaviour and major work has been done by:

- Bandura (1969) – social learning theory
- Barling and Beatty (1983) – self-efficacy
- Hamner (1977) – reinforcement theory.

We have been arguing that the key to personal effectiveness may be behaviour underpinned by some personal qualities, keen perception – particularly people perception and allied to core value systems. The behaviour of individuals can be seen from various perspectives in the next series of Boxes (ESD2.7, ESD2.8 and ESD2.9). We then move to a typology of motivational needs.

BOX ESD2.7

Causes of behaviour: the attribution process

This process sets out to determine the causes of our behaviour and that of other people. Heider[1] believes that it is caused by a combination of our perceived internal forces (abilities, effort, fatigue, etc.) and external forces (rules and policies, the boss's attitudes, etc.). Attributions answer the question of whether the behaviour is controlled largely by ourselves (internal) or by external factors. Causal attributions can be made either consciously or unconsciously depending on the situation.

The causes of behaviour are based on our:

- information about people and the situation (how it is organized and interpreted);
- attitudes, beliefs and values; and
- motivation.

Kelly[2] believes that in making attributions people use three criteria:

- Consensus   To what extent do others, when faced with the same situation, behave in the same way?
- Consistency   To what extent does the person behave in the same manner on other occasions when faced with the same situation?
- Distinctiveness   To what extent does the person act in the same manner in different situations?

According to Harvey and Weary[3] people have a tendency to make two fundamental attribution errors:

- by underestimating the impact of external or situational causes of behaviour; and
- by overestimating the impact of internal or personal causes of behaviour.

People generally attribute their own or others' successful completion of a task to internal factors such as ability and effort whereas failure is usually attributed to external factors such as task difficulty or luck. They accept responsibility for success but not for failure. This is called a self-serving bias and we should be aware of it both in ourselves and other people. In general internal factors tend to be more stable than external factors which are more unpredictable.

Source:
Adapted from
[1] Heider, F., *The Psychology of Interpersonal Relations* (Wiley, New York, 1958).
[2] Kelly, G.A., The Process of Causal Attribution
[3] Harvey, J.H. and Weary, E., 'Current Issues in Attribution Theory', *Annual Review of Psychology*, **35** pp. 431–2, (1984).

BOX ESD2.8

Consequences of behaviour: reinforcement theory (operant conditioning)

In contrast to the content and process approaches to motivation, which try to explain 'why' people do the things they do, reinforcement theory explains behaviour by means of the consequences of the behaviour itself. This theory relies on the concept of Thorndike[1] called the 'law of effect' which implies that behaviour with a pleasant or positive consequence is more likely to be repeated than behaviour having unpleasant or negative consequences. Behaviour modification is based on the techniques associated with reinforcement theory.

Four types of reinforcement help managers to influence behaviour in their employees. Two ways of increasing behaviour involve providing rewards and two ways of reducing behaviour involve removing rewards.

- *Positive Reinforcement* increases a desired behaviour by providing a pleasant reward for that behaviour in order to encourage, e.g. praise, more money, time off, etc. *Shaping* is the successive rewarding of behaviour that closely approximates to the desired response.

- *Negative Reinforcement* provides an unpleasant reward so that an employee will engage in a desired behaviour in order to avoid the unpleasantness. Negative reinforcement may make employees feel negatively towards the manager who provides the negative reinforcement and may also foster immature behaviour.

- *Extinction* is the non-reinforcement or omission of behaviour in the hope that if the behaviour is not rewarded it will reduce over time.

- *Punishment* involves providing an undesirable consequence or reward for an undesirable behaviour.

To be effective the consequences of a behaviour must be known by the person involved before the behaviour occurs. We must also be aware that certain consequences or rewards are preferred by some employees and not others. Therefore, we cannot treat all employees in the same way and this may have consequences in organizations.

To use reinforcement effectively managers should be aware that:

- Immediate reinforcement is best.
- The larger the reinforcement, the more effective it is.
- The more deprived of reward an employee is, the more effective it is.

Source:
Adapted from:
[1] Thorndike, E.L., *Animal Intelligence* (Macmillan, New York, 1911).
[2] Luthans, F. and Kreitner, R., *Organisational Behaviour Modification and Beyond* (Scott, Foresman, Glenview, IL., 1985).

BOX ESD2.9

Learned behaviour: social learning theory

Motivation can be seen as a complex process of social learning. Bandura believes that learning occurs through the continuous interaction of our behaviour, personal characteristics and the environment.[1] Thus we learn to behave in the way we do by observing, copying and interacting with our social environment.

Employees decide to work hard or not to work hard by thinking about and responding to what happens to them in the workplace. The most common influences in this process are personal needs, rewards and reinforcements, job experience, satisfaction and what other employees do.

Three processes are involved in explaining our behaviour:

- symbolic processes
- vicarious learning
- self-control.

Symbolic processes involve the use of language in the form of verbal and non-verbal forms of communication to guide and support our behaviour. We use verbal and symbolic images to process and store our experiences in order for these to serve as guides for future behaviour. By using our imagination in this way we can attempt to solve problems without actually performing all the alternative courses of action.

Symbolic processes include self-efficacy or the belief in one's capabilities to perform a specific task (see Activity ESD2.7). Self-efficacy helps to explain the levels of the goals we set and the effort and persistence we apply to them.

Vicarious learning is our ability to learn new behaviour and/or assess its consequences by observing others behave since we do not actually have to act ourselves in order to learn the consequences of our actions. The process of observing and imitating behaviour is called 'modelling' and is the basis for the mentoring system of management development.

Self-control is the setting of standards and the providing of consequences (rewards and punishments) for our own actions. For example, we can make our self-rewards conditional on reaching a challenging level of performance.

Source:
[1] Adapted from Bandura, A., *Social Foundations of Thought and Action* (Prentice Hall, Englewood Cliffs, NJ, 1988).

Discussing personal goals earlier, we mentioned the work of McClelland (1961). His work on motivation is very useful for our immediate needs.

According to this perspective, people have three basic motivational needs – achievement, affiliation and power. One of these needs tends to dominate in most individuals. Our needs and those of our colleagues and staff can be seen in the following typical behaviours.

Need for achievement These individuals want to out perform others and have an insatiable drive. Their high task behaviour includes:

■ knowing what they can achieve;

■ pushing for responsibility;

■ setting themselves new challenges; and

■ a desire for feedback to do even better.

Need for affiliation These individuals are more concerned with maintaining friendly relationships and can be good team participants. Their low task/high people behaviour may be less results-oriented than those people motivated by the need to achieve as they tend to put people before the task. Their behaviour includes:

■ a need to be popular;

■ a need for company/people to be around;

■ the possible avoiding of difficult situations and decisions; and

■ a sensitivity to situations and people.

Need for power   These individuals are assertive and often charismatic. They utilize the existing power structures in organizations for their political ends. Their behaviour can be effective for the organization but may result in stress-related or the cardio-vascular problems for the individual and includes:

- a desire to lead;

- a desire to volunteer;

- being persuasive if not outspoken; and

- being linked to a managerial cause elsewhere within the organization.

The degree of effectiveness may indeed be related to the dominant motivational need.

We believe that it also links to self-confidence or self-efficacy – which may also be positively correlated to these motivational states.

Self-efficacy

We need to be motivated to succeed in order to meet the processes and goals which make up effective behaviour. This is also linked to aspiration and a perceived level of satisfaction with current behaviour. This perception and aspiration may be linked to self-confidence or self-efficacy.

According to Lane (1992), self-efficacy is the level of confidence an individual has in his or her ability to cope with a situation or to complete a task. (See also Barling and Beatty 1983.) It is normally measured on a scale of 0–100 where each point represents a level of confidence. Self-efficacy is situation- or task-specific since people are more confident with some situations or tasks than others.

To obtain self-efficacy measures, people are asked to state their confidence in their abilities across a range of key task areas. They judge their level of self-efficacy by estimating the demands of the situation or task and then comparing them to a self-assessment of their ability to meet the demands.

Much of our behaviour can be explained in terms of self-efficacy since we are unlikely to start something we cannot finish or do successfully. On the other hand, being told to deal with the situation or complete a task in which we have little confidence or skill will have effects on our motivation and possibly lead to an unsuccessful completion of a task.

Some people make poor judgements about their abilities. Perhaps the best managers are those who are able to get their subordinates to do things which they initially believe are well beyond them, not through using their power position but through careful mentoring.

Lane (1992) shows that the validity of self-efficacy measures is as good as any other in current use. The concept is 'user friendly' and allows people to 'own' their own developmental needs. It is also useful for identifying training/development needs and the changes from before to after will provide a measure of its effectiveness. Let us now try Activity ESD2.7.

ACTIVITY ESD2.7

SELF-EFFICACY

Activity code

✓ Self-development
☐ Teamwork
☐ Communications
☐ Numeracy/IT
✓ Decisions

Task

To get a feeling for the self-efficacy concept you need to either make a list out of your job description or the tasks you do/will have to do and then rate your confidence in completing them out of 100.

Tasks   **Confidence levels**

When you have finished, spend a few minutes reflecting on the process.

- What does it tell you about yourself?
- What new skills, knowledge, contacts, etc. do you require to meet your job description or task successfully?
- How are you going to fulfil these needs?

Learning

Before we move away from the personal aspect of effectiveness, we need to comment briefly on learning (see ESD Unit Four).

Individuals have the capacity to adapt and to adopt: they can change their behaviour. The major mechanism of such behavioural change is through learning which involves the acquisition and use of new knowledge, skills and attitudes. Organizations can facilitate such change through their climate and support mechanisms (see ESD Units Five and Six respectively).

Personal effectiveness in a work organization involves both group interaction and the involvement of the organization as a whole. We examine briefly one or two examples of integration which can make for enhanced effectiveness. Then we turn to competencies.

D.   Personal Effectiveness in a Group Setting

Likert (1961) believes that the organization is made up of a whole series of inter-connected networks of workgroups – co-ordinated by managers. This workgroup idea emphasizes a group format established by the organization to transform inputs into outputs, such as ideas into a new product. But other types of groups exist.

Informal groups or associations of people emerge in a more spontaneous basis and do not come into existence through some formal managerial decree. Instead they tend to be established for the socio-emotional needs of their members.

Formal groups or workgroups primarily exist for task or operational purposes – although the shrewd manager should take account of the socio-emotional or 'maintenance' needs of the group as well.

We could go down the route of 'followership' if the group processes equate to leadership coming from the manager. Personal and group effectiveness are seen to be linked to leadership. Here we shall focus only on formal and informal groups linking them to effectiveness at group and individual level.

One way of harnessing individual and group effectiveness is to examine the variables that impact on workgroup behaviour. Herold (1979), for example, went along this route. Inputs, for example, could include the organizational context, the job in hand, group size, rules, membership characteristics, etc. The processes involve such things as decision making, the rules, the norms and the degree of cohesiveness. The outcome or outputs involve both task performance and people 'maintenance'. In non-work situations, the people maintenance factors are writ large as this becomes the 'task'. Perhaps a personal ability to 'manage' such people maintenance (and tasks for workgroups) in both types of groups goes to the nub of individual and group effectiveness.

Please tackle Activity ESD2.8.

ACTIVITY ESD2.8

TEAMWORK

Activity code

✓	Self-development
✓	Teamwork
	Communications
	Numeracy/IT
✓	Decisions

Think carefully about the following statements.

■ Most teams under perform and do not think about their performance.
■ The performance of teams is usually acceptable rather than outstanding.

Task

Therefore ask yourself:
■ How can a team become outstanding?
■ How do you define outstanding?
■ Who decides whether performance is outstanding?

To Hastings (1986), the issue of building a team out of a workgroup is all about the need to improve task performance. The real difficulty which blocks this improved performance is seen by Hastings to be conflicting expectations. Views outside of the team and inside the team, and the interests of the team members may not coincide. An audit is suggested by the author to facilitate the 'superteam'.

Belbin's (1981) team roles may be more useful for our immediate needs of integrating individual and group effectiveness (see Box ESD2.10).

BOX ESD2.10

Belbin's team roles

Belbin made a long study of the best mix of personal characteristics in a team.[1] A management team can combine all the qualities necessary for success which one individual alone cannot possess. He discovered that a team composed of the brightest managers did not turn out to be the best and that eight roles need to be filled in a fully effective group.

- *Chairman* presides over the team and co-ordinates its efforts – should be disciplined, focused and balanced rather than brilliant or creative – talks and listens well – is a good judge of people and things – works through others.
- *Shaper* is highly strung, outgoing and dominant – is the task leader and in the absence of the Chairman would jump into that role – his/her strength is his/her drive but s/he can be oversensitive, irritable, impatient – s/he is needed to speed the action.
- *Plant* is introverted but intellectually dominant – is the source of original ideas and proposals – is the most imaginative and intelligent member of the team – can be careless of details and may resent criticism – needs to be drawn out or will switch off.
- *Monitor-Evaluator* analytic rather than creatively intelligent – carefully dissects ideas and is able to see the flaws in arguments – often aloof but is necessary as a quality check – is dependable but can be tactless and cold.
- *Resource-Investigator* popular, extrovert, sociable and relaxed – brings new contacts, ideas and developments to the group – contributions need to be picked up by the team.
- *Company-worker* practical organizer who turns ideas into manageable tasks – uses schedules, charts and plans – is methodical, trustworthy and efficient but not excited by visions and is not exciting – an administrator.
- *Team-worker* holds the team together by being supportive to others, listening, encouraging, harmonizing and understanding – is likeable and popular but uncompetitive – is not noticed when present but missed when absent.

■ *Finisher*   needed to enable the team to meet its deadlines – checks details, worries about schedules and chivvies others with a sense of urgency – relentless follow through is important but not popular.

Too many of one type in a team creates a lack of balance; too few roles mean some tasks do not get done. In a small team one person may have to perform more than one role.

The full set is most important when rapid change – in the workforce, technology, market place or product – is involved.

Source:
[1] Adapted from Belbin, R.M., *Management Teams – Why they succeed or fail* (Heinemann, London, 1981).

Another useful classification scheme, which can integrate the socio-emotional aspects of people maintenance roles across a range of formal and informal groups, is that of Benne and Sheats (1948). For the workgroup, the task role should not be ignored; while the relations-oriented roles seem to cover personal effectiveness across all types of groups.

Please tackle Activity ESD2.9. Thereafter we shall turn to personal effectiveness in a broader organizational context.

ACTIVITY ESD2.9

GROUP ROLES[1]

Activity code

✓ Self-development
✓ Teamwork
✓ Communications
☐ Numeracy/IT
✓ Decisions

Task-oriented roles:
■ initiators
■ information seekers
■ information givers
■ co-ordinators
■ evaluators
■ energizers.

Relations-oriented roles:

- encouragers
- harmonizers
- gatekeepers
- standard setters
- followers
- group observers.

Self-oriented roles:

- aggressors
- blockers
- recognition seekers
- dominators
- avoiders.

Effective individuals in groups are those who have covered the task- and relations-oriented roles and this means that group members may have to cover two or more of the sub-roles. Members who cover several sub-roles very well may develop high status. A group dominated by members with self-oriented sub-roles will often be ineffective.

Tasks

- Think about one of the task groups to which you belong.
- Identify the members and the sub-roles they play within the group.
- Describe your sub-roles in the group. Do your sub-roles change when you join other groups? Why?

Source:
[1] Adapted from Benne, K.D. and Sheats, P., 'Functional Roles of Group Members', *Journal of Social Issues*, **4**, pp. 41–49, (1948).

E. Personal Effectiveness in an Organizational Setting

It could be argued that organizations are a collection of groups coming together for some common aim. If this is the case, the personal/group interface would be relevant to this part of the discussion. Organizations are probably more than a series of networking groups though and this is examined in *Effective Organizational Behaviour* (Anderson and Kyprianou, 1994) as is the integrative mechanisms between the individual and the organization.

We could look to effectiveness in organizations and how that concept alters with changes in policy and then extrapolate the ideas on to our views of personal effectiveness. We will not go down this route as this idea is developed elsewhere in the series (Anderson, 1995). Instead, we shall select several thematic examples which can blend together the ideas of personal and organizational effectiveness. These include:

- communications
- career anchors
- ethical responsibilities
- a question of 'fit'.

Communications

Communication is the lifeblood of an organization since it enables people to share information and influence one another's understanding, attitudes and behaviour. Managers need effective communication in order to plan, organize, lead and control their businesses. In performing these tasks they spend most of their time communicating and so communication skills are extremely important. However, we must all be aware of the manager who is a good communicator but a poor manager/leader.

Mintzberg (1973) identified four roles for which a manager depends on communication.

- *The monitor* gathers internal and external information.
- *The disseminator* distributes information internally.
- *The spokesperson* distributes information externally.
- *The decision maker* uses information to make plans, solve problems and explore opportunities.

The causes of many problems of ineffectiveness in organizations can be found in poor communications. Therefore Scott and Mitchell (1979) believe that managers should use their communication skills to:

- influence, i.e. persuade others to work hard and perform tasks;
- inform, i.e. provide information for decision making and job performance;
- control, i.e. provide objectives and monitor performance; and
- inspire, i.e. display values, positive attitudes and build commitment.

Effective communication occurs when the intention of the message of the sender is the same as the interpretation of the receiver. The communication channel used and feedback are important factors for good communication.

Efficient communication occurs when the minimum of resources in terms of time, money and effort are expended. Both effectiveness and efficiency are needed. Listening and feedback are necessary managerial skills here.

A major part of communication is listening and active listening occurs when you:

- stop talking;
- indicate you want to listen;
- listen for both content and feelings;
- empathasize;
- note both verbal and non-verbal cues;
- restate the message to the source;
- are patient and control your temper;
- control your arguments and criticism;
- ask questions; and
- listen carefully without talking.

An active listener encourages the communicator to say more.

Managers are continually being called on to give feedback which should be:

- acceptable
- understandable
- plausible
- supportive
- corrective.

Barriers to effective communication can be caused by:

- semantics
- no feedback
- wrong channels being used
- distractions
- cultural differences
- status.

You must also be aware of the effect of your own emotions and the distrust of the receiver. Both of these have a strong influence on the effectiveness of the message sent.

Non-verbal communication can be a powerful device. Gender, hands, face, voice, posture, eye contact and space can all be used to transmit messages. Some of these are often reflected in our concept of status.

Mixed messages are conveyed when words communicate one message while actions or body language communicate something else. Even organizations can have this effect, for example by demanding long-term loyalty while offering short-term contracts.

There is a silent language associated with the culture of each country and this often distorts cross-cultural communication. Different peoples use the language of contracts, time, space and things in different ways.

There are also barriers to communication in organizations such as:

■ personal characteristics and source credibility;
■ frames of reference and selective perceptions; and
■ resistance to change.

These can be overcome to some extent by:

■ reducing resistance to change;
■ communicating with all employees; and
■ undertaking a communication audit.

Organizations have both formal and informal communication channels and information flows in all directions. Thus managers can control the information flow to a greater or lesser extent. This control can be a powerful tool in the motivation of employees if it is used carefully to allow autonomous work patterns, for example.

Perception is the process of receiving and interpreting information and has been dealt with. Social perception in particular blends in with these interpersonal skills. Refer to Activity ESD2.10.

ACTIVITY ESD2.10

COMMUNICATION STYLES

Activity code

✓ Self-development
✓ Teamwork
✓ Communications
  Numeracy/IT
✓ Decisions

Polsky[1] identified five basic styles of interpersonal communication based on two dimensions.

The five styles of communication are set out as follows.

- Self-denying – has a tendency to isolate oneself, to hide ones ideas, opinions, feelings.
- Self-protecting – gives feedback but is not open to others.
- Self-exposing – is poor at giving feedback but very open with others.
- Self-actuating – gives feedback and is very open.
- Self-bargaining – is willing to give feedback and be open only to the extent that others are willing to do the same.

The two dimensions are:

- openness to others – self-disclosure and receptiveness to feedback; and
- giving feedback – sharing of thoughts and feelings.

Self-disclosure is part of our openness to others and involves communicating verbally or non verbally any information about ourselves to others. Self-disclosure is often a prerequisite for self-development but it may be inhibited by status considerations during the process.

Tasks

- Think about your style of communication.
- Which of the above styles do you use?
- Do you need to improve your style of communication in any way? Why? How?

Source:
[1] Adapted from Polsky, H.W., 'Notes on personal feedback in sensitivity training', *Sociological Inquiry*, **41**:175–82, 1971.

Career anchors

According to Schein (1978), the early career of a manager is a period of mutual discovery between the employee and the organization. Over a period of time each learns more about the other. The employee gains self-knowledge or an occupational self-concept which Schein describes as a career anchor.

A career anchor has three components:

- self-perceived talents and abilities;
- self-perceived motives and needs; and
- self-perceived attitudes and values.

You will notice that this concept is broader than job satisfaction or the motivation to work. In addition, it is not possible to predict career anchors from tests since they are dependent on work experience. Thus the concept emphasizes evolution, development and discovery through experience.

Career anchors are the result of interaction between the person and the work environment. They are 'inside' the person and act as a set of driving and constraining forces on career decisions and choices. If we find ourselves in a situation which is likely to flounder, which fails to meet our needs or which compromises our values, we will be 'pulled back' or anchored to something more congruent. A career anchor therefore is that concern or value which we will not give up easily – if a choice has to be made. However, it is also possible that career anchors will change with new life experiences.

Career anchors are discovered over a number of years in our early career since we cannot know, until we encounter a variety of real life situations, how our abilities, motives and values will interact and so fit the career options available. Thus, a career anchor concept highlights the gradual integration of motives, values and abilities in our total self concept with organizational opportunities and constraints.

The career anchor is intended to identify a growing area of stability without implying that we will cease to change or develop.

Schein (1978) found there were five types of career anchor which can be found in all types of occupations. Each type expects different things from his/her career; measures him/herself differently and therefore needs to be managed differently. Refer to Box ESD2.11 and complete Activity ESD2.11. We then move to consider the theme of ethical responsibilities.

BOX ESD2.11

Schein's five career anchors[1]

Technical/functional competence

Success is indicated by feedback stating that you are an expert in your area and by increasingly challenging work in that area rather than by promotion or monetary reward *per se*. There is a tendency to resist general management or any work that does not permit the exercise of your skills. You will probably leave a company rather than be promoted out of your area of expertise. This may cause internal conflict.

Managerial competence

You believe your competence lies in a combination of three general areas:
- analytical
- interpersonal and
- emotional competence.

Different occupational roles require different kinds of analytical, interpersonal and emotional competences. In other words the person who wishes to rise to higher levels of management must be simultaneously good at analysing problems, handling people and handling emotions in order to withstand the tensions and pressures of the executive suite.

This type of person is concerned about the size of the tasks, the degree of challenge and the amount of responsibility. They measure their success by promotion, rank and income.

Security and stability

People who anchor in security tend to do what is required by their employers in order to maintain job security, a decent income and stable future in terms of pension, benefits, etc.
There are two types of security orientation:

- The source of security and stability rests with membership of a given organization.

- The source of security is geographically based and involves settling down, stabilizing the family and integrating in the community.

There may be the feeling that being anchored in security represents a degree of failure and this can cause internal conflicts in those affected.

Creativity

This anchor is critical to the understanding of the career of an entrepreneur – a person who wishes to be autonomous, managerially competent, able to exercise special talents and build a fortune in order to be secure. However, none of these appear to be the key motive or value. Such people have a prevailing need to build and create something of their own.

The need to be a manager and the need to be an entrepreneur are quite different.[2] Therefore it is quite predictable that a transition crisis will occur for the entrepreneur and/or the organization as the need for management develops.

Autonomy and independence

You find organizations restrictive, irrational and/or intrusive into your private life. Therefore you will leave government or business in order to be more independent and autonomous. You need to be on your own, setting your own pace, schedules, lifestyle and work habits. There is a successful trade-off between status and high income versus freedom to pursue your own lifestyle.

Source:
[1] Adapted from Schein, E.H., *Career Dynamics: matching individual and organisational needs* (Addison Wesley, Reading, Mass, 1978).
[2] Anderson, A.H. and Woodcock, P., *Effective Entrepreneurship* (Blackwell, Oxford, 1996).

ACTIVITY ESD2.11

CAREER ANCHORS

Activity code

✓ Self-development
✓ Teamwork
✓ Communications
☐ Numeracy/IT
✓ Decisions

Tasks

■ Read Box 2.11 and then reflect on your career to date.
■ To which of the five types of career anchors do you conform?
■ Can you identify the career anchor of any of your colleagues?
■ In what ways should that career anchor affect the ways in which they are managed?

Ethical responsibilities

While managers are continually planning, organizing, leading and controlling, etc., to improve performance they must also operate in a socially responsible manner. Managers must accept responsibility for doing the 'right' things – management effectiveness. To do this they may make use of several concepts, including:

■ Morals – distinguishing between right and wrong; and
■ Ethics – conforming to moral standards by a code of morals.

Essentially ethics are principles of behaviour that help us to make choices between alternative courses of action. In a fair and just society we expect ethical behaviour to be part of a legal code. However, just because something is not illegal does not mean it is necessarily ethical. At the same time ethics go beyond legality and extend to our personal values – our underlying attitudes and beliefs which determine our behaviour.

Cavanagh *et al.* (1981) believe four criteria guide our approach to ethical behaviour:

■ utility or the delivery of the greatest good to the greatest number;
■ individuality or the best for long-term interest;
■ moral rights or respect for the fundamental human rights; and
■ justice or impartiality, fairness and equity in dealing with people.

Essentially our ethical behaviour is a dynamic relationship between our personal characteristics, the organization and the environment (see figure 2.2).

This is a dynamic relationship and we have to balance each of the above factors.

Figure ESD2.2   Social responsibility

Bartol and Martin (1994) believe that, in order to become more aware of what is happening in the environment, social demands and expectations can be monitored by:

- social forecasting
- opinion surveys
- social audits
- issues management
- social scanning.

Read Box ESD2.12 on social audits and Box ESD2.13 on guidelines for managers.

BOX ESD2.12

Social audit

Carroll suggested criteria for evaluating performance in organizations which can be used for a social audit.[1]

- economic responsibilities
- legal responsibilities
- ethical responsibilities
- discretionary responsibilities

Source:
[1] Adapted from Carroll, A.B., 'A three dimensional model of corporate performance', *Academy of Management Review*, **4**, pp. 497–505, (1979).

BOX ESD2.13

Guidelines for managers

O'Toole offered the following guidelines for managers.[1]

- Obey the law.
- Tell the truth.
- Respect people.
- Do unto others as you would have them do to you.
- Do no harm.
- Practice participation not paternalism.
- Always act when you have responsibility.

Source:
[1] Adapted from O'Toole, J., *Vanguard Management: Redesigning the Corporate Future* (Berkeley Books, New York, 1987).

A question of 'fit'

The interface between the individual and the organization can be illustrated very well by a study on training practitioners in the Chemical Industry (Pettigrew and Reason, 1979). These researchers highlighted the need for 'congruence' or a 'best fit' between the individual job holder, the job role itself and the 'personality' or culture of the organization. If congruence occurred between these three variables, the trainer was more effective. If this did not occur, ineffectiveness resulted. Perhaps these variables can be extrapolated to include most jobs.

We now turn to competencies.

F.   Personal Effectiveness and Competencies

Boyatzis (1982) sees competency as 'an underlying characteristic of a person'. The definition goes on to talk of 'a motive trait, skill, aspect of one's self image or social role, or body of knowledge which he or she uses'. So this definition includes personal characteristics of the individual which we have developed here as well as an application of skills and knowledge.

Woodruffe (1991) usefully distinguishes between areas of competence and individual competencies with:

> aspects of the job at which a person is competent, (competences) and
> aspects of the person which enable him to be competent (competencies).

In part, we have gone down this route in this unit (competencies) and in the next unit we turn to competences.

However personal competencies also involve degrees of skill and knowledge within the individual. Presumably once they are applied to a given job they become aspects of job competences.

Here we have distinguished the *personal* attributes of effectiveness. This is in line with Anderson's (1995) views expressed in the policy, task, people and functional analysis in *Effective General Management*.

In a sense these personal and task attributes could thus cover both aspects of the job and aspects of what the individual brings to the job. However the personal aspects will transcend the job, while the task aspects will be more dependent on a specific job and their relevance will vary accordingly. Hence the personal attributes could be more universal or *generic* while the task attributes could be more *contingent* on the specific job in the organization. In broad terms, we subscribe to the analysis made by Woodruffe (1991) but make use of the more stringent distinction between the personal and task attributes of the individual and of the job in hand as seen by Anderson in *Effective General Management*.

The mainstream view of competencies is to combine the personal traits with a combined element of the individual's knowledge and skill. We have separated the personal effectiveness aspect from the core knowledge, skill and attitudes held by the individual. We shall now touch upon the knowledge/skill aspect of competencies. Personal qualities and traits brought to the job are also covered in this approach.

Please tackle Activity ESD2.12 and then read Box ESD2.14 which gives some indicative response.

ACTIVITY ESD2.12

COMPETENCIES – TOWARDS CLASSIFICATION

Activity code

✓ Self-development
✓ Teamwork
✓ Communications
  Numeracy/IT
✓ Decisions

Task

What type of competencies would you expect managers to hold in large organizations?

BOX ESD2.14

Towards a classification of competencies

Please refer back to Activity ESD2.12.[1] The competencies could include:
- communications
- groups/awareness of others
- conceptualization/decision making
- strategic insight/commercial awareness
- leadership
- goal orientation
- personal – e.g. impact/self confidence
- managerial elements – e.g. control, etc.
- drive/achievement.

Source:
[1] Derived from the competencies of some UK organizations noted by Woodruffe, C., 'Competent by Any Other Name', *Personnel Management*, September (1991).

The remainder of the unit is based on activities and/or boxes to consolidate ideas on competencies and personal effectiveness.

ACTIVITY ESD2.13

CONSTRUCTING FAST MOVING CONSUMER GOODS COMPETENCIES FOR SALES EXECUTIVES

Activity code

✓ Self-development
  Teamwork
✓ Communications
  Numeracy/IT
✓ Decisions

Task

You are the general manager of a fast moving consumer goods (fmcg) unit of the firm. Your sales executives have not been used to a competencies approach. Outline (individual/group) the type of competencies which you would expect to be seen by your field sales executives.

BOX ESD2.15

Fast moving consumer goods – sales competencies

You may wish to consider such things as:
- concern to meet goals/targets
- research (action) skills
- communication and influence
- impact
- planning/organizing calls/schedules
- customer orientation
- quality approach
- good product/company knowledge
- ability to work in a team and as a group
- ability to handle key accounts/national accounts
- tenacity
- ability to close the sale.

BOX ESD2.16

Competencies – self-analysis

You may be required to analyse and audit your own behavioural patterns. The objectivity and accuracy of the initial inputs will impact on the validity of the behaviours or competencies.

The problem with self-analysis seems to be that it goes to the heart of our self-esteem. We tend to inflate our own positions. One of the authors was involved in job analysis with a major oil/gas company and 'enhancement' usually occurred when discussing jobs for evaluation purposes.

Mabe and West[1] suggest some possible measures to reduce this enhancement.
- It helps if people have prior experience of self-assessment.
- It helps if comparisons are made with others.
- It must be anonymous.
- All assessments should be validated against established criteria.
- The method lends itself to those who have high intelligence and high status.

Source:
Mabe, I. and West, S.G., 'Validity of Self Evaluation of Ability: a review and meta-analysis'. *Journal of Applied Psychology*, **3**, pp. 280–96, (1982).

ACTIVITY ESD2.14

PERSONAL DEVELOPMENT

Activity code

✓ Self-development

☐ Teamwork

☐ Communications

☐ Numeracy/IT

☐ Decisions

Task

To advance we may have to take stock of our existing position – what we can/cannot do in given situations. We do not need some introspective navel gazing experiment but we do need a realistic self-audit with an appropriate action plan following on from our stocktake.

Self-knowledge, self-awareness and self-confidence are all related and can help you adopt and adapt to new situations. You should create a checklist to further this self-awareness. Some possible headings are shown below.

■ Self-audit – e.g. write your autobiography and career/educational history to date. Note opportunities/constraints.

■ Education/training – e.g. note your skills/expertise/developments in this heading.

■ Career – e.g. trace your working life and its paths.

■ Personal – e.g. outline your abilities/interests – at work and outside of work.

■ Goals – e.g. determine how they have altered/moved on – refer back to self-audit.

■ Achievements – e.g. evaluate what you have accomplished at work and outside of work.

■ Stengths/weaknesses – these are self-explanatory.

G. Conclusion

For the sake of analysis, we have separated personal and task effectiveness. In reality they need to fuse and so we turn to the task element in ESD Unit Three.

Self-awareness can lend itself to greater self-insight and hence stimulate self-development.

We examined some key aspects of personal differences and suggested some important areas which impact on effectiveness namely – self-efficacy and self-concept.

We looked to the contexts in which this personal effectiveness could take place by examining some group and organizational influences. We examined the issue of 'congruence' or 'fit' which becomes a central platform to effectiveness and to a conducive self-developmental climate.

We finished this unit by touching upon competencies and personal aspects of effectiveness. Task effectiveness and competences are covered in ESD Unit Three.

Bibliography

Adams, J.S., 'Towards an understanding of inequity', *Journal of Abnormal Social Psychology*, **67** (1963).

Alderfer, C.P., *Existence, Relatedness and Growth: human needs in organisational settings* (Free Press, New York, 1972).

Allport, G.W., *Personality* (Holt, New York, 1937).

Anderson, A.H., *Effective General Management* (Blackwell, Oxford, 1995).

Anderson, A.H. and Kyprianou, A., *Effective Organizational Behaviour* (Blackwell, Oxford, 1994).

Anderson, A.H. and Woodcock, P., *Effective Entrepreneurship* (Blackwell, Oxford, 1996).

Bandura, A., *Principles of Behavior Modification* (Holt, Rinehart and Winston, New York, 1969).

Barling, J. and Beatty, R., 'Self Efficacy and Sales Performance', *Journal of Organisational Behaviour Management*, **5**, (1983).

Bartol, K.M. and Martin, D.C., *Management* (McGraw-Hill, New York, 1994).

Bayne, R., 'Four Approaches to Increasing Self Awareness', in ed. P. Herriot, *Assessment and Selection in Organisations* (Wiley, London, 1989).

Belbin, R.M., *Management Teams – why they succeed or fail (Heinneman, London, 1981).*

Benne, K.D. and Sheats, P., 'Functional rules of group members', *Journal of Social Issues*, **4**, (1948), pp. 41–49.

Bourdieu, P. and de Saint-Martin, M., 'Scholastic excellence and the values of the educational system', in ed. J. Eggleston, *Contemporary Research in the Sociology of Education* (Methuen, London, 1974).

Boyatzis, R.C., *The Competent Manager: A Model for Effective Performance* (Wiley, New York, 1982).

Briggs-Myers, I., *Introduction to Type* (Oxford Psychologist's Press, Oxford, 1987).

Cavanagh, G.F., Moberg, D.J. and Velasquez, M., 'The ethics of organisational politics', *Academy of Management Review*, **6**, (1981), pp. 363–74.

Cattell, R.B., *The Scientific Basis of Personality* (Penguin, Baltimore, 1965).

Child, J. and Macmillan, B., 'Managers and their Leisure', in M. Smith, S. Parker and C. Smith, *Leisure and Society in Britain* (Allen Lane, London, 1973).

Dollard, J. and Miller, N.E., *Personality and Psychotherapy: an Analysis in Theories of Learning, Thinking and Culture* (McGraw-Hill, New York, 1950).

Eysenck, H.J., *The Structure of Human Personality* (Methuen, London, 1960).

Freud, S., *The Ego and the Id* (Norton, New York, 1960).

Gahagan, D., 'Attitudes', in eds J. Radford and E. Govier, *A Textbook of Psychology* (Sheldon Press, London, 1980).

Goldthorpe, J.H., Bechhoter, F. and Platt, J., *The Affluent Worker in the Class Structure* (Cambridge University Press, Cambridge, 1969).

Gross, R.D., *Psychology: The Science of Mind and Behaviour* (Arnold, London, 1987).

Hamner, W.C., 'Reinforcement Theory and Contingency Management in Organisational Settings' in eds H.L. Tosi and W.C. Hamner, *Organisational Behaviour and Management: A Contingency Approach* (Wiley, New York, 1977).

Hastings, C., *Superteams* (Fontana, London, 1986).

Heider, F., *The Psychology of Interpersonal Constructs* (Wiley, New York, 1958).

Herold, D.M., 'The effectiveness of work groups', in ed. S. Kerr, *Organisational Behaviour* (Grid Publishing, Columbus, Ohio, 1979).

Herzberg, F., *Work and the Nature of Man* (World, Cleveland, Ohio, 1966).

Hirsch, S.K. and Kummerow, J., *Introduction to Type in Organisations* (Oxford Psychologist's Press, Oxford, 1990).

Huczynski, A. and Buchanan, D., *Organisational Behaviour* (Prentice Hall, Hemel Hempstead, 1991).

Jung, C.G., *Analytical Psychology: Its Theory and Practice* (Routledge and Kegan Paul, London, 1968).

Kelly, G.A., *The Psychology of Personal Constructs* (Norton, New York, 1955).

Lane, J., 'Methods of Assessment', *Health Manpower Management*, **18**, 2, (1992).

Likert, R., *New Patterns of Management* (McGraw-Hill, New York, 1961).

Locke, E.A., 'Nature and causes of job satisfaction', in ed. M.D. Dunnette, *Handbook of Industrial and Organisational Psychology* (Rand McNally, Chicago, 1967).

Lupton, T. and Wilson, S. 'The Social Background and Connections of Top Decision Makers', in J. Urry and J. Wakeford, *Power in Britain* (Heinemann, London, 1973).

McClelland, D.C., *The Achieving Society* (van Nostrand, Princeton, NJ, 1961).

Maslow, A., *Motivation and Personality* (Harper, New York, 1954).

Mintzberg, H., *The Nature of Managerial Work* (Harper & Row, New York, 1973).

Mitchell, T.R., *People in Organizations International Edition* (McGraw-Hill, Tokyo, 1982).

Mullins, L.J., *Management and Organisations* (Pitman, London, 1993).

Parsons, T., 'The Social Structure of the Family', in ed. R.N. Anshen, *The Family: Its Functions and Destiny* (Harper & Row, New York, 1959).

Peters, T.J. and Waterman, R.H., *In Search of Excellence* (Harper & Row, New York, 1982).

Pettigrew, A.M. and Reason, P.W., 'Alternative Interpretations of the Training Officer Rule: A Research Study in the Chemical Industry', (Chemical and Allied Products Training Board, Staines, Middlesex, March 1979).

Polsky, H.W., 'Notes on personal feedback in sensitivity training', *Sociological Inquiry*, **41**:175–82, 1971.

Porter, L.W. and Lawler, E.E., *Managerial Attitudes and Performance* (Dorsey Press, Holmewood, IL, 1968).

Schein, E.H., *Career Dynamics: matching individual and organisational needs* (Addison Wesley, Reading, Mass, 1978).

Scott, W.G. and Mitchell, T.R., *Organisation Theory* (Irwin, Holmewood, IL, 1979).

Spranger, E., *Types of Men* (Niemeyer, Halle, Germany, 1928).

Stevens, C., 'Assessment Centres: The British experience', *Personnel Management*, IPM, London, July, (1985).

Stodgill, R.M., 'Personal factors associated with leadership: a survey of the literature', *Journal of Psychology*, **25**, (1948).

Townsend, A., *Developing Assertiveness* (Routledge, London, 1991).

Vroom, V.H., *Work and Motivation* (Wiley, New York, 1964).

Waterman, R.H., *The Renewal Factor: How the best get and keep the competitive edge* (Bantam, New York, 1987).

Woodruffe, C., 'Competent by Any Other Name', *Personnel Management*, (September, 1991).

ESD Unit Three

Competence and Task Effectiveness

Learning Objectives

After completing this unit you should be able to:

- determine the parameters of task (non personal) effectiveness;
- outline key approaches to task effectiveness – including the view of the series;
- analyse the value of the capability debate to task effectiveness;
- conduct a thorough critique into the value of competence as a basis of task effectiveness;
- conduct a thorough critique of the value of National Vocational Qualifications as a basis of task effectiveness;
- relate task effectiveness back to personal effectiveness; and
- apply the generic skills of the series.

Contents

A. Overview

B. Task Effectiveness

▶ Elements

▶ Elements plus

▶ Management roles

▶ Essential elements of the management process

▶ Policy – tasks, people, functions (TPF)

C. Capability

D. Competence

▶ Background

▶ The development of the Management Charter Initiative

▶ The MCI approach

▶ The MCI – assessment schemes

E. National Vocational Qualifications (NVQs)

▶ Background

▶ NVQs – their relevance to self-development

▶ NVQs – a critique

F. Conclusion

ESD Unit Three

> " . . . The essence of our experience here is summed up in the popular phrase, 'A fair day's work for a fair day's pay!' Knowledge workers, however, should be expected to do 'an exceptional day's work – and they should then also have a chance to earn exceptional pay! "
>
> (Drucker, 1969)

A. Overview

Self-development is not a navel-gazing exercise. While we believe in an humanistic approach to developing people, at the place of work, such processes must be linked to some task being achieved.

We spend the first section looking at this concept of task effectiveness. Then we turn to the grander concept of 'capability' which fuses traditional educational goals of developing the inner person to task demands of the workplace. We have empathy for this approach.

A harder nosed approach is given greater consideration through the use of competence. The Management Charter Initiative (MCI) approach in particular is analysed in depth. In spite of its warts, it has great value to our idea of task effectiveness. The NVQ system is seen in a less bright light but again it has some merit for our self-developmental approach to task effectiveness.

Finally we come full circle and relate the task element back to the personal element in ESD Unit Two.

B. Task Effectiveness

Elements

Traditionally, management can be seen as a process of achieving organizational goals through planning, organizing, leading and controlling. These four elements are closely related and involve the continuous maintenance and improvement of quality. It is a manager's job to create an environment in which people can use resources efficiently and

93

effectively to reach stated objectives. The manager is also responsible for meeting the social needs of the workforce as well.

Planning

This is a process of determining what is to be achieved, setting the objectives and identifying the tasks for achieving them. Quality objectives must be a priority since if these are achieved, the related objectives such as cost reduction, market share and return on investment, will be easier to achieve.

Plans are guides for:

■ obtaining and committing the resources required to reach the objectives;

■ identifying people to carry out the tasks; and

■ monitoring and measuring progress.

The goals of the organization must be feasible and acceptable and lead to objectives for the sub-units. In turn they lead to programmes for achieving the objectives in a systematic manner.

Organizing

This involves allocating and arranging human and other resources so that plans can be completed successfully. Managers determine which tasks have to be done; how they can be broken down into jobs and who is going to do them. That is, the 'organization turns plans into action'.

Organizing also involves the organization structure. This must enable the organization to operate effectively as a cohesive unit and so achieve the quality objectives. Different objectives will require different kinds of structure.

Leading

The earlier functions of planning and organization deal with the more abstract aspects of management but leading is concrete in that it involves dealing directly with people. It requires strong interpersonal skills, communicating a vision to others, providing direction, motivating people to achieve goals and inspiring people to work hard for the benefit of the organization, namely building commitment. Leading is 'the art of making things happen'.

Controlling

This process makes sure that actual performance is equal or better than planned performance.

Managers need to:

■ establish standards;

■ measure current performance;

■ compare to standards; and

■ make corrections as necessary.

They also need to follow work progress by maintaining contact and communications directly with the people involved. Controlling guides the organization towards quality performance.

Managers maybe more inclined to one function than another and organizations may require more emphasis on one function than another at a particular time. Thus the process of management is dynamic and ever changing.

Elements plus

In practice, the management process may not simply consist of four separate elements. Carroll and Gillen (1987) reviewed major studies on managerial work and found that there were several additional factors to be taken into consideration:

■ work agenda

■ work methods and roles

■ knowledge and management skills.

The relationship is illustrated in figure ESD3.1

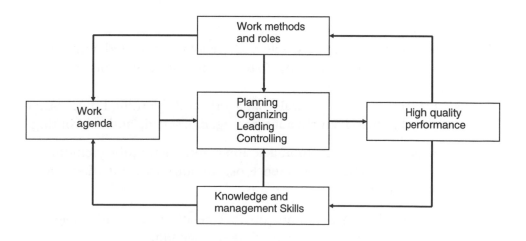

Figure ESD3.1 How the factors involved in managerial work are interconnected

Source: Adapted from Carroll and Gillen, 1987.

Management roles

In *The Nature of Managerial Work*, Mintzberg (1973) found that managers work:

- long hours;
- at an intense pace;
- at fragmented and varied tasks;
- with many communication media; and
- mainly through people.

He was able to relate a manager's work to the roles which managers perform in organizations:

- Interpersonal roles – interactions with other people:
  - figurehead
  - leader
  - liaison.
- Informational roles – exchanges and processes information:
  - monitor
  - disseminator
  - spokesperson.
- Decisional roles – uses information in decision making:
  - entrepreneur
  - disturbance handler
  - resource allocator
  - negotiator.

These roles form a dynamic whole and are all inter-related and vary in importance from person to person, job to job, organization to organization and through time.

Kotter (1991) studied general managers and identified two other activities critical to management success – agenda setting and networking.

Agenda setting is about developing action priorities for jobs including their time scales. These are often loose to start with but they are always kept in mind.

Networking builds and maintains positive relationships with people whose help may be needed to complete the agenda.

Stewart (1992) identified the following factors which influence work agendas:

- job demands – activities managers must do;

- job constraints – factors which limit what managers can do; and

- job choices – activities which managers can do but do not have to do.

There seems to be a division amongst those who adhere to 'elements' and those who favour roles.

Essential elements of the management process

To develop work agendas, perform roles, and plan, organize, lead and control, managers need a sound knowledge base and certain management skills/competencies.

The knowledge base is important but remember that Kotter (1991) found that one of the reasons why certain managers could achieve so much in such a short period was that they could take action using only small amounts of information. Does this imply simply luck or some as yet undefined mental skill?

Katz (1974) classified the essential skills of managers into:

- technical – the ability to perform particular tasks;

- human – the ability to work well with people; and

- conceptual – the ability to think analytically.

A managerial competency is both a skill and applied knowledge that contributes to high performance in a manager's job.

However we must constantly differentiate between competences and competencies. For instance, Schermerhorn (1993) suggests the following examples:

Competences
- planning
- organizing
- leading
- controlling
- information gathering
- decision making.

Competencies
- leadership
- self-objectivity
- analytical thinking
- behavioural flexibility
- oral presentation
- written communication
- personal impact
- resistance to stress
- tolerance for uncertainty.

As we have argued in ESD Unit Two, competencies are personal inputs while competences are task related.

Policy – tasks, people, functions (TPF)

As we briefly mentioned in ESD Unit One, the series as a whole follows a model of effectiveness based on managerial jobs. This is summarized as 'policy – TPF'. In effect this means an awareness of the external environment and of business *policy*, a *task* orientation, a *people* orientation and understanding of the main *functions* of management, marketing, personnel management, operations and enterprise and accounting/finance.

Box ESD3.1 gives a brief summary of the task elements of this scheme.

The issue may not just resolve task effectiveness and the capability argument broadens out the debate.

BOX ESD3.1

Task elements of the TPF scheme[1]

Task elements

■ *Planning* is the key aspect of the task elements and dovetails into the policy and functional approaches.

■ *Goal setting and performance* are the action plans which put things into practice.

■ *Control* can be systems- or people- or machine-led mechanisms to ensure that events conform to plans.

■ *Decision making* is at the heart of management problem solving capacity.

■ *Co-ordination and organization* ensure a coherent plan of campaign.

In addition the 'softer' aspects need to be considered via the people elements:

■ motivation

■ communication

■ leadership

Source:
[1]Anderson, A.H., *Effective General Management* (Blackwell, Oxford, 1995).

C. Capability

In the UK in 1980 a new initiative 'Education for Capability' began with the publication of a manifesto by the Royal Society (RSA) for the encouragement of arts, manufactures and commerce. This called for an end to the dichotomy between education and training and envisaged a new culture of learning which combined academic excellence with excellence in creativity, undertaking and completing tasks, working with others and coping with everyday life.

Activity ESD3.1. sets out some ideas. Try the tasks which follow.

ACTIVITY ESD3.1

CAPABILITY

Activity Code

✓ Self-development
✓ Teamwork
✓ Communications
☐ Numeracy/IT
✓ Decisions

. . . There is a serious imbalance in Britain today in the full process which is described by the two words 'education' and 'training'. The idea of the educated person is that of a scholarly individual who has been neither educated nor trained to exercise useful skills; who is able to understand but not to act. Young people in secondary or higher education increasingly specialize, and do so too often in ways which mean that they are taught to practise only the skills of scholarship and science. They acquire knowledge of particular subjects, but are not equipped to use knowledge in ways which are relevant to the world outside the education system.

This imbalance is harmful to individuals, to industry and to society. A well-balanced education should, of course, embrace analysis and the acquisition of knowledge. But it must also include the exercise of creative skills, the competence to undertake and complete tasks and the ability to cope with everyday life; and also doing these things in co-operation with others.

There exists in its own right a culture which is concerned with doing, making and organizing and the creative arts. This culture emphasizes the day to day management of affairs, the formulation and solution of problems and the design, manufacture and marketing of goods and services.

Educators should spend more time preparing people in this way for a life outside the education system. The country would benefit significantly in economic terms from what is here described as education for capability.

Source:
Manifesto of the Education for Capability Campaign, Royal Society for the Encouragement of Arts, Manufactures and Commerce, London, 1980.

Tasks

By individual or group initiative:

1 discuss whether this viewpoint is still valid in the UK;
2 compare and contrast this approach to that of the government which is trying to raise the qualifications of the working population through NVQs; and
3 decide whether your arguments also apply to the field of management? Explain your reasons.

Stephenson (1994) believes that although capability may be one of those human characteristics more easily recognized than measured, it does not release us from our obligation to develop our understanding of its nature. (Stephenson is Project Director for Higher Education for Capability which provides direct assistance, support, information and expertise for the introduction and enhancement of capability approaches to learning and development). He says that Higher Education for Capability argues that capability is an integration of knowledge, skills and personal qualities used effectively and appropriately in response to varied, familiar and unfamiliar circumstances.

The Higher Education for Capability movement believes this is best developed by giving learners the opportunity to take on the challenge of managing their own development, within what may seem to be the unfamiliar world of education. Learners should be able to articulate the relevance of their learning to their personal, academic and vocational development.

Weaver (1994) identified six capacities that educated human beings ought to be able to develop, namely:

- comprehension – acquiring and understanding the necessary knowledge;
- cultivation – acquiring a proper sense of values;
- competence – applying specialized knowledge;
- creativity – developing new ideas, innovations, concepts;
- co-operation – people being able to work together; and
- coping – the capacity to manage oneself, cope with the environment and profit from experience.

According to Stephenson (1994), capability is as much about knowledge, values, self-esteem and the capacity for autonomous development of the self and context as it is about the possession of skills alone. Thus the Government's drive to raise the qualification level of the working population through National Vocational Qualifications (NVQs) may assess achievement but they do not necessarily indicate potential or even capacity. Narrowly defined competences are only a part of human capability. So we need to be aware of an over-rigid prescriptive approach if we wish to develop the 'inner person'.

Of course, task effectiveness has been isolated for analysis only, as it dovetails into people effectiveness. Indeed the TPF approach indicated in Box ESD3.1 widens the base of the task-only orientation. Hence we take a broad view of development across the series combining attitudes, the cognitive base and skills. This may be a form of 'capability'. Yet we must underpin this capability by being competent at a given set of tasks, so we shall now turn to competence. Ultimately we cannot paint a chapel in Florence unless we have mastery over the paintbrush.

D.   Competence

Background

For organizations to survive and develop there is an increasing need for their managers, and indeed all employees, to adapt to change. This implies continuous improvement and attention to quality and the need to be adaptable and flexible. New skills, new work relationships, new ways of working and thinking have to be developed. To undertake such development requires highly skilled management and employees. Therefore, in order to gain competitive advantage, organizations will have to develop their human resources. Apart from this task orientation there are increasing demands on people to develop themselves.

During the last ten years in the UK there have been a number of government-driven initiatives which have contributed to the growth of competency-based education and training in the UK. There is now a continuously updated national framework of qualifications which is agreed across all sections and occupations. The competency of an individual can be identified and assessed against nationally agreed standards. The competences can be achieved through formal education, training or experiential learning throughout life.

Please refer to Box ESD3.2.

BOX ESD3.2

Can competence be measured?

Traditionally, evidence assessed at a university tends to be knowledge based and takes the form of assignments and formal examinations, whereas, assessment of skills tends to be regarded as part of the world of work. If universities now aim to recognize 'non-traditional learning' and in particular 'life-long learning' the divide between the world of work and the university has to break down. What is common to both is learning.

Here we come to the crux of the matter since this is where vocational and academic approaches may part company. In vocational training one can learn by 'sitting next to Nellie' or as a colleague recently told one of us, 'I may be able to bake a cake having learned by rote in the kitchen but I cannot read a recipe. How do I learn to read at the work place?'. At the same time, simply putting together a portfolio of evidence which meets the standards does not prove a candidate has learned anything. If there is a proposal for vocational qualifications and academic awards to be recognized as equivalent we must find a way for a person holding an NVQ to be able to join an academic course at the next level above, if that person so wishes.

One connection between the academic world and the world of work which we can easily appreciate is learning. In both situations success can be measured in terms of what one has learned. Therefore, if we can agree about criteria for measuring learning then it must be possible to equate academic and work-based achievements. This implies the sophisticated use of language to demonstrate learning which will identify those capable of gaining from Higher Education.

Another concept which may be useful in our search for a method of measuring the extent of learning is Kolb's Learning Cycle which has been used as an aid to curriculum design for many years.[1] He believes that the effective learner spirals upwards through a repetition of – experience – observation and reflection – conceptualization – experimentation and then round again. The critical reflection, self-assessment and analysis of observations implied in the model have been used in professional contexts to develop more effective behaviour for many years.

There are six ways of demonstrating that learning has taken place in the academic world which can also be used in the world of work. These are based on Bloom.[2]

There will be an increase in:

■ information and knowledge – which are expressed by terms like 'list', 'state', 'name';

■ understanding of the intellectual skills for dealing with materials and problems (comprehension, translation and interpretation, and extrapolation) – which can be expressed by terms like 'discuss', 'explain', 'clarify', 'identify', 'what if?' and 'if . . . then';

■ the ability to apply knowledge and understanding – which is expressed by terms such as 'demonstrate', 'illustrate' and 'apply';

■ the ability to analyse information and situations – which is expressed by terms such as 'distinguish', 'contrast', 'compare' and 'calculate';

■ the ability to synthesize – which is expressed by terms such as 'organize', 'plan', and 'set up'; and

■ the ability to evaluate – which is expressed by terms such as 'evaluate', 'appraise' and 'assess'. The use of both internal and external evidence is expected.

There is an additional term which we would like to use at this point – the ability to innovate – which is the practical application of new ideas.

Therefore, if we accept the criteria for learning suggested by Bloom and the need to reflect on our experience suggested by Kolb, we can propose a method for equating the academic world with the world of work. This will involve managers in reflecting on their experience and identifying their resultant learning.

Sources:
[1] Kolb, D.A., Rubin, J.M. and McIntyre, J.M., *Organisational Psychology* 4th edn. (Prentice Hall, Englewood Cliffs, NJ, 1984).
[2] Bloom, B.S., *Taxonomy of Educational Objectives: The Classification of Educational Goals* (Longmans, London, 1956).

The framework is controlled by the National Council for Vocational Qualifications (NCVQ) through a portfolio of National Vocational Qualifications (NVQs). Scotland has its own framework – SCOTVEC and SNVQs. Lead Bodies have been established to identify the competencies and standards required in each occupational area.

Qualifications in the form of S/NVQs are statements confirming that a person can perform to national standards and therefore possesses the skills, knowledge and understanding necessary for performing in the work place.

These S/NVQs will be available in every recognized occupational area. There are five levels of S/NVQ – basic, craft, technical, low-level professional and high-level professional.

A credit accumulation and transfer scheme (CATS) has been developed to help non-traditional entrants to Higher Education and eliminate unnecessary repetition of learning by giving credit for learning achievement. At the same time there is also the possibility of transfering credits from one educational institution or programme to another. This provides the possibility of exemption from relevant parts of a course. Assessment of prior learning (APL) gives credit for previous learning whether certified or uncertified and assessment of experiential learning (AEL) gives credit for learning from life and work experience.

Alongside these developments for individuals there is the Investors in People Initiative (IIP) of the Technical Education Councils (TECs). This is producing new national standards to improve performance in organizations through investing in people. An investor in people organization commits itself to:

■ developing all employees to achieve its business objectives;

■ reviewing regularly the training and development needs of all employees;

■ taking action to train and develop individuals on recruitment and throughout their careers; and

■ evaluating the investment in training and development to assess achievement and improve future effectiveness.

Successful organizations which achieve this standard use human resource development approaches and avoid the trap of simply following bureaucratic rules. The Management Charter Initiative (MCI, 1991) is a useful illustration of the competence approach. But first we need to understand where it came from as this gives an interesting context to the need for self-development.

The development of the Management Charter Initiative

During recent years a series of factors have led to an increasing awareness of management education, training and development (METD). According to Deloitte, Haskins and Sells (1989), these factors have included:

■ the management lessons of the depressions of the 1980s;

■ structural and demographic changes in employment;

■ increasing demands on managers;

■ greater awareness of market influences on employment; and

■ the threats and opportunities of a single European market in 1993.

Although it was the focus of national debate from time to time during the post war period, METD did not achieve what might be described as critical momentum until the late 1980s. At that time the poor performance of industry and commerce and the publication of a number of reports focused attention on the need for METD.

A key report by the Institute of Manpower Studies (1984) investigated vocational education and training in Japan, USA and West Germany. The conclusion was that in these countries there was a clear link between investment in education and training and competitive success. This link was lacking in the UK. These countries also developed effective performance at work in its widest sense rather than concentrating on narrow skills development.

A year later, Coopers and Lybrand (1984) investigated the state of training in British industry. They found that top managers were unaware of how their company's training performance compared with their competitors. Senior executives did not know what resources were directed at training, and training was not seen as a contributor to competitiveness and profitability but rather as an overhead to be cut when under pressure.

However, following a survey, Mangham (1986) found that the majority of companies saw little connection between performance and management training and preferred to invest their resources elsewhere. There was also no evidence of a link between the incidence of training and the actual performance of the organizations. On the other hand none of the companies claimed that training provided an inadequate return on investment. Mangham believes that this dichotomy reflects our lack of precision in defining what are the qualities, attributes and skills of effective managers.

Handy (1987) examined METD in France, Japan, UK, USA and West Germany. He found that managers in these countries were educated to a higher level and benefited from formal and systematic policies for continuing education and development. He suggested a ten point plan that drew on the best practice in other countries but blended with UK culture and traditions. The top companies were to act as role models of good practice and managers would be better educated.

Constable and McCormick (1983) reviewed management education and training in the UK and concluded that Britain's managers lacked the education, training and development of their competitors. Although management recognized that education and training could enhance performance, the average UK manager received only about one day's training per year and many received none at all. Constable and McCormick called for a policy for management education and training.

These reports led to a major initiative by the Confederation of British Industry (CBI). In October 1987, John Banham, the Director General of the CBI, declared that the CBI, the British Institute of Management (BIM) and the Foundation for Management Education were to support a new body, the Council for Management Education and Development (CMED) to be headed by Bob Reid, Chairman of Shell UK. CMED then created the Management Charter Initiative (MCI) and drew up a charter of good practice. A Code of Practice was launched in July 1988 and support was sought from employers of all sizes. Currently over 800 organizations, both public and private, support the code. The objectives of the MCI is to increase the quantity, quality, relevance and accessibility of management education and development.

The MCI is an employer-led organization which brings together all parties to management development. It is the 'Lead Body' for management and supervisory occupations and is intended to be responsive, non-bureaucratic and support and encourage the best practice. A local focus is introduced in the form of networks and public, private, small, medium and large organizations are involved. Its objective is to promote national standards for management, that is, management education should not be based solely on academic study but on what managers do in the workplace. Before the MCI was formed there were no nationally accepted competence-based standards for management performance.

Competence is the ability to perform activities within an occupation or function to the standards expected in employment. This implies effective performance over time including dealing with the unexpected and maintaining performance in different contexts. Relevant knowledge and understanding are required to underpin effective performance so that skills can be transferred to new situations and performance maintained. Essentially, knowledge is the factual content for an occupational area and understanding is the 'internal organization of knowledge' in order to apply it appropriately in different contexts. We shall now turn to the MCI approach in more detail.

The MCI approach

The MCI is pioneering new approaches which meet the needs of a wide range of organizations which are calling for improvements in quality, quantity, relevance and accessibility to management education and development in the UK. These approaches are based on six key principles.

Open access   This removes unnecessary barriers which prevent managers embarking on development programmes or which restrict access to assessing their competence. In the past the UK has had an elitist attitude to qualifications which tended to create barriers to access rather than encourage the development of potential. The common barriers to access are academic qualifications, age, duration of course, place and mode of learning.

Corporate and individual development   This provides a coherent framework to meet both the organization's and the manager's needs. Corporate development plans identify employer needs and involve both the provider and the employer in designing programmes to satisfy those needs. A learning contract between the employer, provider and manager enable the manager's development needs to be built into the programme. Corporate development plans can demonstrate the commitment of employers to programmes and motivate the managers. In this way managers find a direct relationship between the programmes and the work situation.

Personal development plans involve competence based standards, the learning process, a timescale and support mechanisms. Sometimes these plans can be associated with a firm's appraisal system.

Flexibility and innovation in delivery   This ensures both a wide choice of learning approaches and effective use of the workplace. This flexibility is complementary to open access since managers are not limited to attending courses at some location for a particular period. The approach encourages innovation and work-based learning.

Competence-based approaches   These require effective assessment of performance, with evidence of the necessary underpinning knowledge and understanding. These approaches raise questions about the sufficiency of evidence, the credibility of a qualification without normal examinations and the need for work-based assessment.

Credit accumulation   This enables managers to work towards qualifications by gaining credits for competencies they can demonstrate, no matter how they were acquired. For this process to work, the programmes need to be unit or modular in design and some way of integrating the parts must be found.

The accreditation of prior learning (APL) has value for managers in that they gain credit for competencies already demonstrated and therefore their progress is accelerated. For providers, APL removes the need for earlier education and development to be repeated.

Employer involvement   This approach increases the effectiveness of development practices by using mentors and line managers as resources. Involvement needs commitment by employers and not all firms are prepared to do this.

A clear need has developed for a coherent hierarchy of management qualifications based upon the ability to manage and a process of career development for managers. Currently the certificate level provides for first level managers and the diploma level for middle managers and those with more complex managerial responsibilities. This structure enables the development of the relevant competencies concurrently with the development of specialist professional and occupational expertise at the appropriate time in a manager's career.

The management standards, the personal competence model and the required knowledge and understanding, defined by the MCI (MCI 1;2), have been developed and tested during in-depth discussions with hundreds of employers and 3000 managers. The MCI believe they are firmly based on the essentials for performance and achievement throughout the economy.

Management standards define what a manager should be able to do, and describe the results and outcomes a competent manager should be able to produce. The standards are set out in a hierarchy of key roles, units of competence and elements of competence. At the top of the pyramid is the overall key purpose of managers, namely 'to achieve the organization's objectives and to continuously improve performance'.

The key roles represent the different areas in which managers are expected to operate in – finance, information, operations and people. For each of the key roles there are a number of units of competence, which describe what is expected of a competent manager in particular aspects of the job. Each unit contains a number of elements of competence, which define what a competent manager is expected to achieve. Every element contains a number of performance criteria and a set of range indicators. The performance criteria describe the outcomes a manager has to achieve in order to demonstrate competence, and the range of indicators give the range of circumstances to which the element applies. Please see Box ESD3.3 for an example of the key roles.

BOX ESD3.3

Key roles

Key Role – Manage Operations

Unit 1   Maintain and improve service and product operations.
Element 1.1   Maintain operations to meet quality standards.
Performance Criteria e.g. All supplies necessary for operations are available
                           and meet organizational/departmental requirements.
Range Indicators   Several are provided starting with:
                           Operations are all those activities within the manager's
                           line responsibility.

The MCI standards are linked to a personal competence model, underpinned by the required knowledge and understanding and operate within an environment or job context. The personal competence model (MCI 3) identifies the key personal competencies for achieving results under headings such as:

- planning to optimize the achievement of results by:
  showing concern for excellence
  setting and prioritizing objectives
  monitoring and responding to actual against planned activities
- managing others to optimize results by:
  showing sensitivity to the need of others
  relating to others
  obtaining the commitment of others
  presenting oneself positively to others
- managing oneself to optimize results by:
  showing self-confidence, personal drive
  managing personal emotions and stress
  managing personal learning and development
- using the intellect to optimize results by:
  collecting and organizing information
  identifying and applying concepts
  taking decisions.

The standards and personal competencies have also been used in various other ways:

- analysis of training needs
- recruitment of personnel contractors
- appraisal
- development and training

- job description/evaluation
- succession planning
- matching skills to objectives.

Please refer to Activity ESD3.2 and then complete Activity ESD3.3.

ACTIVITY ESD3.2

TOWARDS COMPETENCE

Activity code

- ✓ Self-development
- ✓ Teamwork
- ✓ Communications
- ☐ Numeracy/IT
- ✓ Decisions

Task

Using your knowledge to date, by individual/group initiative, construct a task/competence profile for a job holder specializing in co-ordinating self-development for managers and staff.

ACTIVITY ESD3.3

EFFECTIVE PROFESSIONAL MANAGEMENT

Activity code

- ✓ Self-development
- ☐ Teamwork
- ☐ Communications
- ☐ Numeracy/IT
- ☐ Decisions

Task

Please indicate, using ticks, the areas where you believe you are competent and the areas you need to develop. (In the course of your work you need to be constantly developing all of these skills.)

	Competent	Needs Developing
Planning Showing concern for excellence Setting and prioritizing objectives Monitoring and responding to actual against planned activities		
Managing others Showing sensitivity to the needs of others Relating to others Obtaining the commitment of others Presenting oneself positively to others		
Managing self Showing self-confidence and personal drive Managing personal emotions and stress Managing personal learning and development		
Using Intellect Collecting and organizing information Identifying and applying concepts Taking decisions		

Source:
MCI *Assessment Guidelines* (MCI, London, n.d.).

Underpinning the competence approach is a body of knowledge and the understanding of facts, figures, theories, methods, procedures, possibilities, opportunities and threats. Effective task action (MCI 3) is not possible without this knowledge and understanding which covers three broad areas:

1   purpose and context which identifies the manager's objectives and the relevant organizational and environmental influences, opportunities and values;

2   principles and methods which covers any theories, models, principles, methods and techniques that provide the basis for managerial performance; and
3   data which are the specific facts likely to be important in meeting the standards.

Some views of the MCI's approach to 'new' and 'traditional' education can be seen in Box ESD3.4. However in many education institutions some aspects of the traditional approach is no longer prevalent as the dominant approach.

Please refer to Box ESD3.5 and then tackle Activity ESD3.4.

BOX ESD3.4

MCI: learning

MCI Approach		Traditional Approach
Open access	v	Rigid entry
Individual needs	v	Course syllabus
Unit basis	v	Whole programme
Flexible delivery	v	Rigid structure
Innovative approach	v	Traditional approach
Learning at work	v	Classroom focus
Practical experience	v	Theoretical approach

BOX ESD3.5

Assessment and qualifications

MCI Approach		Traditional Approach
Performance	v	Theory
Evidence	v	Examinations
Credit for competence	v	No credit given
Credit transfer simple	v	Credit transfer difficult
Focus on end results	v	Analysis of courses

ACTIVITY ESD3.4

CRITIQUE

Activity code

✓ Self-development
  Teamwork
  Communications
  Numeracy/IT
✓ Decisions

Task

Refer back to Boxes ESD3.4 and ESD3.5. Make a critique of the MCI approach both to learning and to assessment including qualifications.

Perhaps both approaches to learning noted by the MCI are credible. Certainly the traditional approach has stood the test of time so far as standards are concerned. It will be interesting if the same thing can be said about the new approaches in some 20 years time.

There is clearly some innovation here so we will develop the MCI ideas before embarking on a critique.

The MCI – assessment schemes

The MCI believes it has identified the common core which goes through all managerial jobs and which forms the foundation for the skills which people take with them from one job to another. The standards are competence-based, focusing firmly on what a manager should be able to do in the work place. Essentially it involves the assessment of management competences against national standards, using appropriate assessment methods. The standards are generic and apply across all industry and different work environments. This is a radical departure from traditional examination and award assessment procedures.

Each manager works backwards from the standards to determine the development required to meet the standards, that is, the gap is the key and will vary from manager to manager. In effect the managers manage their own learning and development. This is a needs-driven approach which works from the individual point of view. Hence knowledge and understanding begin to develop where the manager begins to develop.

Also involved in the process are assessors and advisors/mentors. The assessor is the judge who uses the standards as criteria either in the company or academia. In both places, checks and balances are in place to maintain standards. The advisor is academic whereas the mentor is work-based. The roles can very enormously but essentially consist of empowering, directing and enabling young managers to develop their competencies.

The purpose of the assessment is to determine when a manager is competent and entitled to accreditation. It is based on the gathering together and interpretation of evidence about a manager's performance of the activities of each element. These are then judged against standards defined by performance criteria. The evidence must be actual performance and relate to the underpinning knowledge and understanding necessary to sustain effective performance in other situations. The manager must also be able to deal effectively with the unexpected and maintain performance standards in the present organization or any other in the future.

In contrast to the norm-referenced assessment where marks are graded around a norm for the population, this assessment is criterion referenced. This means that the assessor can only make one of two decisions – competent or not competent – based on the evidence presented.

The assessor uses the following key principles to make decisions:

- Sufficiency of evidence   Is enough evidence available to judge competence?

- Currency of evidence   Is the evidence generated from activities in the past appropriate to judge current competence?

- Authenticity   Does the evidence relate to the manager's own work?

- Confidentiality   If the evidence is confidential, it can produce problems in assessment.

- Validity   Are the links between standards and evidence clear and explicit?

Managers find the self-assessment and the development of the portfolio a valuable learning process. It involves a considerable amount of reflection about work experience and personal abilities and develops an awareness of personal strengths and weaknesses. This self-assessment against the standards acts as a strong motivator to complete the qualification by developing areas where the manager is not yet competent.

Before we turn to NVQs, another task initiative which may stimulate self-development, please refer to Boxes ESD3.6 and ESD3.7 which give us some pluses of the MCI approach.

BOX ESD3.6

The Driver Vehicle Licensing Authority (DVLA)

The DVLA is a monopoly since people do not have a choice to go elsewhere and this imposes on the DVLA an enormous responsibility which they take seriously. At the same time, the government has made the DVLA an executive agency with corporate and business plans. This involves innovation, taking risks, being receptive to new ideas and good management. They encourage staff development with a structured training programme geared to their business objectives. The MCI competence-based approach was chosen for the management development programme.

The DVLA started with the MCI Level 1 in 1990 and later in the year began a Level 2 programme. The MCI computer-based assessment system (CAS) was used from the beginning. CAS is a simple system which enables a manager to assess him/herself against the management standards and personal competence model in order to identify individual strengths and weaknesses and therefore development needs.

Every manager in the programme completed a CAS self-assessment of their competences against the management standards. The process was repeated by their line managers who also assessed them against the same standards. In this way both parties are able to consider all the elements and take into account the relevant performance criteria and range indicators. The process produced the two profiles which were displayed on the screen.

The DVLA found that the line managers usually rate their subordinates higher than the subordinates rate themselves. This boosts their confidence and enables both parties to discuss both profiles and any further development which is needed. A tutor is also involved and where the joint assessment is high, that is, the manager is currently competent against those units and elements, then the manager is encouraged to gather appropriate evidence for the accreditation of prior learning (APL).

If the joint assessment is low in any elements or units then a programme of development and work experience is explored in order for the manager to reach the required standard.

Source: Adapted from:
MCI Conference Reports (MCI, London, 1991).
Middle Management Dynamics (MCI, London, 1991).

BOX ESD3.7

The Safeway experience

Some years ago Safeway found that during a manager's career there were swings from competence to incompetence as they were promoted from job to job, that is, it took some time for managers to learn their new job and become efficient. Therefore Safeway decided to assess their managers against the management standards in order to reduce this incompetence factor. The assessment process identifies possible incompetencies which can then be remedied; highlights a manager's perception of their own competence level and makes that perception more realistic.

The Safeway management development programme takes up to two years and covers all facets of retail management. Trainee managers are only placed into a junior management position in a store with the full accompanying responsibilities after the management development programme. Assessment is continuous and managers receive a certificate for satisfying the MI standards at the end of the programme.

It take 2–3 years to progress to deputy store manager where managers enter the middle manager programme. They are reviewed against MII standards and are promoted to store manager once these competences are satisfied.

This approach overcomes the problem of promoting people above their level of competence which reduces the efficiency of the organization for some time until they catch up.

Assessment covers the usual management roles of operations, finance, people, information and personal management effectiveness, plus the management skills required in the Safeway environment. Safeway have established their own professional and job specific competences for these skills. Credits are awarded for gaining each of the competences. As managers progress through the organization, they take with them a competence log which is completed and signed off by their manager.

This approach generates a high degree of motivation amongst the young managers so that the number of credits and speed of gaining them have become talking points.

Source: Adapted from:
MCI Conference Reports (MCI, London, 1991).
Middle Management Dynamics (MCI, London, 1991).

One of the advantages for organizations which take up this MCI approach is the ongoing development of their staff by being involved in the process of staff development. Thus the organization is directly involved in developing its managers. This can only be good for them since they can identify strengths and weaknesses which they might never have noticed under normal circumstances and which can be made use of or addressed as necessary.

The managers are more in control of their development since they have to reflect on experience and be responsible for their own future development. They become proactive rather than reacting to their environment. Managers also learn about their organizations and how they work and this contributes both to the firm's and their own effectiveness.

In the first phase of the review of the management standards, several issues have been identified such as:

- mixing units or elements from different levels and or other standards in order to reflect actual roles more accurately;
- combining units or elements from other Lead Bodies' standards (e.g. Marketing) with some but not all from a given level of the management standards;
- developing and using much more user friendly versions;
- amending the language of the standards to reflect better the jargon and culture of a given organization or sector;
- developing a unified framework of management standards working with a single set of units but showing increasing competence/skill and responsibility at the element level;
- reviewing the language of the standards
- shifting the emphasis in management activity towards a customer focus, quality and teams;
- acknowledging the shifting values in society regarding managerial ethics, equal opportunities and the environment; and
- noting the apparent clash between the needs of the management standards and the S/NVQs in Management.

Hopefully, many of these issues will be resolved by the second phase of the review, but turn now to Box ESD3.8.

BOX ESD3.8

A critique of the MCI

This box refers back to Boxes ESD3.4 and ESD3.5.

Learning

Access

The traditional education model has rigid entry requirements in the UK but this has been diluted of late with rising state quotas on entry levels. The problem with too open an access could mean that the end result, if it is a qualification, becomes devalued – or perhaps, as in higher education, more bodies means lower standards.

Needs

The objective syllabus content must be considered against the subjective needs of individuals. Standards of learning may suffer although an experiential-based form of learning needs to be balanced against systems of learning.

Unit/Whole

Learning in most traditional approaches has to be broken into segments for ease of delivery and understanding. By making small units the task becomes perhaps less demanding intellectually.

Delivery

The traditional approaches allowed for more than a lecture/tutorial format – although greater flexibility in time/distance, etc. seems to be occurring in the new university sector in the UK for example.

Approach

Innovation does and did occur under the traditional approaches to learning and there is no monopoly on innovation.

Work/Classroom

The classroom provides more of a controlled environment whereas opportunities must be initiated and created – with organizational assistance which is often lacking – for real learning to occur at the workplace.

Practice/Theory

This is an artificial distinction anyway – knowledge and skills, theory and practice are required under any form of learning.

Assessment/Qualifications

Performance

The real distinction here is between performance on the job which is difficult to monitor, and performance in simulations, such as assignments and in formal examinations.

Evidence

Again examinations do give some evidence of the ability to answer questions in depth. They test understanding and application. Evidence gathering at the place of work can be equally problematic in gauging the level of expertise.

Competence

This view is probably correct but testing, assignments and continuous assessment under traditional modes of delivery can test degrees of competence.

Credit transfer

Traditionally this was the case but again in modular schemes, etc. transfer has become easier.

Results

This comparison is an error of judgement. The traditional method of formal management education is very results-oriented: you pass or fail. It is also process-oriented. The means of getting there ought to be part of the learning experience hence a too results-oriented approach, not only depends on which results we are attempting to achieve but also it fails to take account of the process of development in attaining these results.

We should not over simplify the divisions between the MCI approach and 'traditional approaches'. The route of assessment and qualification may differ but we should not paint a caricature of 'traditional' approaches. Whether the new approaches are as valid must also be debated.

E.   National Vocational Qualifications (NVQs)

Background

In 1986 a review of vocational qualifications in England and Wales was followed by a government white paper which proposed the formation of the National Council for Vocational Qualifications (NCVQ) – a move which was widely supported by the political parties, the Confederation of British Industry and the Unions. This political weight is to be backed by a new directive which will ensure that NVQs are based on world-class standards. Thus they will be more transportable than other equivalent qualifications since they will have trans-European recognition. A Scottish equivalent (SVQ) is also in place.

Most occupations in the UK now have NVQs up to Level 3 (broadly equivalent to GCE A level standard) and NVQs at Levels 4 and 5 are also available in some occupational areas such as management. Candidates for NVQs are assessed in the work place against national standards. These are a statement about what the job holder should be able to do in the work place.

The NVQ framework (NCVQ, 1991) identifies the relationships between vocational qualifications and makes it easier for people to map out their career pathways. The five levels of NVQs allow progression from routine and predictable work activities to complex and unpredictable activities. Level 3 is the entry level to first degree courses in universities whereas graduates will be expected to perform at Levels 4 and 5 on entering employment.

Please refer to Boxes ESD3.9 and ESD3.10.

BOX ESD3.9

Levels

The Guide to National Vocational Qualifications summarizes the levels relevant to Higher Education as follows:

- Level 3 – implies competence in a broad range of work activities performed in a wide variety of contexts, most of which are complex and non-routine. There is considerable responsibility and autonomy, and the control or guidance of others is often required.

- Level 4 – implies competence in a broad range of complex, technical or professional work activities performed in a wide variety of contexts, and with a substantial degree of personal responsibility and autonomy. Responsibility for the work of others and the allocation of resources is often present.

- Level 5 – implies competence involving the application of a significant range of fundamental principles and complex techniques across a wide and often unpredictable variety of contexts. Very substantial personal autonomy and often significant responsibility for the work of others and for the allocation of substantial resources feature strongly, as do personal accountability for analysis and diagnosis, design, planning execution and evaluation.

Source:
Adapted from *The Guide to National Vocational Qualifications* (NCVQ, London, 1991).

BOX ESD3.10

NVQ – Accreditation

For a National Vocational Qualification (NVQ) to be accredited it has to be:

- based on the national standards required for performance in employment, and take proper account of future needs with regard to technology, markets and employment patterns;

- based on assessments of the outcomes of learning, arrived at independently of any particular mode, duration or location of learning;
- awarded on the basis of valid and reliable assessments made in such a way as to ensure that performance to national standards can be achieved at work;
- free from barriers which restrict access and progression, and available to all those who are able to reach the required standard by whatever means; and
- free from overt or covert discriminatory practices with regard to gender, age, race or creed and designed to pay due regard to the special needs of individuals.

NVQs identify a package of specialized skills and broad competences which enable people to find employment, adapt to changing conditions, identify additional skills and move to other jobs. Full NVQs can be expected to be the target for young people entering employment and for the unemployed.

Those who are in work may be better served by a mix of units which do not add up to a full NVQ but are more suitable for the role in question. This is a cost effective option for both employee and employer.

Some competences, such as management, are common to many occupational areas, therefore a number of Lead Bodies, such as the MCI for managers, have been set up to develop 'generic units' in the competences which can be incorporated into other NVQs.

We need NVQs because there is a view that vocational qualifications are not as good as having academic qualifications. Also, most people agree that we need good quality training for people at work so the National Council for Vocational Qualifications (NVQs) was set up to reform the system. It is a quality assurance body rather like the British Standards Institute (BSI) and acts as a catalyst to bring together all the interested parties. NVQs are based on standards developed by industry and commerce and are about doing a job well.

There are Lead Bodies which define the standards required in various occupations, for example, in Training and Development, Hotels and Catering or the Motor Industry. The MCI is the Lead Body for the Management and Supervisory occupations. Alongside the Lead Bodies are Examining and Awarding Bodies which operate the assessment procedures. These include the Business and Technical Education Council (BTEC), City and Guilds (C&G) and the Royal Society of Arts (RSA). Now tackle Activity ESD3.5.

ACTIVITY ESD3.5

COMPETENT/NON-COMPETENT

Activity code

☑ Self-development
☐ Teamwork
☐ Communications
☐ Numeracy/IT
☐ Decisions

The concept that a person is judged competent/non-competent is a difficult one to appreciate for most people. Here, we set out a five stage model of the process of acquisition of skill developed by Dreyfus:[1]

■ Novice — follows context-free rules with the components of the task defined.

■ Advanced beginner — begins to recognize the contextural elements of the task and perceive similarities between new and previous experiences.

■ Competent — begins to recognize a wider range of cues and is able to select and focus on the most important. Reliance on rules lessens and experimentation occurs.

■ Proficient — performs unconsciously, fluidly and effortlessly. Thinking is still analytical but an evolving situation can now be read.

■ Expert — has an intuitive understanding of a situation and can cope with uncertainty and unforeseen situations.

How does the NVQ approach of competent/non-competent fit in with this model? At which of these stages should a person be judged competent? There is some confusion over the way the term competent is interpreted at different levels and in different occupations.

Most people like to know how well they are performing and competent/non-competent tells them very little. At the same time organizations would like to identify top performers in order to improve quality.

Task

Discuss the terms competent/non-competent and how quality can be improved in the workplace.

Source:
[1] Adapted from Dreyfus, H.L., *Mind over Machine* (Blackwell, Oxford, 1986).

NVQs – their relevance to self-development

Employers

NVQs have some relevance to organizations conducting management and staff development.

Essentially, NVQs:

- increase business efficiency through more effective and efficient staff;
- identify training needs more easily leading to training being targeted and so being more cost effective;
- may raise motivation leading to reduced turnover; and
- improve the quality of recruitment and selection.

The development of NVQs has made some employers more aware of the need for training and of its value. Many organizations have not fully embraced NVQs for a number of reasons, but have used the standards as a guideline for in-house training schemes. An example of this is British Home Stores (BHS) who, because of a perceived lack of relevance to their industry, have developed an in-house training programme 'BHS opts for an in-house alternative to NVQs' specifically for their needs but modelled on NVQ standards.

NVQs have a real value for training as the standards act as a benchmark for needs analysis and as criteria for evaluation. Again the problem of transferability to the actual job which has often dogged training is no longer an issue as the NVQ approach is geared to on-the-job performance.

The predefined modular system of NVQs may not facilitate the design of programmes, but the training and development events may be cheaper owing to the predefined structures which are available through NVQs.

Job analysis with key description and people requirements can be stimulated by the NVQ system – for the benefit of all concerned with the job.

Customers and staff

As part of a quality and customer care programme, NVQs can benefit both staff and self-development as well as customer satisfaction. For example, companies such as the Royal Mail have used NVQs in their customer service function and have noticed results such as:

- enthusiasm of staff for the opportunity for formal recognition;
- a greater sense of teamwork;

- higher standards because staff have been 'empowered' to use more initiative; and

- happier customers.

The strength and perhaps the weakness of NVQs is that they enable employees to become qualified without an academic base. Their past achievements and the successful attainment of standards in the workplace are accredited.

This could lead to a very narrow focus though with skills dominating at the expense of a cognitive base, and skills may be less transferable to other jobs and to other situations.

However NVQs do provide a route for career development and progression by specifying competence for every level of work in organization. This can only be beneficial for career development in the past has been the preserve of an élite of managers.

Continuous self-development can be stimulated through the NVQ system. NVQs are currently in place for over 80 per cent of the workforce below professional level. This provides employees from the factory floor to the boardroom with the opportunity to develop their skills continually and gain formal recognition. The individual gains in terms of increased motivation, improved job prospects, and concrete evidence to support an application for a job or course.

From a purely self-developmental purpose, NVQs may have considerable value – irrespective of their intrinsic merits or otherwise – which we develop in Box ESD3.11. Afterwards, work through Activities ESD3.6. or ESD3.7

BOX ESD3.11

NVQs and self-development

NVQs
- are flexible in terms of time, place or model of learning;
- provide clear targets to aim for;
- are based on standards relevant to employment;
- provide ongoing learning and assessment in the workplace; and
- enable the qualifications to be achieved over a period by credit accumulation.

ACTIVITY ESD3.6

NVQ LEVEL 4 IN MANAGEMENT

Activity code

- ✓ Self-development
- ☐ Teamwork
- ☐ Communications
- ☐ Numeracy/IT
- ☐ Decisions

NVQ Level 4 in Management is designed for first level managers such as:

- experienced staff who have progressed through an organization
- recent entrants to management
- specialists who have management responsibilities
- people returning to management after a break.

Such managers will be responsible for the direction and control of other people; the achievement of results and the efficient and effective use of resources.

They will be expected to be proactive within the narrow limits of the function or area for which they are responsible and reactive in terms of the organization in general.

They will need the skills of:

- managing the flow of work
- setting performance targets
- developing their staff
- providing instructions
- monitoring and controlling progress against objectives
- negotiating and discussing with colleagues and reporting to more senior managers.

Task

Work through the questions below based on the Management Standards at NVQ Level 4. Tick off those for which you know you can find evidence.

Tick

Key role – manage operations

Have you maintained operations to meet quality standards?

Have you created and maintained the necessary conditions for productive work?

Have you contributed to the evaluation of proposed changes to services, products and systems?

Have you implemented and evaluated changes to services, products and systems?

Key role – manage finance

Have you made recommendations for expenditure?

Have you monitored and controlled the use of resources?

Key role – manage people

Have you defined future personal requirements?

Have you contributed to the assessment and selection of candidates against team and organizational requirements?

Have you developed and improved teams through planning and activities?

Have you identified, reviewed and improved development activities for individuals?

Have you developed yourself within your job role?

Have you set and updated work objectives for teams and individuals?

Have you planned activities and determined work methods to achieve objectives?

Have you allocated work and evaluated teams, individuals and yourself against objectives?

Have you provided feedback to teams and individuals on their performance?

Have you established and maintained the trust and support of your subordinates?

Have you established and maintained the trust and support of your immediate manager?

Have you established and maintained relationships with colleagues?

Have you identified and minimized interpersonal conflict?

Have you implemented disciplinary and grievance procedures?

Have you counselled staff?

Key role – manage information

Have you obtained and evaluated information to aid decision?

Have you recorded and stored information?

Have you led meetings and group discussions to solve problems?

Have you contributed to discussions to solve problems and make decisions?

Have you advised and informed others?

This process will require time and thought to identify your main strengths and achievements. You may need to consult your manager, a mentor or colleagues. Try to complete this section when you are relatively free from pressure.

Any elements which are left un-ticked will help you identify your areas of weakness. Focus on these in preparing your personal development plan. You can discuss them with your manager, mentor and colleagues in order to find ways of gaining the necessary evidence and develop an acceptable timetable for the achievement of competence.

Source: Adapted from various MCI concepts.

ACTIVITY ESD3.7

NVQ LEVEL 5 IN MANAGEMENT

Activity code

✓ Self-development

☐ Teamwork

☐ Communications

☐ Numeracy/IT

☐ Decisions

NVQs at Level 5 are designed for the middle manager who could have a generalist or a specialist role and normally a well defined set of targets and objectives. These managers tend to operate at a tactical level within the organization. They are often managers of managers with a pivotal role in the lines of communication and authority. Their approach to management issues is expected to be proactive and there could be some involvement at strategic level.

Task

Work through the questions below based on the Management Standards at NVQ Level 5. Tick off those for which you know you can find evidence.

Key role – manage operations

Have you identified opportunities for improvements in services, products and systems?

Have you evaluated proposed changes for benefits and disadvantages?

Have you negotiated and agreed the introduction of change?

Have you implemented and evaluated changes to services, products and systems?

Have you introduced, developed and evaluated quality assurance systems?

Have you established and maintained the supply of resources into the organization/department?

Have you established and agreed customer requirements?

Have you maintained and improved operations against quality and functional specifications?

Have you created and maintained the necessary conditions for productive work activity?

Key role – manage finance

Have you controlled costs and enhanced value?

Have you monitored and controlled activities against budgets?

Have you justified proposals for expenditure on projects?

Have you negotiated and agreed budgets?

Key role – manage people

Have you defined future personnel requirements?

Have you determined specifications to secure quality people?

Have you assessed and selected candidates against team and organizational requirements?

Have you developed and improved teams through planning and activities?

Have you identified, reviewed and improved development activities for individuals?

Have you developed yourself within the job role?

Have you evaluated and improved the development processes used?

Have you set and updated work objectives for teams and individuals?

Have you planned activities and determined work methods to achieve objectives?

Have you allocated work and evaluated teams, individuals and self against objectives?

Have you provided feedback to teams and individuals on their performance?

Have you established and maintained the trust and support of your subordinates?

Have you established and maintained the trust and support of your immediate manager?

Have you established and maintained relationships with colleagues?

Have you identified and minimized interpersonal conflict?

Have you implemented disciplinary and grievance procedures?

Have you counselled staff?

Key role – manage information

Have you obtained and evaluated information to aid decision making?

Have you forecast trends and developments which affect objectives?

Have you recorded and stored information?

Have you led meetings and group discussions to solve problems and make decisions?

Have you contributed to discussions to solve problems and make decisions?

Have you advised and informed others?

This process will require time and thought to identify your main strengths and achievements. You may need to consult your manager, a mentor or colleagues. Try to complete this section when you are relatively free from pressure.

Any elements which are left un-ticked will help you identify your areas of weakness. Focus on these in preparing your personal development plan. You can discuss them with your manager, mentor and colleagues in order to find ways of gaining the necessary evidence and develop an acceptable timetable for the achievement of competence.

Source: Adapted from various MCI concepts.

NVQs – a critique

A perusal of the current literature on NVQs will quickly identify several critical issues. It has been argued that although funded by the government, NVQs are still being viewed with great criticism, indifference, scepticism and resistance from employees and employers – including the majority of Chief Executive Officers and a surprisingly large number of training professionals. Perhaps this is because of the issues outlined below.

Bureaucracy and costs

There is a fear that the NVQ system is too bureaucratic and too costly. Trainers have complained about the magnitude of NVQ documentation and the complexity of the wording. There are costs in terms of time, materials, training assessors and lost productivity during assessment. These costs put NVQs low down on a training shopping list with a limited budget. Implementation procedures and internal resistance also unsettle employers.

The structure of industry with a high proportion of small businesses make it questionable whether the requirements of the assessment process can be met. Too high a degree of simulation is required in some cases since too wide a variety of activities are included in an NVQ. At the same time the range of competences in any one business, because of specialization, may not be wide enough to gain a full qualification. For a small business the costs involved may be prohibitive.

Relevance

Some companies are unconvinced about the relevance and benefits of NVQs for their organization. Companies fail to see the benefit to them because the generic standard does not fit into their specific business. There is a perceived lack of relevance to individual or company needs and circumstances. BHS abandoned its NVQ programme in 1994 as it was not meeting the company's needs. They developed an in-house training programme which is more specific to their needs but is modelled on NVQs.

Gardner Merchant, a leading catering company, has committed itself to training 25 per cent of its workforce to NVQ Level 3 by the year 2000 – only half of the target set by the government. Philpott (1994) argues that government targets are 'excessive' and 'inconsistent' with industry needs. She says that training 50 per cent of staff to NVQ Level 3 would produce 'too many chiefs and not enough indians'. They would qualify too many staff with no suitable positions available.

Assessment in the workplace

There is emphasis on performance assessment in the workplace to the exclusion of all other types of assessment. This is unique to the UK and flies in the face of European experience where vocational qualifications are assessed on two dimensions, work-based criteria plus academic examinations.

Prais (1989) argues against the underlying principles of competence-based assessment: 'Most Europeans would agree that their own systems are imperfect . . . but they would be astonished to find that radically new principles for the award of vocational qualifications were being adopted on the basis of notions that are still in the debatable stage, at best.' He goes on to offer a solution by building on what is best from the UK and the rest of Europe. Prais's main criticism is that NVQs are based on internal assessment of performance at work. However, European countries incorporate a balance of practical tests and written theoretical tests which probe deeper into the underlying knowledge of a candidate. There is a lesson here for the UK.

NVQs do not compare favourably in relation to vocational qualifications in other European countries. For example, our Level 1 is lower than first stage qualifications of other countries. Also European vocational qualifications often include other subjects such as the native language, mathematics, social science or a foreign language.

More fundamentally, the exclusion of written exams in NVQs disregards the importance of literacy and numeracy. For instance, Steedman and Hawkins (1994) argue that NVQs provide 'occupational training at the expense of general education'. Hence in the 1980s, the building trades took City and Guilds exams in maths – a practice which ceased with NVQs. This has led to our French and German counterparts (who have maths exams) being more qualified and thus gives the continental Europeans a possible competitive edge.

To conclude this review on NVQs the following statements seem valid.

- A national standard of competence exists across all sections of the workforce.
- Access is broader but dissemination is less.
- NVQs do capitalize on job experience.
- NVQs do have some positive elements particularly for our immediate needs here for self-development – examples include recognition of success at work, a possible incentive to succeed, progression routes and recognition of a qualification.

There are problems though.

- The skill orientation is at the expense of cognitive development.
- The job orientation is too narrow and NVQs are more akin to training than education.
- The lack of formal examinations may give us second rate qualifications – or at least the continued perception that vocational qualifications are not in the same academic league as qualifications from an independent and accredited college or university.

At the end of the day, they are better than nothing but they have clear limits. Our approach within the series is more akin to the 'Education for Capability' ideas with a culture of learning combining academic excellence, creativity, the abilities to complete the task, to work with other people and to cope with everyday life. NVQs form only some of the first rungs of this capability ladder – but at least they are rungs and we feel that the NVQ system goes some way to meeting task effectiveness at the place of work.

F.   Conclusion

We argued in ESD Unit One that self-development is linked to greater personal and organizational effectiveness. In ESD Unit Two we examined personal effectiveness and looked at how competencies met these criteria.

Here we have looked at task effectiveness and have focused both on MCI competences and the NVQ system.

The main difficulty, as in ESD Unit Two, is to determine what we mean by task effectiveness. A range of proposals were put forward. In particular the series view of policy, task aspects, people elements and functions was noted as a common denominator of managerial performance – some of which included task aspects.

We then turned to capability which is perhaps more of a humanistic educational model than a task/training type of approach. This however is seen as a strength for we should be able to move beyond the immediate task in order to be effective.

Competence was debated at length alongside the NVQ system. It is easy to be critical – perhaps too easy – but there are some serious problems in both approaches. Yet there are also benefits to self-development in both approaches.

The real concern is that the frameworks and standards can be reductionist in nature – almost with a hint of Taylorite principles at work. Both the MCI and NVQ routes give us a base line on task competence but they must be allied to the personal effectiveness covered in the last unit. Furthermore, they need to take a wider vision and move to some capability-type approach which is more akin to a developmental model than the overly prescriptive routes of the MCI and of the NVQs.

For pure task effectiveness (excluding personal effectiveness) the MCI system – warts and all – does give us something to work on. This series can be related in part to the MCI ideas of functions, for example, but there must be less of a prescriptive approach and more room for personal initiative. We develop this in the next few units.

As a final thought for this unit, understanding task effectiveness is essential to self-development. Please tackle the last activity of ESD Unit Three which involves a personal task log for hotel staff and consolidates the ideas in this unit.

ACTIVITY ESD3.8

PERSONAL LOG BOOK FOR THE STAFF AT THE CAMBRIDGE BLUE HOTEL

Activity code

✓ Self-development
✓ Teamwork
☐ Communications
☐ Numeracy/IT
✓ Decisions

Task

You have been asked to create a personal task log book for the staff of the Cambridge Blue Hotel.

A log book is a record of a personal learning plan. It acts as an ongoing indicator of the personal development of the staff. In particular it should emphasize task progress and highlight areas of skill and knowledge training. This could form a traditional route of induction and focus on a range of tasks for staff from dealing with customers, product/company knowledge, health/safety aspects, front office/barwork skills to dealing with sales and management. Alternatively you may wish to use a competence type of list.

Bibliography

Carroll, S.J. and Gillen, D.J., 'Are the classical management functions useful in describing managerial work?' *Academy of Management Review*, **12**, (1987), pp. 38–51.

Constable, R. and McCormick, R.J., *The Making of British Managers, A Report of the BIM and CBI into Management Training, Education and Development* (BIM, London, 1983).

Coopers & Lybrand Associates, *A Challenge of Complacency* (NEDO/MSC, London 1984).

Deloitte, Haskins, and Sells, *Management Challenge for the 1990s* (Training Agency, Sheffield, 1989).

Drucker, P.F., *The Age of Discontinuity* (Heinemann, London, 1969).

Handy, C., *The Making of Managers* (NEDO/MSC/BIM, London, 1987).

Institute of Manpower Studies, *Competence and Competition* (NEDO/MSC, London, 1984).

Katz, R.L., 'Skills of an effective administrator', *Harvard Business Review*, **52**, (Sept/Oct 1974), p. 90.

Kotter, J.P., 'Managers as Leaders', *Harvard Business Review*, (Boston, MA, 1991).

Management Charter Initiative (MCI) *Good Practice Guide* (MCI, London, 1991).

Mangham, I.L., 'In Search of competence', *Journal of General Management*, (1986), pp. 5–12.

MCI 1, *Certificate Level Guidelines* (MCI, London, ND).

MCI 2, *Diploma Level Guidelines* (MCI, London, ND).

MCI 3, *Assessment Guidelines* (MCI, London, ND).

Mintzberg, H., *The Nature of Managerial Work* (Harper & Row, New York, 1973).

National Council for Vocational Qualifications, (NCVQ), *Guide to National Vocational Qualifications* (NCVQ, London, 1991).

Philpott, M. 'Catering NVQ targets criticised', *Personnel Management*, (June 1994).

Prais, S.J., 'How Europe would see the new British Initiative for Standardising Vocational Qualifications', *Nat. Inst. Econ. Rev.*, (August, 1989).

Schermerhorn, J.R., *Management for Productivity* (Wiley, New York, 1993).

Steedman, H. and Hawkins, J., 'NVQs are too narrowly focused to be useful for young people, says report', *Personnel Management*, (Sept, 1994).

Stephenson, J., 'Capability and competence: are they the same and does it matter?' *Capability*, **1**, (1994).

Stevens, C., 'Assessment Centres: The British Experience', *Personnel Management* IPM, London, (July 1985).

Stewart, V., 'Human Capital Issues in Organisational Change', selected papers from the IPMA National Conference, Asia Pacific Journal of Human Resources. (Australian Human Resource Institute, 1992).

Weaver, T., 'Knowledge gets you nowhere', *Capability*, **1**, (1994), pp. 6–12.

ESD Unit Four

Learning: the Motor of Self-development

Learning Objectives

After completing this unit, you should be able to:

- understand that learning is the basis of self-development;
- be aware of a range of learning theories and characteristics;
- apply experiential learning to self-development;
- be aware of different learning experiences – particularly action learning;
- link individual learning to conducive learning environments; and
- apply the generic skills of the series.

Contents

A. Overview

B. Learning

▶ Nature of learning

▶ The outcomes of learning

▶ Some theories of learning (outline)

– Behaviourists

– Cognitivists

– The Gestalt School

– Humanists

– Phenomenologists

– Social learning theorists

– Experientialists

▶ How adults learn

▶ Learning and development

▶ Learning barriers

▶ Learning systems

C. Self-learning

▶ Experiential learning

▶ Individual styles

▶ Self-development and learning

D. Learning Experiences

▶ Academic/Educational

▶ Personal

The learning diary

▶ Organizational learning

▶ The learning contract: individual and organizational agreements

E.   Action Learning – The Key To Self-learning?

F.   Conclusion

ESD Unit Four

> " . . . (Learning is) a relatively permanent change in behaviour that occurs as a result of practice or experience. "
>
> (Bass and Vaughan 1966)

A. Overview

The nature of learning must be understood as it is seen as the backbone of the whole subject of self-development. Perhaps it is also the life-blood of the process as well. We touch upon learning theories but only as they impact upon our subject matter. The process of how adults go about learning provides an important context to our subject. Before looking at barriers to learning, we broaden the debate by examining learning and development.

The next section moves on to self-learning styles and a range of learning characteristics that can stimulate self-development.

The penultimate section concerns learning experiences – at academic/educational, personal and organizational levels. Learning contracts fuse these streams together.

We conclude by having an in-depth analysis of action learning which may meet many of our ideas on learning to date.

B. Learning

Nature of learning

As we have seen from the quotation at the beginning of the unit, learning or behavioural change, tends to be seen in terms of experience. Indeed learning from experience is regarded by many people as something that happens automatically by performing various activities. People do modify their actions in the light of the experience they undergo. However learning from experience means more than reacting to events. One can also learn from contrived learning experiences which include on-the-job activities. In this way, work and learning can be integrated. Anything remote from the adult/managerial experience is believed by some to block rather than stimulate learning but this is debatable.

141

'Learning refers to the acquisition of skills, knowledge, abilities and attitudes through patterned actions and practice, which changes our behaviour.'

(Anderson and Kyprianou, 1994)

How does this concept of learning affect our current needs? Learning is seen by the authors as the key vehicle of self-development, if not of organization development.

Harrison (1992) usefully puts the concept of learning into three clear applications:

■ Development is that process through which individual and organizational growth can reach full potential.

■ Education contributes to that process because it directly and continuously affects the formation of knowledge, ability, character, culture, aspiration and achievements.

■ Training is the short-term systematic process of mastering tasks, skills and knowledge to predetermined standards.

All of these activities are involved in management and are supported by various learning theories.

Before we touch upon some of these key theories, we should look to the outcomes of learning which are important to any notion of self-development.

The outcomes of learning

There are three major outcomes to learning which may be observed after it has occurred:

■ skills
■ knowledge and understanding
■ beliefs, attitudes and values.

As we have seen (ESD Unit Three), increasing use is being made of the term competence.

Skills of many kinds are required by managers such as:

■ perceptual motor
■ cognitive
■ linguistic
■ communication
■ social
■ statistical, etc.

See Box ESD4.1 which identifies a hierarchy of thinking skills and Box
ESD4.2. which outlines a model for skills acquisition.

BOX ESD4.1

A hierarchy of thinking skills

Bloom identifies a hierarchy of thinking skills through which learning can take place.[1]

- Knowledge – simple knowledge of facts, terms, theories, etc.
- Comprehension – understanding the meaning of the knowledge
- Application – the ability to apply this knowledge and comprehension in new situations
- Analysis – the ability to break down the material into its constituent parts and to see the relationship between them
- Synthesis – the ability to re-assemble the parts into a new and meaningful relationship, thus forming a new whole
- Evaluation – the ability to judge the value of material using explicit and coherent criteria, either one's own or derived from the work of others.

Source:
[1]Adapted from Bloom, B.S., *Taxonomy of Educational Objectives: The Classification of Educational Goals* (Longmans, London, 1956).

BOX ESD4.2

A model for skills acquisition

- Novice – follows context-free rules, with the relevant components of the situation defined but may lack any sense of the overall task.
- Advanced beginner – begins to recognize the contextual elements of the task through practical experience and perceive similarities between new and previous experiences.
- Competent – begins to recognize a wider range of cues and is able to select and focus on the most important; relies less on rules and may experiment and go beyond the rules using trial and error.
- Proficient – achieves unconscious, fluid, effortless performance of skills/competencies.

> ■ Expert – has an intuitive understanding of situations and can cope with uncertainty and unforeseen situations.
>
> *Source*:
> Adapted from Dreyfus, H.L. *Mind over Machine* (Blackwell, Oxford, 1986).

According to Gardner (1985) knowledge and understanding can be divided into 'know how' – being able to do something, and 'know that' – a statement about the procedures required to do something. This is, perhaps, a reflection of the clash between the academic and vocational viewpoints.

However, Sternberg (1985) adds to the definition of 'know how' when he says:

Underlying successful performance in many real world tasks is *tacit knowledge* of a kind that is never explicitly taught and in many instances never even verbalised.

Tacit knowledge, therefore, is acquired through experience rather than instruction and this leads on to the idea of *tacit skills*. This means that the skills are learned through practical experience or 'learning by doing'.

Our attitudes grow out of our beliefs and develop as we live our lives. Some attitudes may turn into core attitudes which are very resistant to change. Other attitudes, however, may change with our experience. As we have seen in ESD Unit Two, our beliefs are based on 'what is' whereas our values are based on 'what should be'.

Gross (1987) believes that one can turn a belief into an attitude by adding a value statement about what is good, desirable, valuable or worthwhile. He says that a person can have thousands of beliefs, hundreds of attitudes but only a few dozen values.

Management education is now often being described in terms of management competence which has been variously defined. The concept of competence integrates knowledge, understanding and skill and these elements are assessed by performance. The last two units differentiated between competences and competencies and these definitions perhaps emphasize the two views.

The following definitions give a flavour for the concept of competence:

an underlying characteristic of a person which results in effective and/or superior performance in a job

(Boyatzis, 1982)

or

the ability to perform the activities within an occupational area to the
levels of performance expected in employment.

(Training Commission, 1988)

We now turn to some key theories of learning. We shall not develop these
to any great extent as we cover them elsewhere in the series (Anderson
and Kyprianou, 1994).

Some theories of learning (outline)

Behaviourists

This school of thought links stimulus and response. Reflex responses
or behaviours are emphasized. Classical conditioning, with its
salivating dogs, seems to have little to help us in understanding
self-development.

Operant or instrumental conditioning focuses more on the consequences of behaviour and takes us away from a crude stimulus/response
approach. However its 'reward' system is also mechanistic – although
some extrinsic reward, promotion, more salary, etc. may follow on from
self-development. Perhaps intrinsic or inner motivation may be more
relevant to self-development. Reinforcement is another aspect of
operant conditioning and positive reinforcement, by the organization for
example, can certainly maintain a momentum of development – self or
otherwise.

Cognitivists

The 'inner mental map' in relation to external stimuli is more important
to the cognitivists who move us away from crude stimulus – response
approaches. In particular, their view of insight learning is important to
self-development as understanding and reflection are important to the
whole process of learning.

New information should have some meaning for the learner – if it is to
be acted upon. This process involves the teacher/trainer in structuring new
information and making it meaningful in terms of existing understanding.
Thus the learner's needs are the focus of the relationship.

In pure self-developmental terms with little or no facilitation or
assistance this could mean that the learners are given the responsibility to
structure their own realities – which will enhance learning. Either way, the

cognitive map is developed in the context of existing understanding which may be derived from prior knowledge/experience, etc.

The Gestalt school

This approach takes an holistic approach to learning. Derived from the German word for 'form' or 'pattern', the approach concerns itself with the organized form of perception and of cognitive development. In this approach, an active relationship is seen between objects being perceived and the whole organizing processes within the perceiver.

The Gestalt approach is summed up well by Gabriel (1986).

> Gestalt psychologists were to refer to atomistic, associationistic psychology as 'bricks and mortar' pyschology, the bricks being the atoms or elements and the mortar the associations between them. They believed that the important part of the matter was the wall.

So perceptions from outside are seen to be synthesized by the mind into a gestalt or pattern. The whole becomes greater than the component parts because of what has been added internally by the 'organization'. Hence a learning experience is very much an interaction between the external event and the internal cognitive processes.

This approach sees the totality and learning linked to seeing the whole as a problem. Insightful learning and spontaneity are also emphasized by this approach which may have some relevance to our self-developmental needs.

Humanists

Advocates of this learning theory draw on a variety of religious, philosophical and psychological theories. This view of the tutor – learner relationship is that the tutor/trainer role should facilitate the learning process by helping the learner to clarify goals, to design learning situations and to evaluate outcomes (see figure ESD4.1).

Phenomenologists

Those who accept the premises of phenomenology are concerned with experience. The person has an immediate unanalysed experience – prompted by some stimuli (it is not a crude stimulus/response). The approach is used particularly in the study of perception and of how people come to terms with events – as they occur irrespective of the inner self giving contrary viewpoints.

Traditional View

Tutor (important)	Flow	Learner
• embodies knowledge and expertise • decides what is to be learned and how it will be learned • tests extent of learning	⟶	• receives knowledge, skills, etc. • memorizes and regurgitates as required
Active		Passive

Humanistic View

Learner (important)	Flow	Tutor
• decides learning goals • designs learning strategies and methods • evaluates learning experiences	⟵ ⟶	• helps to diagnose needs • helps to design learning • helps to evaluate and gives feedback
Active		Active

Figure ESD4.1   The tutor–learner relationships

Source: Adapted from Jones, 1981.

In personality theory, it has found favour because of the onus on the immediate experience which gives rise to some vision of self-actualization. Like the humanists, this desire to unlock our full expression, if not actualization, may go to the root of 'pure' self-development.

Social learning theorists

This approach touches upon the cognitive theory with its cognitive imagery but it is linked to a view of behaviour imitation or modelling.

For self-development, it would mean gathering information, developing this mental imagery of behaviour and its outcomes (which is linked to the earlier stimulus/response approach) and then trying out the behaviour. It is linked to self-efficacy which we developed in ESD Unit Three.

Perhaps the competence model itself is seen as a behavioural model which we use as a means to improve performance with its elements and appropriate behaviours and management practices linked to the whole model of say the MCI approach.

Experientialists

This is a popular approach in education and in training. The view here is that experiential learning makes events meaningful to learners as they sort things out for themselves.

Effective learner spirals are seen to occur through a repetition of experience, observation, reflection, conceptualization and experimentation, etc. This is an important and popular approach to learning which fits into the learner orientation of self-development, so we shall devote more time to this approach in due course. In the interim, we need to turn to the specific learning needs of mature adults as they underpin any view of self-development. But before we leave these theories, tackle Activity ESD4.1.

ACTIVITY ESD4.1

THEORIES

Activity code

- ✓ Self-development
- ✓ Teamwork
- ✓ Communications
- ☐ Numeracy/IT
- ✓ Decisions

Task

As an individual/group initiative, summarize the main tenets of the learning theories in the text and determine the relevance of each to self-development.

How adults learn

Unless they are inmates of total institutions like prisons or monasteries or whatever, or are banished to some desert island with no real lifeform apart from themselves, most adults bring a rich tapestry of acquired knowledge, skills and practical experience to the process of modifying their behaviour through some learning experience. As adults, in order to cope with everyday pressures, they need to be independent and self-directed (hopefully with some community or collective interest as well). In the main they are not dependent children. Please tackle Activity ESD4.2.

ACTIVITY ESD4.2

HOW DO YOU LEARN?

Activity code

- ✓ Self-development
- ☐ Teamwork
- ☐ Communications
- ☐ Numeracy/IT
- ✓ Decisions

Task

Reflect on a personal learning experience, note the features and the context of how you went about learning. This could be from academic, work or leisure interests.

Knowles (1970) found that the education of adults tends to follow the art and science of teaching children (pedagogy) which is based on the old concept of education, the transmission of knowledge. He believes this approach should be restricted to children and a theory of education which recognizes the attributes and needs of adults in the learning situation should be developed. He terms this 'andragogy' and he suggests that andragogy should replace pedagogy for adults.

Knowles outlined four assumptions about adult learners which are different from assumptions about child learners. He suggested that with maturity a person:

- moves from being dependent to self-directing;
- accumulates experience which becomes a resource for learning;
- becomes increasingly orientated to the tasks of his/her roles in life; and
- shifts his/her orientation towards learning from being subject-centred to being problem-centred.

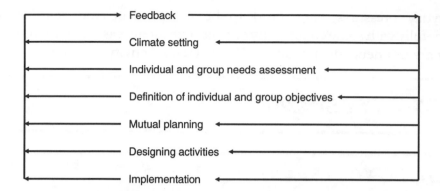

Figure ESD4.2   Andragogy

Source: Adapted from Knowles, 1970.

In andragogy all parts of this learning process involve the active participation of the learner (see figure ESD4.2).

Learning and development

Much of the literature on training, development and education uses the terms 'learning' and 'development' synonymously. However, Davies and Easterby-Smith (1984) showed that managers make a clear distinction between the two terms. For these managers, 'learning' referred to the products of training, and the knowledge and 'tricks of the trade' that a manager can pick up over the years. This occurs over a short time span. 'Development' referred to the acquisition of greater general competence, or 'capacity', and was normally linked in the managers' minds with promotion. This occurs over a long time span.

On the other hand, Kolb and Fry (1975) and Revans (1982) think of 'learning' as a process of interaction with the environment; whereas 'development' is associated with the stage people have reached in their ability to learn.

Development is the process through which learning brings about significant changes in a person over time. Thus an organization will expect its members to develop and so the organization itself will develop because of its deliberate policy of development.

People develop throughout their lives since they are continually engaged in learning processes as they balance changes in themselves with changes in the environment. The changes in the environment have caused many professions in recent years to require their members to undertake continuing professional development (CPD). This is because the changes in the environment rapidly render obsolete both skills and knowledge (see ESD Units Five and Six).

CPD requires both learning to learn and continuous learning and so will benefit all kinds of individuals and organizations. Indeed Whittaker (1992) believes that:

- professionals should actively seek improved performance i.e. continuous development;

- development should be owned and managed by the learner;

- learning needs are individual;

- learning objectives should be clear; and

- investment in the time required for CPD should be regarded as being as important as investment in other activities.

Therefore, according to CPD logic, if managers consider themselves to be professionals they must take responsibility for their own development and learning by identifying their learning needs and the various ways of meeting them. This may be done through study or through every day work. They must be capable of monitoring their own progress, assessing the outcomes and adjusting their goals as necessary. We develop this idea in Activity ESD4.3.

ACTIVITY ESD4.3

TRAINING/DEVELOPMENT NEEDS

Activity code

✓ Self-development

  Teamwork

  Communications

  Numeracy/IT

✓ Decisions

Task

- Outline your training needs within your existing post.

- If in full-time education, outline your developmental needs before you embark on a career in industry.

Davies and Easterby-Smith (1984) adopted a long-term view of the development of managers and therefore used the term 'development' rather than 'learning'. They examined the impact of the organization's environments on the manager's development and looked at the relationship between a manager's development and his/her past career experience. They found it interesting that not one of the managers considered that he/she had 'developed' as a result of training. Nevertheless, some did say they had learned some things from it!

Please refer to Box ESD4.3.

BOX ESD4.3

What is training?

The International Labour Organization (ILO) suggest the following scan of training – which may also cover development – in the example of driving a motor car.

- **Knowledge**   This would include such things as the position of the various controls; how to operate them and what happens when you do.

- **Skills**   This would include such things as how to start up the car, how to move off, how to steer it around obstacles, how to change gears, how to reverse, etc. All of these things could be practised at the beginning in a field where there is no danger or inconvenience to other people.

- **Techniques**   This would include the ability to apply all this knowledge and these skills to real life conditions on the open road and in the busy city.

- **Attitudes**   The training course would clearly need to try to develop in the trainees the proper attitudes towards such things as road safety, vehicle maintenance, etc.

> ■ Experience   According to the objectives of our training course, it may be necessary for our trainee driver to have experience of driving under special conditions, e.g. on very rough mountain roads or even in another country where they drive on the other side of the road.
>
> *Source*:
> Adapted from *Teaching and Training Methods for Management Development* (ILO, Geneva, 1972).

Over a third of the managers recalled some form of development in their own capacities and skills and in all cases this had occurred during their normal work.

Please tackle Activity ESD4.4; thereafter consult Box ESD4.4.

ACTIVITY ESD4.4

JOB MOVEMENT

Activity code

- ✓ Self-development
- ✓ Teamwork
- ☐ Communications
- ☐ Numeracy/IT
- ✓ Decisions

Job change within or between jobs is seen as an important self-learning route.

Task

How would you ensure that this learning was consolidated in such a change of jobs? You may wish to outline key features associated with this development.

BOX ESD4.4

Developmental experiences

The developmental experiences were associated with either a job move elsewhere or within an existing job.[1] Three features were found to be significant for development after a job move.

■ Each job had a significant element completely new to the manager.

■ The manager was given responsibility for a specific area of business.

■ Most of the managers felt that they had initiated their developmental moves themselves rather than being part of a planned progression system.

Source:
[1]Adapted from Davies, J. and Easterby-Smith, M., 'Learning and developing from work experiences', *Journal of Management Studies*, **21**, pp. 167–83, 1984.

Within the job, development was associated with change in various forms, or with projects and assignments.

From the evidence Davies and Easterby-Smith (1984) concluded:

managers develop primarily through confrontations with novel situations and problems where their existing repertoire of behaviours are inadequate and where they have to develop new ways of dealing with these situations.

We now turn to barriers involved with learning.

Learning barriers

The main blockage to learning depends on the theory of learning being applied. To some extent, each theory will have its own limitations and potential learning barriers. For example, to the behaviourist, if the stimulus or reinforcement is inadequate or lacking, the response will not occur. For the social learning theorists, if the model is not adequate or is not 'transmitted' behaviour replication will not occur in full etc.

Please tackle Activity ESD4.5 then refer to Box ESD4.5 which moves away from the theory to more pragmatic examples of barriers.

ACTIVITY ESD4.5

BARRIERS TO LEARNING

Activity code

- ✓ Self-development
- ☐ Teamwork
- ✓ Communications
- ☐ Numeracy/IT
- ✓ Decisions

Task

We all experience blockages or barriers to learning.

- Take five minutes and note any barriers to learning that you have personally experienced.
- Now attempt to classify these learning barriers.

Learning systems

In this unit we looked at Bloom's (1956) learning taxonomy – a key educational system for learning. Other systems, or taxonomies of learning, which attempt to codify learning exist as well (see Anderson, 1993).

For our immediate needs here the example of Long's (1969) spectrum may be worth citing. Interestingly the more tangible, 'harder' parts of the spectrum deal with skill acquisition while the 'softer', abstract, people-oriented aspects occur at the other end of the spectrum. Perhaps our 'competency' of the 1990s lies near his use of skills and knowledge (application). Please refer to figure ESD4.3.

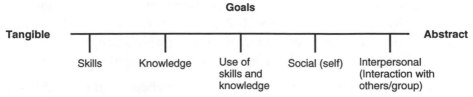

Figure ESD 4.3 Long's spectrum
(Adapted from Long, 1969)

BOX ESD4.5

Barriers to learning

Mumford[1] identified several barriers to learning and development such as:

- cognitive   previous learning experience
- cultural   the way things are here . . .
- emotional   fear or insecurity
- expressive   poor communication skills
- intellectual   limited learning styles and/or poor learning skills
- motivational   unwillingness to take risks
- perceptual   not seeing that there is a problem
- physical   place, time
- situational   lack of opportunities
- environment boss/colleagues/family being unsupportive.

Source:
[1]Adapted from Mumford in Pedler, M., Burgoyne, J., Boydell, T. and Welshman, G., *Self Development in Organisations* (McGraw-Hill, London, 1990).

Interestingly the development of 'self' is further over towards the abstract aspect of the chart – perhaps emphasizing the difficulty of self-learning. We now turn to this by examining experiential learning in greater depth.

C. Self-learning

Experiential learning

According to one of the main advocates of this type of learning, Kolb's (1982) experiential learning offers:

> something more substantial and enduring. It offers the foundation for an approach to education and learning as a lifelong process that is soundly based in intellectual traditions of social psychology, philosophy and cognitive psychology. The experiential learning model pursues a framework for examining and strengthening the critical linkages among education, work and personal development.

Experiential learning has its focus on experience as the modifier of behaviour. Perhaps this assumes that experience and learning are synonymous – which may not be the case. If the focus does lie on experience, other aspects are also involved in experiential learning. Kolb, Rubin and McIntyre developed a four stage cycle where concrete experience is followed by observation and review from reflection and then the formation of abstract concepts and generalization (see Kolb *et al.* 1984). Testing out the implications should then occur in new situations.

Experiential learning has clear benefits. It is closely linked to the work situation – drawing upon everyday experiences – and it facilitates ease of transfer to everyday reality. It can be enriching as individual learners can be self-motivated on their voyage of discovery. It can allow experimentation. As it is based on experiences (both current and past) it may build up the learners' confidence – particularly in new situations. It may be linked with 'learning how to learn' – which goes to the heart of self-development.

Of course 'pure' experiential learning is not without its critics, including one of the authors. The individual experience may not tally with organizational needs. If the experience or cognitive structure is not established by previous learning, experiential learning may be inhibited. It needs a context so the particular experience facilitates generalization. It may be too *ad hoc* without structures of reinforcement and feedback and it may give too many hard knocks to the learner through too many trials and errors. There is concern with its potential for randomness and its scope for chance which can nullify developmental initiatives.

So experiential learning is a key aspect to management development and to self-development. Experience is important: thinking, doing and reflecting can only be helpful to self-development and the ability to make insightful analyses and transfer them to other situations can only underpin self-development.

At the same time, the individual learner needs a support system, from resources to an organization committed to the cause of development. Others would argue that other theories of learning are equally applicable to facilitating management development. Either way, experiential learning, warts and all, is seen here as a useful underpinning theory of learning for stimulating and understanding self-development.

We now move on to learner styles which owe much to the principles of experiential learning.

Individual styles

With the emphasis on the learner, the individual's style or approach to learning is given great emphasis by the adherents of experiential learning.

For example, the work of Honey and Mumford (1982) can be cited. They further defined and refined Kolb's (1982) categories to give us a range of learner styles. Moreover, these predominant styles would be most likely to be of benefit and to develop in a given type of situation. Activists, reflectors, theorists and pragmatists were put forward as key learner types.

You may wish to tackle Activity ESD4.6 and then consider Box ESD4.6, and then do the 'mini project' in Activity ESD4.7, depending on time.

ACTIVITY ESD4.6

LEARNING STYLE

Activity code

- ✓ Self-development
- ☐ Teamwork
- ☐ Communications
- ☐ Numeracy/IT
- ✓ Decisions

Task

Outline your personal style or approach to learning (150 words maximum). You may wish to consider:

- the role of concrete facts and experiences;
- the degree of reflection before action;
- the level of analysis and the use of theory; and
- the level of activity or application/experimentation.

BOX ESD4.6

Styles

- **Activists** — adopt task-oriented approaches
  - like new experiences
  - like concrete/here and now activities.

- **Reflectors** — mull over ideas
  - think before acting
  - review ideas, etc. before decision-making.

- ■ Theorists   – like to be stretched intellectually
                  – like to question premises/assumptions
                  – like to explore theoretical links between issues/subjects.

- ■ Pragmatists – are practical
                 – need to relate the task back to the job
                 – like practice and feedback.

Source:
Adapted from Honey, P. and Mumford, A., *A Manual of Learning Styles* (Honey, Maidenhead, 1982).

ACTIVITY ESD4.7

MINI PROJECT

Activity code

✓ Self-development
✓ Teamwork
✓ Communications
☐ Numeracy/IT
☐ Decisions

Task

Discuss the advantages and disadvantages of experiential learning with particular application to adults pursuing a self-developmental programme at the place of work. (Suitable for group discussion/debate or individual/group report.)

Self-development and learning

Certain features or characteristics of learning are seen to prevail. Of course different theories of learning will emphasize different aspects of these features, but some degree of commonality may be possible. (See

Anderson's article in the *Independent Journal for the Professional Trainer*, 1993.)

The key characteristics of learning which we develop in the next activity are seen as:

- motivation
- knowledge of results
- reward
- trial/error
- learning by doing/experience
- scale of learning
- time periods
- structured learning
- interference
- individual differences.

Please refer to Activity ESD4.8 and thereafter to Box ESD4.7.

ACTIVITY ESD4.8

LEARNING AND SELF-DEVELOPMENT

Activity code

✓ Self-development
✓ Teamwork
✓ Communications
☐ Numeracy/IT
✓ Decisions

Task

Below you (or your group) will find a list of general learning principles and their characteristics.[1] The activity involves examining the implications of these principles for self-development.

Assume that the developmental learning is taking place in either an academic environment or in a corporate training situation. For example, this series or an MBA programme could be used.

Learning principle	Characteristics	Implications for self-development
1 Motivation	■ This is a critical aspect of learning. ■ It is goal-directed behaviour. ■ The learner is ultimately responsible for his/her level of commitment.	
2 Knowledge of results	■ Feedback allows for 'corrective' action. ■ The rate of learning should increase when the learner is advised of his/her progress.	
3 Reward	■ A reward increases the possibility of repeating desired behaviour.	
4 Trial and error	■ This is not practice as it has no real structure. ■ It is expensive and time-consuming.	
5 Learning by doing/ experience	■ An active role is involved rather than just passive reading.	
6 Scale of learning	■ 'Whole' learning is learning a complete section ■ 'Part' learning is learning in units.	
7 Time periods	■ Do not expect a steady upward line of learning. ■ You will tend to have a good period and then it flattens out. You feel you are not learning anything. This is normal so stop for a while and return later.	
8 Structured learning	■ This is not just repetition. ■ It is putting the learning into some scheme of things.	
9 'Interference'	■ If learning can build on prior experience, all the better for you. ■ 'Noise' and interference should be avoided.	
10 Individual differences	■ We are all different. Our learning styles and approach may also differ.	

Source:
[1] Anderson, A.H., *Successful Training Practice* (Blackwell, Oxford, 1993).

BOX ESD4.7

Learning, self-development and an educational environment

This box refers back to Activity EDS4.8. [The numbering equates to that of the activity.]

1 You must have clear goals for what you want to achieve, e.g. a degree for its own sake of gaining knowledge; accomplishment or as a passport to a new career, etc.
2 The tutorial system is geared to meet this principle.
3 This is linked to motivation and your commitment. You need to build in some 'rewards' for yourself, e.g. 'I'll complete two lessons this week and go to the pub on Friday night – provided I complete the sessions'.
4 You should really avoid this method wherever possible. The whole learning programme should be structured to your needs.
5 Taking notes, summarizing points in your own words, completing the exercises and essays/case studies, etc. all contribute to this successful process of 'activity'.
6 The course is not simple and so part learning is used in each lesson plan which, in turn, contributes to the *whole* module and to the *whole* programme.
7 The timing of self-study is critical. Use the lesson plans. You should take one lesson/one module at a time. Some lessons cannot be crammed in a day's study – don't overdo it. Pace yourself and allow periods of study up to an hour. Break and return. Do *not* study for eight hours solid!
8 Normally this scheme of things has been carried out for you through lectures/lesson plans.
9 You need a quiet corner to study in your home, at lunchbreak or in the local library.
10 This is correct but the principles outlined here are fully transferable although *you* must apply them to you as an individual.

Source:
[1] These comments are derived from the Effective Management Training/development programme run by Anderson Associates, Personnel and Management Advisors (AAPMA) and are related to the Distance Learning Masters Degree Material prepared by M. Anderson (7 Water Lane, Melbourn, S. Cambridge SG8 6AY, England).

D.   Learning Experiences

Academic/Educational

Traditional teaching methods start with abstract concepts, whereas, experiential methods begin with real experience.

There are six ways of demonstrating that learning has taken place in the academic world which can also be used in the world of work. These are based on Bloom (1956) (see also Box ESD3.2). They are:

- information and knowledge

- understanding

- the ability to apply knowledge and understanding

- the ability to analyse

- the ability to synthesize

- the ability to evaluate.

If Bloom (1956) is right, we should be able to identify learning in both the academic world and the world of work by looking for evidence of the six learning outcomes together with changes in personal attitudes, awareness, values and/or effectiveness. This implies making use of Kolb's (1982) learning cycle – emphasizing particularly personal observation and reflection.

Personal

Clearly much of the onus for self-development is going to lie with you – the individual manager. Later (ESD Units Five and Six) we touch upon support systems and organizational learning. However the skills of observation and in particular reflection may underpin the whole action-orientation of management.

We shall touch briefly upon organizational learning as we cover this area more appropriately in ESD Unit Six and then we shall pull together the self-learning concept by an in-depth examination of action learning.

First of all consider Box ESD4.8 on the importance of reflection and complete the Activity ESD4.9. We shall then conclude this section by looking at learning diaries and learning contracts.

BOX ESD4.8

The importance of reflection

If we accept the criteria for learning suggested by Bloom[1] and the need to reflect on our experience suggested by Kolb,[2] we can propose a method for equating the academic world with the world of work. This will involve managers in reflecting on their experience and identifying their learning from it. For example they should be able to answer questions such as those which follow.

■ What information or new knowledge have your learned? What have you discovered?

■ Can you discuss and/or clarify difficult points, identify key issues, answer 'what if' and 'if . . . then' scenarios? Can you explain key principles and theories or the techniques you have used to solve a problem?

■ Can you demonstrate, illustrate, apply your learning? Can you apply principles to new situations? Can you solve different types of problems by applying theories?

■ Can you compare, contrast, appraise information, principles and theories in relation to your situation?

■ Can you discuss the sources of information (books, journals, people, organizations, etc.) which you have consulted in exploring the major issues and carrying out the tasks?

■ Can you appraise the evidence you have supplied and the information you have obtained for its usefulness, reliability, validity, etc?

■ Can you teach, design, develop new ideas, theories and solutions, organize, plan, set up?

■ Can you then evaluate key theories, principles and situations implicit in your evidence? Can you decide the effectiveness of various approaches in practice?

■ Can you outline a strategy and identify the resources you would need to resolve any key issues you have identified? How would you evaluate your plan?

■ What changes have occurred in your effectiveness, awareness, beliefs, attitudes and values?

Such a report can be easily and quickly assessed.

Source:
[1] Bloom, B.S., *Taxonomy of Educational Objectives: The Classification of Educational Goals* (Longmans, London, 1956). [2] Kolb, D.A. and Fry, R., 'Towards an applied theory of experiential learning', in ed. C.L. Cooper, Theories of Group Processes (Wiley, London 1975).

ACTIVITY ESD4.9

REFLECTIONS

Activity code

✓ Self-development

  Teamwork

  Communications

  Numeracy/IT

  Decisions

Task

In order to develop your skill in reflecting on your experience, use the checklist in Box ESD4.8 to write a report outlining your learning from one of the following:

1 your work during the last few months or
2 the last project you completed.

The learning diary

We can all learn something everyday. The key difference between those who learn everyday and those who learn nothing is perhaps 'reflection'. This is not usually a formal process, just something that some of us do instinctively. However, it is possible at regular intervals, to look over the past and deliberately reflect on what we have experienced and what that experience means.

The learning diary is a way of developing the habit of reflection which will help you to make the most of your daily experience. Many managers find the learning diary of great value in their jobs. In addition it will help you to recognize the evidence which will demonstrate competence. The steps to follow are set out here.

1 Think of the most important, unusual or troublesome things that have occurred during the day. What did you learn from them?
2 Now try to think of two or three reasons why the learning was important. In what ways will it improve your performance?

3   In what ways does this new learning fit into the rest of your knowledge, skills or activities? If you can put your learning into context it will make it much more powerful.

This may seem odd at first but you will soon get used to it and find that it takes only a few minutes every day. Alternatively, you can develop also a critical incident diary. Please refer to Boxes ESD4.9 and ESD4.10 respectively. Then consult Activity ESD4.10.

BOX ESD4.9

A learning diary

Learning Diary

Date: Position:

The most important things I have learned today are:

1

This is important because:

This is related to:

2

3

BOX ESD4.10

A critical incident diary

A critical incident diary is a development of a learning diary.

Critical Incident Diary

Date: Position:

Nature of incident

Questions raised / decisions taken:

Who was involved?

Activities undertaken to deal with the incident:

Outcome:

Knowledge needed to deal with the incident:

Skills required to deal with the incident:

Reflections on outcome (e.g. I was able to / unable to . . .)

ACTIVITY ESD4.10

DIARIES

Activity code

✓ Self-development
☐ Teamwork
☐ Communications
☐ Numeracy/IT
☐ Decisions

Task

Start keeping a learning diary or a critical incident diary.

There is no need to make entries every day; try weekly to start with until you find how useful it can be. Be brief.

Organizational learning

We develop the ideas of how organizations can develop themselves and their relationships with self-development in ESD Unit Six.

In the interim, the organizational view of self-development can be approached by reference to Boxes ESD4.11 and ESD4.12 and Activity ESD4.11.

BOX ESD4.11

A hierarchy of management development

Burgoyne has developed a model of management development which aims to display what is involved by being a 'mature' organization in terms of management development.[1] This may have implications for self-development (see Activity 4.11).

Burgoyne's view of management development is quite structured and career oriented being 'the management of managerial careers (the biographies of managerial working life) in an organizational context'.

This maybe a little too career management-oriented but it does link the development of individuals to that of the prevalent organizational milieux.

According to Burgoyne there is a ladder of maturity or a hierarchy of development. Organizations can climb up the rungs, occasionally slip down, and hopefully rise to the top. The steps are as follows:

Phase 1   There is no systematic concept/idea.

Phase 2   There are sporadic/isolated outbursts of management development.

Phase 3   A more structured approach exists.

Phase 4   A management development policy exists in line with corporate policies.

Phase 5   Now management development has inputs into the formation of corporate policy.

Phase 6   Management development and corporate policy are mutually enhancing and we find strategy developing through management development.

Source:
[1] Adapted from Burgoyne, J., 'Management Development for the Individual and the Organisation', *Personnel Management*, (June 1988).

ACTIVITY ESD4.11

ORGANIZATIONAL MATURITY AND SELF-DEVELOPMENT

Activity code

✓ Self-development
✓ Teamwork
✓ Communications
☐ Numeracy/IT
✓ Decisions

Task

Please refer back to Box ESD4.11.

By group or individual initiative, examine the six phases of maturity and note their implications for self-development.

BOX ESD4.12

Organizational phases and self-development

Burgoyne's Phase 1 means that there is no systematic management development, so development must come only from some inner directed effort.[1] Some *ad hoc* assistance may occur, through reactive 'inputs' from customer care to financial awareness, but the organization provides little support.

Phase 2 involves a lot of developmental activities being 'done to' people. This phase often shows inconsistencies between the formal systems of management development and everyday learning. Again there is a focus on individual self-help if you wish to develop – and it may be difficult to reconcile organizational efforts with personal development.

At Phase 3 the systems are better and more finely tuned. Sudden changes in policy or product markets or whatever may leave the systems far behind. All too quickly we can revert back to Phases 1 or 2. In a relatively stable environment self-development and organizational inputs can tally up; when the stability alters, the onus may well be placed on the individual again.

Phase 4 involves having a clear management development strategy to implement corporate policy. This can involve both self-development and corporate development but the people input is very much subordinate to corporate goals. This level assumes that management development (self- and organization-structured) can be used to implement containable corporate goals.

Phase 5 sees more of a people input with such consideration being given in corporate plans. Individual talent and ability as well as organizational need seem to flourish under these conditions – which may be few and far in organizational reality.

At Phase 6, management development including self-development, actually changes and improves corporate policy formation. This is the apex of the pyramid and looks to be the culmination of real organizational learning. Again few firms may reach the dizzy heights.

Source:
Source of phases: [1]Adapted from Burgoyne, J., 'Management Development for the Individual and the Organisation', *Personnel Management*, (June 1988).

The learning contract: individual and organizational agreements

A recent development for the stimulation of learning has been the learning agreement/contract. Learning contracts provide several benefits according to Boak and Joy (1990).

For participants the contracts:
- are of their own choosing;
- are relevant to their needs; and

■ improve their learning abilities.

Their managers;

■ become involved in training and development; and

■ can influence the activities of trainer and participant.

Trainers:

■ focus on a wide variety of real problems; and

■ see real development in skills and attitudes.

The learning agreement/contract should state the exams or units and elements of competence for which, either in part or whole, you will be seeking credit. Those units or elements for which you have little or no evidence are covered by the development plan.

In your agreement/contract you should also include a development plan.

For each of your areas of weakness answer the following questions:

■ State the area of weakness – what are your training needs?

■ State your objectives – what do you want to be able to do or be like after taking action?

■ How will you know when you have achieved this? What will be with signs?

■ What are you going to do to achieve this?

■ Which are your start and finish dates, review dates?

The agreement/contract should then be signed both by you and your adviser.

Please refer to Activity ESD4.12.

ACTIVITY ESD4.12

A LEARNING CONTRACT

Activity code

✓ Self-development

☐ Teamwork

✓ Communications

☐ Numeracy/IT

☐ Decisions

Task

Assess your past experience and future needs then write out a learning agreement/contract. (This builds on Activity ESD4.3)

E. Action learning – The Key To Self-learning?

Many people believe that management education is the key to economic performance but it is also possible that economic performance results from management education. Good economic performance generates the slack which enables development in managers. On the other hand, good economic performance and good management education may be caused by a third factor which is a change in attitudes. This is the approach which is beginning to occur in the UK.

Managers often say they learned to do their jobs by experience, that is, they learn from the jobs they have done. However, recent reports, e.g. Handy (1987) and Constable and McCormick (1983) have argued that this is not sufficient in the present environment. Managers in the USA, West Germany, France and Japan are more likely to have developed to a higher level than UK managers because they have more training.

The way managers and organizations behave could also be dependent on culture and fashion. Therefore it does not follow that methods which are successful at one particular time are better but are more effective within that period of time and situation. For example, we find very successful companies in one decade but which, in the following ten years, have dropped out of the top of the charts only to be replaced by others.

The natural reaction to management deficiencies is to provide courses to improve areas such as marketing or planning, for example, or to attempt to change an organization's culture. Some firms use a form of job rotation in order to provide a wide variety of experience. On the other hand, managers often say that a significant learning experience is being involved with a project which is outside the normal routine and job. Projects are tasks with clear boundaries and an end result and they are being used increasingly as a method of learning and planned development. In this way a wide spectrum of development processes has developed under the broad heading of action learning.

The importance of discovery to learning should not be underestimated. This is probably the reason why action learning in the form of problem solving, projects or a new job can be so important to management development.

Margerison (1980) and Pearce (1992) describe how to start using action learning in management development. According to Margerison, the traditional approach to management was locked into 'a skills development and personal growth mindset rather than a job improvement, profit centred, action orientated, task results mindset.'

Outlined in the following table are the differences between traditional learning and action learning.

Traditional	Action
Classroom-based learning	Work-based learning
Individual orientation	Group orientation
Input orientation	Output orientation
Knowledge orientation	Action orientation
Passive learning	Active learning
Historical focus	Concern with here, now and future
Cost investment	Requirement for investment return
Producer orientation	Market/customer orientation

Source:
Adapted from Margerison (1980).

Margerison (1980) believes action learning is confronting reality rather than studying a hypothetical situation. It involves the use of skills *in situ* rather than learning them in one place and transferring them to another place.

> We have got to get our philosophy, our methods, our structures, close to the manager's life, existence and reality. In this way we will make an impact on performance and help facilitate improvement in personal and organizational action.

Pearce (1992) believes, 'action learning's uniqueness lies in the fact that it does not prescribe any one solution as best, or any one way as the correct way. It creates conditions where people can learn the best way to achieve results within the constraints which are imposed. In doing so each person discovers and tests out his strengths and develops new ones.'

Since action learning is the interaction between people and problems/opportunities, it can occur at several levels of complexity. The matrix in figure ESD4.4 illustrates the kind of situation which can be arranged.

The types of situations are, according to Pearce, as follows:

Type 1   Your own job develops current competence, future capabilities and clarifies roles and problems associated with the job. Quality circles develop new ideas and create better work relationships as members' views are taken into account and acted upon.

Situation	Task	
	Known	Unknown
Known	I Own job	II Highlighted projects
Unknown	III Same job in another part of the organization or in a different organization	IV Project in another part of organization, or in a different organization

Figure ESD4.4   The learning matrix

Source: Adapted from Pearce (1992).

Type 2   Highlighted projects increase a person's vision and abilities in a bigger organizational context.

Type 3   The same job elsewhere tends to concentrate on technical problem solving, for example, Revans' (1984) first example from the UK coal mines (see Box ESD4.13).

Type 4   A project in a strange organization is useful for personal development and for helping the 'client' organization to value different experience and viewpoints.

Action learning is based on a project which is a real management task/problem/opportunity/issue on which action must be taken.

Each project should be 'owned' by a client who wants the problem solved and each participant/set should have a supervisor/advisor. (A set is a group of managers, usually 4–6, plus an advisor, who work together on a problem.) Typical programmes run for 2–12 months.

In action learning, questioning is more important than programmed knowledge according to Margerison (1980). If we ask the right questions the knowledge can be obtained – the expert is not central to the proceedings. To Margerison, 'too many experts make learners dependent and undermine thinking and effort.' The expert is only useful when the right questions have been formulated, that is, ' . . . you say where you wish to go before you receive any guidance on how to get there.' A timetable should be set against which managers can measure their performance in terms of reports/presentations.

Please refer to Box ESD4.13.

BOX ESD4.13

The Revans experience

The first example of action learning occurred just after the 1939–45 War when Reg Revans was given three months to decide how to find the managers to run a thousand collieries. His war experience had made him very distrustful of experts with ready made solutions which had worked in the past. He believed the coal industry required managers who could think afresh about the problems ahead. No one knew what these might be and most managers would misunderstand them when they arrived. One of his ideas was to provide a staff college in order to equip those who went there with the ability to pose new questions in conditions where no one could tell what might happen next. However, he did not want to teach them anything. How could he do this?

Revan's recommendation included the first description of action learning:

> Those who went there would be expected to be thoroughly familiar with the principal problems of the industry and to have their own suggestions about their solutions . . . It would bring together groups interested in common problems, who would spend a weekend, a week, a fortnight or even longer, on the fullest exchange of their ideas and experiences of those problems . . . We do not envisage the permanent employment of a staff of qualified tutors, to deliver lectures or conduct seminars

This was an educational approach in which the syllabus was the current situation; the tutors were other managers with similar problems; the campus was the pits with their problems. The learning came from posing the relevant questions and the criticism of other mangers.

The staff college did not materialize and so the approach had to change. The managers gathered together in small sets of four or five close to their own pits. They worked on their own problems and visited one another's pits.

> This had a dramatic effect: managers began to think afresh about their own past experiences and to reorganise, sometimes quite fundamentally, how they saw their jobs, how they saw their subordinates and even how they saw themselves.

To demonstrate the effectiveness of his approach, Revans quoted the experience of five managers in another area who tried out the idea on their own.

> At no extra expense, and within three years, they had increased their annual output per person employed by over 30 per cent against an average improvement in the coalfield as a whole too small to detect.

When Revans moved to the University of Manchester as Professor of Industrial Administration, he turned his attention to the Royal Infirmary. His study of the retention of nurses in hospitals went ' . . . beyond the idea of a small group as a learning microcosm, and hit upon the notion of a complete institution . . . as a learning community.'

According to Revans, management education in this country was overtaken by a disaster in 1965. Vast sums of money were poured into business schools dedicated to the spread of management science. Therefore Revans moved from Manchester to the Fondation Industrie – University of Belgium.

The inter-university programme for advanced management involved the five universities of Belgium and 21 of its largest firms which controlled 40 per cent of the country's investment. This programme was based on Revan's belief that

> an educational policy, therefore, must contrive that the manager like the clinician, will develop a skill in asking specific questions relevant both to himself and to each unique and unstructured situation. The development of this diagnostic skill is possible only if the managers seeking it are, like the doctors in the medical school, brought into direct and responsible contact with open ended cases having no approved answers. They must attack the current problems of the enterprise and meet realistically, if not always successfully, the challenge that the unknown makes, not only to their technical knowledge but also to their non-intellectual qualities.

There were three parties to this project: the participants, companies and university staff. The formal programme consisted of a two month introductory course, a three month diagnostic phase, a month's visit to the USA and a four month action phase. Each participant was assigned a policy problem in an enterprise other than his own. Thus top managers in one industry were assigned to work full-time on a strategic problem in a different industry.

It was the experience of the majority of the participants that the formation of long-term plans, (strategy), was more frequently hindered by inadequate definitions of value systems than by information about prospects and means. Three general points were made. There seemed to be:

■ little open discussion of the collective and personal value systems of top management;

■ a general belief that profit and efficiency are an adequate expression of final goals; and

■ an absence of a sensitivity to values reflected at all levels of the organization.

Sources: Adapted from:
Easterby-Smith, M. and Burgoyne, J. 'Action Learning: an Evaluation' in ed. M. Pedler *Action Learning in Practice* (Gower Press, London, 1983).
Revans, R., *Developing Effective Managers* (Longmans, London, 1971).
Revans, R., *The Sequence of Managerial Achievement* (MCB University Press, Bradford, 1984).

The evaluation of action learning is very subjective when it is done retrospectively. This is especially so since action learning is to be found in so many situations. Essentially these can be divided into two groups – business/industrial and academic.

The business/industry approach is able to demonstrate success in terms of the development of managers and a successful outcome to the project, for example, in terms of solving a problem or increasing efficiency. The strengths of action learning for an organization are that no training school is necessary. The managers are doing something, whether wealth creating or not. Also, it seems to be sensible for managers to focus on problems with the support of a group.

The weaknesses are that managers when working in a group are limited by their specialist knowledge and they tend to use the skills of their functional area. Therefore, the manager does not necessarily gain new knowledge, experience or skills. Indeed, it would appear that managers using action learning could obtain a narrow education: the skills needed to solve a particular problem could be very limited. For example it may be difficult to design an action learning programme which would encompass learning across the major functional areas of a business. Thus, it may well be that several projects need to be undertaken in order to obtain this broad-based expertise. This implies a long time span and a long learning curve.

Is there a more efficient way of achieving the same end?

Without some form of consultancy or support it is possible that new ideas, shortcuts and even well-tried methods could be missed. Action learning may be situation-specific. It could be that able learners are better at action learning, or they may even reach the same point quicker just by using a different method.

So much depends on the environment: the organization may be in crisis and any method could produce results, or the organization may have slack in management time. It depends also on the extent to which the organization makes itself receptive to the action learning approach, since it needs commitment in terms of management time and this is not available in many organizations.

Coopers and Lybrand (1984) emphasized the importance of evaluation as a means of changing attitudes to training. We have to show in measurable ways the value to an organization of an investment in training and development to justify costs; to establish the effects on learners, to measure impact on job performance or on the profitability; effectiveness; and flexibility or survival of the organization itself. Each of these reasons will entail a different approach. Therefore evaluation looks at the total value of the learning programme. A mixture of learning, behavioural and organizational objectives have to be satisfied.

The question now arises: to what extent is action learning training? If action learning is a planned process to modify attitudes, knowledge or skill, then it can be thought of as a form of training and criteria such as the ones mentioned above might be used to measure its effectiveness.

However, managers differ in various ways, for example, in learning styles, motivation, culture, value systems, on-the-job performance, life traumas and background experience. Each of these factors will affect the way in which managers will behave in educational programmes.

When the literature of action learning is examined, it is obvious that evaluation at this sophisticated level has not taken place. The evaluation is largely anecdotal and is concerned largely with the advantages to the organization. In some cases the fact that the manager has also learned something and can continue to use that knowledge in new situations is also mentioned.

From the evidence provided it appears that action learning does raise the performance of both the manager and the organization. However, we are not aware of any experiments that have taken place to compare action learning with a control group or with managers being developed in other ways, or to measure its efficiency or effectiveness compared to other methods.

Another aspect that should be explored is the organization itself. In any organization there are numerous problems looking for solutions and a lot of solutions looking for problems. The change to action learning could be stimulated by numerous triggers, for example, management has more free time; problems are so great that a different approach is needed; or the climate is right or the culture is changing.

Please refer to Boxes ESD4.14 and ESD4.15. Activity ESD4.13 should then be tackled.

BOX ESD4.14

GEC and action learning

In the UK, Revans's ideas were taken up by GEC because during the 1960s the company went through a painful series of mergers which slimmed the workforce from 250,000 to 170,000. However, in cutting costs GEC stopped sending its managers to business schools, and management development became a matter of survival in a rigorous environment.

By the 1970s the chief executive, Weinstock, realized that he had to do something about his pool of top management. A TV programme featuring action learning and Reg Revans fired his imagination so that by 1974 he had four action learning sets in operation. Even though GEC had a wide diversity of companies, the opportunity was taken to include union people and managers from other companies.

Several problem areas were identified by Foy[1]:

■ Support from the participants' own top management is essential.

■ Choosing and assigning participants without participation from them can adversely affect morale.

■ In every action learning programme the most prevalent problem appears to be re-entry.

GEC suffered three defections from its first 21 graduates, probably through poor selection methods.

The benefits to the GEC

. . . appeared to be more confident and competent managers, some progress toward resolution of major problems, and often, diffusion of a technique that is useful for gathering information and solving other organizational problems. The individuals who have invested time and commitment receive a more personal payoff.

Source:
[1] Adapted from Foy, N., 'Action learning comes to industry', *Harvard Business Review*, **5**, pp. 158–68, (1977).

BOX ESD4.15

Action learning and the State of Victoria

McNulty reported that the Premier of the State of Victoria in Australia realized in 1977 that his Cabinet Office was in a mess.[1] Therefore the Premier introduced action learning to all 26 departments of the state government. This took the form of an external exchange programme of four months full-time and a part-time internal exchange programme over four and a half months.

The success of the full-time programme was illustrated by an example in the Crown Lands and Survey Department, where there was a six-month backlog in the production of survey maps. The manager wanted more staff but got a mechanical engineer from the private sector through the action learning programme. The engineer was able to eliminate the backlog by cutting out unnecessary steps in production and getting staff involved in the changes and implementation.

The success of the part-time internal programme was shown by an officer in the Department of Agriculture who was in charge of the fruit fly campaign. His set questioned the need for this campaign, and as a result eliminated a major part of it. This produced a saving of over 80 per cent in costs.

The success of the programme caused the Premier to promote his Education and Recruitment Director to run the State Housing Commission with the aid of action learning groups. Now the tenants looked into the troubles of the maintenance and repair men; the security corps looked into the problems of adolescents and the adolescents looked into the torments of the security men. The police, residents, renting officers and architects looked at plans for development and so on. It then became unnecessary to employ security men, the crime rate fell by nearly two thirds and the standards of the local amenities attracted attention from all over Australia.

McNulty also provided examples from Nigeria, Egypt, Israel, India and France.

Source:
[1]Adapted from McNulty, N.G., 'Action Learning around the world' in ed. M. Pedler (Gower Press, Aldershot, 1983).

ACTIVITY ESD4.13

Action learning – an evaluation

Activity code

✓ Self-development
✓ Teamwork
☐ Communications
☐ Numeracy/IT
☐ Decisions

Task

Derive your (or group) conclusions from the reported cases on action learning.

F. Conclusion

Learning goes to the core of self-development. We examined some learning theories and teased out their relevance to our needs. We then touched upon barriers to learning and placed self-development in the context of learning taxonomies. Self-learning was then examined.

Learning experiences, including academic, personal and organizational situations were touched upon. Finally we cemented many of our ideas by putting them into effect via action learning. Now we turn to other resources in ESD Unit Five to implement policies of self-development.

Bibliography

Anderson, A.H., 'Learning characteristics and learning theories,' *Training Officer – The Independent Journal for the Professional Trainer*, **29**, 9, (November 1993).

Anderson, A.H., *Successful Training Practice* (Blackwell, Oxford, 1993).

Anderson, A.H. and Kyprianou, A., *Effective Organizational Behaviour* (Blackwell, Oxford, 1994).

Bass, B.M. and Vaughan, J.A., *Training in Industry: The Management of Learning* (Tavistock Publications, London, 1966).

Bloom, B.S., *Taxonomy of Educational Objectives: The Classification of Educational Goals* (Longman, London, 1956).

Boak, G. and Joy, P., 'Management Learning Contracts: The Training Triangle' in M. Pedlar, J. Burgoyne, T. Boydell and G. Welshman, *Self Development in Organisations* (McGraw-Hill, London, (1990).

Boyatzis, R.C., *The Competent Manager: A Model for Effective Performance* (Wiley, New York, 1982).

Constable, J. and McCormick, R., *The Making of British Managers* (BIM/CBI, London, 1983).

Coopers & Lybrand Associates, *A Challenge of Complacency* NEDO/MSC, London, 1984).

Davies, J. and Easterby-Smith, M., 'Learning and developing from work experiences,' *Journal of Management Studies*, **21**, (1984), pp. 167–83.

Gabriel, C., 'Psychology as a Science' in eds J. Radford and E. Govier, *A textbook of psychology* (Sheldon Press, London, 1986).

Gardner, H., *The Theory of Multiple Intelligence* (Paladin, London, 1985).

Gross, R.D., *Psychology, the Science of Mind and Behaviour* (Arnold, London, 1987).

Handy, C., *The Making of Managers* (MSC/NEDO/BIM, London, 1987).

Harrison, R., *Training and Development* (IPM, London, 1992).

Honey, P. and Mumford, A., *A Manual of Learning Styles* (Honey, Maidenhead, 1982).

Jones, M., *Management Development: A Participative Approach* (Manchester Training Handbooks, Dept. of Administrative Studies, Manchester University, 1981).

Knowles, M., *The Modern Practice of Education* (Follett, London, 1970).

Kolb, D.A., *Experiential Learning* (Prentice Hall, New York, 1982).

Kolb, D.A. and Fry, R., 'Towards an applied theory of experiential learning,' in ed. C.L. Cooper, *Theories of Group Processes* (Wiley, London, 1975).

Kolb, D.A., Rubin, J.M. and McIntyre, J.M. *Organisational Psychology*, 4th edn. (Prentice Hall, Englewood Cliffs, NJ, 1984).

Long, C.G.L., 'A Theoretical Model for Method Selection', *Industrial Training International* **4**, (1969), pp. 475–8.

Margerison, C. 'How chief executives succeed', *Journal of European Industrial Training*, **4**, 5, (1980).

Pearce, I., 'The Development of First Line Managers at ICL', *Management Development Review*, **5**, 1, (1992).

Revans, R., *The origins and growth of action learning* (Chartwell Bratt, London, 1982).

Revans, R., *The Sequence of Managerial Achievement* (MCB University Press, Bradford, 1984).

Sternberg, R.J. *Beyond IQ; A Triarchic Theory of Human Intelligence* (Cambridge UP, Cambridge, 1985).

Training Commission, 'Classifying the components of Management Competence' (Training Commission, Sheffield, 1988).

Whittaker, J., 'Making a policy of keeping up to date,' *Personnel Management*, (March, 1992).

ESD Unit Five

Resources to Help your Development

Learning Objectives

After completing this unit you should be able to:

- plan how to get what you want from external courses/training events;

- carry out an audit of resources available to you, both within your organization and outside, which you can use for your own development;

- use a range of techniques to structure learning at work and create a network of contacts to support your development;

- compile a portfolio which makes explicit what you have learned and select out specific 'profiles' of evidence for the purpose of getting recognition; and

- apply the generic skills of the series.

Contents

A. Overview

B. Training versus Development – Getting the Most out of Courses

C. Choosing the Most Appropriate Method for your Development

D. Structured versus Unstructured Methods of Development

E. Structured Learning Off-the-job

▶ Structuring your own learning off-the-job

▶ Learning resource centre

▶ Open learning

▶ Space for group development

▶ Action learning

F. Principles of Effective Management Education and Training

G. Structured Learning On-the-job

H. Techniques for Structuring and Recording Work-based Learning

▶ Mapping your learning network

▶ Learning from networking: some process skills

▶ Having a mentor

► Critical incident diaries

► Planned or unplanned experiences

► Using a portfolio for development to build up specific profiles

I. Conclusion

ESD Unit Five

❝ Self-development is bound to be a risky business, involving as it does facing up to one's own weaknesses and trying to work on them. It is therefore extremely important to provide a learning climate that helps people to examine their own weaknesses, to discuss them, to practise new behaviours, to take risks, to give and receive feedback, and generally become deeply involved in the exciting, if sometimes painful process of growth. This requires a high level of trust, mutual understanding and respect, and commitment both to one's own learning, and to that of others. ❞

(Pedler *et al.*, 1993)

A. Overview

The aim of this unit is to help you take 'ownership' of your own learning in the context of your organization and to recognize and exploit opportunities for learning for your own development. You will be encouraged to draw heavily on what you have discovered to date from your own learning style and personal learning contract to become the kind of manager you want to be.

So far we have concentrated on helping you recognize what it means to be effective in your organization. But in the last unit you had the opportunity to find out how best you learn and to put together a learning contract in which you should have committed yourself to achieving specific targets. You should also have completed an overall plan of the resources you would need to help you meet these targets. This is the subject area that we are covering in detail in this unit, as a result of which you may want to go back and revise your learning contract.

B. Training versus Development – Getting the Most out of Courses

Think back to the last time you attended a training course. Was it you who requested the training or were you asked to attend? It is not unusual at the beginning of the course for delegates on a programme to respond to the trainer's question 'Why are you here?' with a shrug and confession that they were only told about it last Friday! In other words they hadn't got a clue why they were on the programme or what was expected of them at the end of it – they were just told to come.

A distinction that can be made between training and development (Boydell, Leary and Pedler 1993) is that training is something that is done to you whereas development is something you do for yourself. This is not to say that attending a training course could not be part of the development process but you are the one who must initiate it, or at least co-determine your needs. Garratt (1991) defines development as 'the process of revealing and bringing out what already exists within an individual, adding to it where appropriate by training and education, and then making the results manifest through their being seen to be used and to celebrate what is developed'.

The other side of development is that it cannot happen in a vacuum; a person develops in the context of a job and of an organization. This is relevant because as a manager you cannot develop by yourself. Your learning contract should have helped you identify significant people at work who can be resources for your own learning as well as provide valuable feedback. We shall look at this in some detail in this unit.

Please tackle Activity ESD5.1. A deeper more reflective experience then occurs in Activity ESD5.2 after you have consulted Box ESD5.1.

ACTIVITY ESD5.1

YOUR DEVELOPMENT

Activity code

✓ Self-development

☐ Teamwork

☐ Communications

☐ Numeracy/IT

✓ Decisions

Task

Think back to when you first started your current job and the stages of development you have undergone since then. Compare the stages with the six stages of development described in Box ESD5.1

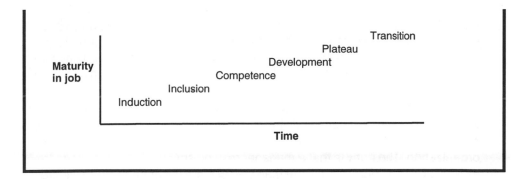

BOX ESD5.1

Stages of development

- *Stage 1 – Induction*   Garratt[1] admits this is often done well in organizations. It involves the introduction of a newcomer as much into the culture of the organization as to the environment in which he/she is going to work.

- *Stage 2 – Inclusion*   This is a stage which, in Garratt's opinion, is rarely identified or well managed by organizations yet is crucial if a manager is to be seen to be effective. This stage 'is not so much about your technical abilities, for which you were presumably selected for the job, but more about your personality and behaviour, and whether they will fit with those that already exist in the workplace'.

- *Stage 3 – Competence*   It is interesting that the term 'competence' is often regarded as being a set of behaviours which somehow exist in their own right. The whole rationale behind NVQs is that any occupation can be specified according to a set of performance criteria which can be assessed by an independent assessor in the workplace. What is often forgotten is that competence is a:

   wide concept which embodies the ability to transfer skills and knowledge to new situations within the occupational area. It encompasses organi- zation and planning of work, innovation and coping with non-routine activities. It includes those qualities of personal effectiveness that are required in the workplace to deal with co-workers, managers and customers (italics added).[2] [We see this latter point as forming competencies, of course.]

   In principle all these qualities should be built into the performance criteria and (more crucially) within the range indicators. But practice suggests not enough attention is given to the 'social' context within which competence must be assessed. One of the authors has explored this in another book[3]. It is also the point that Garratt makes – that a manager is unlikely to be competent unless he/she has gone through Stage 2 in the development process, i.e. he/she has been 'included'.[4] The moral is that regardless of all the skills you have (for which you were selected in the first place) these skills will be noticed and you will be judged as 'competent' only when you are in a position of being accepted within the organization culture.

■ *Stage 4 – Development*   It is only when a manager has been 'included' and his/her competence recognized that there is the opportunity for a genuine programme of development which is legitimized and recognized by the organization. The irony is that a manager may be sent by the company on the most expensive courses but if the manager has not yet gone through the rites of passage described above, he/she really will not be able to develop further.

Garratt makes the point that at this stage, a manager moves from 'a job' to 'a role'.

> A job is specified through the job description. When a personality and set of competences are attached to that job and developed, then an organizational 'role' is created.[5]

■ *Stage 5 – Plateau*   As its name suggests, this is a stage when the manager is perceived competent, he/she has had all the development perceived necessary and all is right with the world. Garratt notes that 'In a turbulent society this idyllic stage rarely lasts long' though the demography of managers and the economy over the last decade has meant that many managers have reached their plateau and/or are reluctant for moves. This is a situation, though, that is unlikely to last!

■ *Stage 6 – Transition*   As the description suggests, this is the final stage of development which may occur at retirement or it may be the transition to another job or career/promotion, etc. in which case the cycle begins all over again.

Garratt puts the development cycle into historical context:

> Whilst for the last two decades a lot of managerial focus has been on the latter stages of plateaued and transitional managers, because of the demography of Europe we are now seeing a swing back to the early stages, with a particular concern for retaining competent people at all levels. This is where development and personal development contracts can prove so useful.[6]

Sources:
1. Garratt, B., *Learning to lead: Developing your organisation and yourself* (Fontana, London, 1991).
2. The Training Agency, *Training in Britain – A Study of Funding Activities and Attitudes*, (HMSO Books, Class No. 658. 3124 TRA, 1989).
3. Critten, P., *Investing in People: Towards Corporate Capability* (Butterworth Heinemann, London, 1994).
4. Garratt, ibid.
5. Garratt, ibid.
6. Garratt, ibid.

ACTIVITY ESD5.2

DEVELOPMENT PHASES

Activity code

✓ Self-development

☐ Teamwork

☐ Communications

☐ Numeracy/IT

✓ Decisions

Task

Using the development stages in Box ESD5.1, apply each one to your current job role or to a past job.

- Stages 1 and 2   Think back and consider how long it took you to be 'included' in your organization, i.e. accepted by colleagues and superiors alike, invited to group meetings (outside as well as inside work-time).

- Stage 3   Think back to when your abilities as a manager first became recognized. Did it follow a time when your colleagues had tested out whether or not you were 'one of them'? Is the jury still out on whether or not you are competent?

- Stage 4   Can you relate to this stage? Are there circumstances where you have 'technically' been developed, i.e. attended the right kind of programme, but where this has failed to lead you anywhere?

- Stage 5   Do you identify with the condition described at this stage? If so, why do you consider you have reached a plateau and what circumstances might change this position in the coming years?

C.   Choosing the Most Appropriate Method for your Development

The message of the last section is that before you start selecting appropriate methods for your own development, you must:

- be clear about your own goals, what is expected of you by your manager (see your learning contract)
- be clear about your position within the organization (see Box ESD5.1)

- be aware of the possible methods;
- be aware of the 'inner merits' of each possible method;
- be aware of any relationship between your aims and the value of the method;
- be aware of the need for evaluating the effect of the method – after the event;
- above all, be clear about your own agenda, i.e. what it is you want to develop (this should also be spelt out in your learning contract – see ESD Unit Four.); and
- finally you should take account of your learning style (see ESD Unit Four).

In Box ESD5.2 is a reminder of how each type of learner prefers to learn. Please refer to it as it reinforces the learning styles found in the last unit.

BOX ESD5.2

Styles

- If you are an *activist* you will learn best from situations where you can get involved with other people in solving an immediate problem.

- If you are a *reflector* you will learn best from situations which allow you to stand back and take your time to carry out research into a particular problem and reflect on the outcome.

- If you are a *theorist* you will learn best from situations where you can thoroughly analyse a problem and arrive at a general model which fits the data.

- If you are a *pragmatist* you will learn best from situations where you have a chance to test out ideas and recommend further action to be taken.

As you work through the rest of this unit you may wish to check out each approach that satisfies your own learning style.

D.   Structured versus Unstructured Methods of Development

Honey and Mumford (1982) suggest a framework within which most development activities can be fitted. According to this model (see figure ESD5.1) opportunities for learning and development can be categorized according to two dimensions:

- Do they occur in a work situation or outside?

- Are they entered into consciously (i.e. they are structured) or unconsciously (unstructured)?

1500–1545	Opportunity to examine different techniques, packages and to watch videos on quality
1545–1630	Panel answers questions from the floor
1630–1700	Consolidation – the way ahead

If you were a manager with an interest in or need for guidance on how to manage quality in your organization, which of the three events in Activity ESD5.3 would you choose? Of course it all depends on your particular needs. If you were particularly interested in research on the subject and in Dr X's work in particular you might opt for Event 1.

The description of Event 2 suggests the prospect of a much broader programme. The learning outcomes give you a clear idea of the likely practical value of the course. In contrast to Event 1 which had no learning outcomes and gave the impression that the day would be devoted to Dr X's lecturing, there is greater variety. For one thing there will be an opportunity to learn about the practical experience of another company. At the end of the day you will come away with a particular system you can then try out. From this point of view the programme might appeal to the theorist and pragmatist.

But it is the third event which has something for everybody.

- The theorist will have the opportunity to compare different systems, ask questions and come to a 'considered' view as to which methods will work best.

- The reflector has an opportunity to take his/her time and observe different techniques without being forced into any one direction. They would also appreciate the visual support of the videos.

- The pragmatist will like the essentially 'practical' spirit of the event and the opportunity to apply and test out ideas and techniques in relation to problems and issues back home.

- The activist will appreciate the opportunity for discussion and for testing out ideas with others.

Notice that all three events take the same amount of time but consider how much more the third event manages to cover. It achieves this by shorter input sessions as well as by giving people their own 'space' to consolidate ideas. This is particularly useful at the session after lunch – the traditional 'grave yard session'. It also gives the delegates the feeling that they are in control – compare this with Event 1.

Of course, if you have a picture of a course as a typically closed session where you take on board information presented to you by the course leader, you may well question whether Event 3 is a course. Is it not more like a day conference or workshop? Maybe it is but if it proves to be a more effective method for enabling you to learn and develop, that is a good thing.

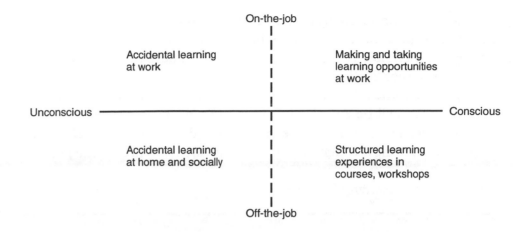

Figure ESD5.1 Frameworks for development

E. Structured Learning Off-the-job

Attendance at a course is the most usual form this takes. The course could be either a standard programme run by a college, university or professional body which may or may not lead to a recognized national qualification. It could also be a programme specially tailored to the needs of your own organization, again run by an external body or run in-house by your own training department.

What is common to all these types of course is that you have the opportunity for a period of time, which could be as short as half a day or as long as a month, away from the day-to-day pressures of work to do nothing else but learn. The kind of learning in which you are engaged will depend on the design of the training event. On the one hand, it could be a theoretical type of programme where you are expected to take on board information and have very little chance to apply it or challenge what is said. On the other hand it could be a very participative course where you are able to test out ideas and are encouraged to question and challenge.

Depending on your learning style you will find one type of course more preferable to the other. If you are an activist or pragmatist, for example, you would not be happy to be simply 'talked' at. You would want to be involved and test out ideas for yourself.

How do you check out if a particular course is appropriate for you?

The starting point is to be clear about the learning outcomes of the course. Most courses will publish statements as to what you should expect to do or to know. But unless you have a clear idea of what particular needs you have you will not be in a position to decide whether the learning outcomes are appropriate or not. Therefore you need to go back to ESD Units Three and Four and look at what you have learned about yourself, your development needs and your learning style. These will give you a clue as to the resources best suited to you.

The published details of a course should also give you some idea of the way the course will be run. Will there be opportunities to discuss ideas with fellow delegates? Will you be expected to demonstrate the effectiveness of your learning through presentations to others? What are the periods of study?

Please refer to Activity ESD5.3.

ACTIVITY ESD5.3

COURSES FOR HORSES?

Activity code

✓ Self-development
✓ Teamwork
☐ Communications
☐ Numeracy/IT
✓ Decisions

Task

By individual or group effort, have a look at the following descriptions of three training events all related in some way to helping managers update themselves on aspects of quality. They are all one day events.

Event 1 The Management of Quality

This is a one day event aimed at managers with specific responsibility for quality and run by Dr X, a national authority on the subject, who will draw on research he has carried out in his recently published book *Quality at the cross-roads*. Each delegate will receive a copy of Dr X's book.

Programme:
0900–1030	Definitions of quality: leading thinkers in field
1100–1230	Summary of research carried out in seven different companies
1330–1500	What is meant by TQM?
1530–1700	The way ahead.

Event 2 The Management of Quality

This is a one day event aimed at any manager who wants to find out more about the latest techniques on quality and how they can help improve performance.
At the end of the day managers will be able to:

- draw up a company wide policy on quality;
- select most appropriate techniques from a range of tested methods to implement policy; and
- draw up an action plan to identify goals to be achieved and resources needed.

Programme:
0900–1030	What is quality and what should be our policy?
1100–1230	Twenty ways to bring about quality – a review of current approaches
1330–1500	TQM at Boswell's: one company's experience of introducing 'total quality'
1530–1700	Preparing an action plan for the future.

Event 3 The Management of Quality

This is an opportunity for managers to learn about different approaches to quality and share their own experiences. This one day event will provide a forum for discussion and debate. Managers will have an opportunity to examine different commercial packages on display and view a selection of videos which will be shown throughout the day.
At the end of the day managers will be able to:

- test out their own ideas about quality against various models and techniques;
- form a view as to the kind of quality programme that best suits their own company culture;
- identify obstacles to change and how they can be overcome; and
- produce an action plan for testing out selected techniques in their own company and for influencing others.

Programme:
0900–0915	Introduction to programme and facilities available
0915–1000	Some definitions of quality
1000–1030	Discussion groups : How would we recognize quality in each other's company?
1045–1115	Ajax : Examples of introduction of a quality programme
1115–1145	Basildon Consultancy Group : stages in the development of a quality programme
1145–1230	Opportunity to examine different techniques, packages and to watch videos on quality
1330–1415	Discussion groups : What are the obstacles to introducing a quality campaign and how can they be overcome?
1415–1500	A model for bringing about change

Over the last decade the traditional manager's course has changed dramatically as trainers and educators have realized that, by definition, managers are in business to get results. What they need is help to develop skills which they can apply and test out for themselves. This may well require background knowledge and information but these should be kept to the minimum with most time given over to testing out ideas either in discussion groups or in role play.

The value of structured learning off-the-job lies in the space it gives managers to stand back from the day-to-day operations and take a holistic view supported by new ideas introduced through the training event. Unfortunately some course leaders take the view that having a captive audience of managers for a day gives them a licence to cram as much information into the day as possible. We are sure you have been on courses where at the end of it, you are saturated with so much knowledge that you cannot see how it can be used.

The moral is to choose courses and training events which give you sufficient time to think things through by yourself and in collaboration with others. They should also give you sufficient information beforehand so that you can form a very good picture of how you are going to be able to put the information, knowledge and skills covered into operation.

Please refer to Activity ESD5.4.

ACTIVITY ESD5.4

ANDERSON ASSOCIATES, PERSONNEL AND MANAGEMENT ADVISORS (AAPMA)

Activity code

✓ Self-development
✓ Teamwork
✓ Communications
☐ Numeracy/IT
✓ Decisions

Task

Using the wider criteria noted in Section C of this unit – 'Choosing the most appropriate method for your development' – make an evaluation of the developmental programme outlined below.

The Effective Management Programme[1]

Concept

Our effective management programme is a unique learning resource for management development. It is an international programme of 16 modules based on the successful Anderson 16-volume series of books, *Effective Management, a skills and activity-based approach*, published by Blackwell of Oxford. This business-led, goal-centred programme is designed for managers undertaking corporate training and for those who are studying at a masters level in management.

Aims

The overall objectives of the programme (see separate modules for specific aims) include:

- to develop interactive functional skills of management through activity-based learning;
- to define and develop underpinning knowledge;
- to give an in depth and integrated approach to the four main functions of management: people, marketing/sales, finance/accounting and enterprise/ operations;
- to demonstrate the application of universal or generic skills of management; and
- to place management in context including individual, organizational and external influences over a period of time.

Content (Features)

- An emphasis is placed on *activity* and *skills*.
- These 'doing' aspects of managerial work reflect reality and are underpinned by *knowledge* inputs.
- Most professional managers have a *specialist function*. We integrate this specialism with other business functions.
- We need managers who have *generic* or *universal skills* as well as functional expertise.
- We encourage the *generalist's perspective* to mobilize all these skills and functions.
- This whole programme is permeated by *enterprise* and entrepreneurial qualities which must form the basis of effective management.

Format

- The programme is interactive and learner-oriented and based on a combination of experiential learning, self-development and action learning allied to semi-structured inputs.
- Each of the 16 modules is divided into six units.
- A unit lasts for some 6–7 hours, so the whole module takes 4–5 days, depending on hours worked.
- Each unit can be used for a one-day input.
- The modules are classified into a *cluster* – people management, finance, marketing and enterprise.
- In each of the four clusters we have an introductory module which should be tackled first to give an understanding of the areas (depending on prior knowledge).

Delivery

Options include:

- open seminars with our tutors;
- in-company or in-house seminars with our tutors;
- once trained, in-company or in-house seminars with your tutors and our specialists; and,
- once well established, a 'franchise' arrangement whereby the organization can deliver the programme with our advice and guidance.

For further information on the programme and the fee structure etc. contact:

M. Anderson
7 Water Lane
Melbourn
S. Cambridge
SG8 6AY
ENGLAND

Source:
[1] © Anderson Associates, Personnel and Management Advisors.

Structuring your own learning off-the-job

If you know what experience you want, you may be able to organize it for yourself? Off-the-job does not have to be miles away from your factory or office. It could be in a room next door to your office.

One of the authors has been working with nurses in helping them put together evidence of their learning in the form of portfolios. One of them described how she had commandeered an office that was not being used all the time to be the ward's 'learning space'. Out went the desk and in came easy chairs, book shelves, a white-board. On the door she put this notice 'This room is only to be used for learning and development!'

All of us need a learning space which is sufficiently removed from the action to give us time for reflection and inner growth.

Have a look round your organization for a space that can be used in this way.

Libraries have been used for this purpose – though in our view they tend to be associated with passive learning. By definition you have to be quiet so as not to disturb others' private learning! But learning is also social: it may require others to challenge your thinking and it may require discussion, debate and argument. Ideally, then, you need a space for private learning which might well be the library, though you might need to create other facilities within it to encourage learning rather than simply reading. You also need a space where small groups can meet and discuss issues. It will be like a small classroom with whiteboard, maybe an overhead projector and ideally a video recorder/player and a TV. It should have easy chairs and a pleasant, bright ambience.

Let us see how you can now use these facilities to structure your own learning off-the-job.

Learning resource centre

This is just a fancy name for the room dedicated to private study. We would hope that any of your staff could use these facilities but for the purposes of this book let us assume the focus of study is management development. It should have the following resources:

- books on management development – including the latest works of popular authors; and

- in-company reports on management issues. Every company has a rich source of information about its culture and management style in the reports and memos that are continually circulating. But rarely does it ever examine them and use them as documentary evidence of the principles of management development that apply to a particular company.

Have a look at this memo in Box ESD5.3.

BOX ESD5.3

Consultation

From: The Managing Director   To: All Heads of Department

Consultation in preparation for next year's business plan

It is the Board's view that there should be wider consultation among all staff prior to the development of next year's business plan. Accordingly, before our next meeting on October 5, you will have set up a meeting with your staff at which you will:

1 give them each a copy of last year's Business Plan
2 explain the format and what are the key areas
3 ask them what they consider should be the priorities for the company in the coming year.

Prior to our meeting, I will expect a written summary of your staff's response which I will circulate to all Heads of Department. At the meeting on October 5, we will then have an opportunity to discuss the summary report and to agree on what recommendations we will be making to the Board.

This says a great deal about this particular company's culture and management style. The theme of consultation does not exactly match with the tone of the memo which is in the nature of an instruction from the top down! It would be a valued document in the learning resource centre. A 'structured' exercise might be to have managers read a series of articles on 'consultation' and 'empowerment' (all available in the centre) and then to read the company's own memos and reports on the same subject.

At least this would be more honest than sending managers on external courses on consultation at great expense without revealing to them the incompatible culture that exists within the organization. This way the new manager can learn the theory on the one hand but also appreciate the reality of putting it into practice on the other. The next structured exercise will be to help them work out the best strategy for working towards a more participative, 'empowered' culture. This will take more than an external course or two!

Open learning

A popular definition of 'open learning' is any system or material that enables anyone to learn what they want, when they want, where they want and how they want. The Open University in the 1970s pioneered a way of 'opening' up higher education to a much wider audience than could be met through the traditional entry to University via A levels. Through the application of modern technology in text and broadcasting it is possible for almost anyone to study for a higher level qualification no matter what their age or circumstances.

In the 1980s the Government provided funding under a scheme called Open Tech to develop a vast repertoire of materials that could enable anyone to develop a vast range of occupational skills (the OU concentrated on academic learning). In fact the UK leads the world in the provision of Open learning materials.

The forms it can take are various. At one level it could be a text, for example, on budgetary control, which would have introductory text and then pose a question to which the student would have to respond. The text follows this with a commentary on what would be an appropriate response and then goes on to another idea which is similarly tested out. Very often there would be support material which the student would have to consult. Box ESD5.4 shows an example from a forthcoming open learning module aimed at health care practitioners to help them put together a portfolio. In this extract, the health care professional is being introduced to the MCI management competences.

BOX ESD5.4

Open learning

In this section we are going to examine in detail the first line management standards which may be appropriate to you. But the method of collecting evidence is appropriate to whatever level of manager you happen to be . . . As you put evidence together you may find you can meet the criteria of Level M2 and, in some cases, you may even be eligible for assessment at the senior management level. What is important is for you to collect evidence at whatever level and in whatever role or capacity you are able. In the new world of management, as Charles Handy reminds us,

'Management ceases to be a definition of a status, of a class within an organization, but an activity which can be defined and its skills taught, learnt and developed'[1]

Action

Think back over the last week and reflect on the key activities that come to mind. Use the diary format you used in Section 6 for reflecting on critical incidents at work (Form DYP22).

Commentary

In the activities you have listed, it is very likely you have included activities such as the following:

■ 'Compiled the staff rota'

■ 'I had to intervene in a dispute between two members of staff'

■ 'Ordered supplies for the next week'

■ 'Supervized compilation of care plans'

■ 'Attended case-load meeting'

In every case each activity either directly or indirectly has a consequence for someone else. The 'management' element is the extent to which you can describe just what part you played in initiating any change that took place.

So much for the theory now, let us look at the practical consequences for you of benchmarking your own experiences against the kind of activities that appear in the MCI standards.

Source:
[1] Handy, C., *Understanding Organisations* (Penguin, Harmondsworth, 1983).

The style of the whole effective management series reflects an 'open learning' approach where you are encouraged to carry out exercises and compare your response with that in the text. In this way you are encouraged to develop yourself. This is then developed through our new MBA.

At another level, open learning could use technology, videos, audio-tape and computers to deliver learning material to enable the student to respond and to provide appropriate feedback. Over the next decade, developments in technology will provide what has been called a digital and electronic 'highway' on which images, dialogue or information will be communicated from any part of the world (or boardroom) at the pressing of a key on a computer terminal.

But you do not have to have hi-tech to turn the most commonly available technology, like videos for example, into an open learning format. All you need is to provide a series of questions, issues for speculation, which can be answered by viewing a particular video recording. Afterwards you can provide the answers to the questions posed so that the students can check them out for themselves or you can follow up with a group discussion in your tutorial room.

Space for group development

This is an area at work which is your classroom but technically it is 'off-the-job' in that, in the words of the nurse quoted above, it is to be used only for learning and development'. Above all it should not be linked by telephone so participants are not interrupted. Within this room you can facilitate all the methods that you would find in a well-run course:

- Role play

  Managers can explore their responses to simulated problems and receive feedback on the way they handled the situation (sales presentation, conflict between members of staff, a grievance, negotiation, etc.) Feedback will be even more effective if all transactions are video-recorded – on the understanding that the manager gets to keep the video which he/she can use as evidence of management development.

- Presentations

  Speakers from outside or inside the organization can be invited to give presentations, run seminars, tutorials, etc. Of course such presentations could take place elsewhere (e.g. in the boardroom) but having them take place in your 'development space' gives them a different dimension and quality. Any presentation should be seen as an opportunity for debate and challenge and not for a one-way monologue from the MD!

- Group discussions

  Again, these could take place anywhere in the organization but the fact that they take place in the 'development' room should signal to all that the discussion process is expected to lead to some form of learning outcome, which should be recorded as such. You could have a 'development log book' permanently in the room which you expect to see updated following any learning event that takes place.

Action learning

Another key development area you might encourage is action learning (Anderson, 1994). As we noted in ESD Unit Four, this was a process pioneered by Revans which is based on the principle that managers, above all else, learn best from tackling problems and projects for which they are individually held responsible (Revans, 1982). Furthermore, they are held responsible for taking action and learning from it by a group of fellow managers who are themselves likewise committing themselves to solving problems and learning from the experience. The group is often called an 'action learning set' and is usually facilitated by a 'set leader' whose job it is to help the group to focus on the problems or issues presented to learn from them.

However, Revans did not dismiss the need for formal 'programmed' knowledge (which he calls P). He felt, however, that it should be preceded by 'questioning and insight' which he calls Q. Learning (L) = P + Q. In the kind of set up we are encouraging you to consider in your organization, namely to 'structure' learning off-the-job, you can use your learning resource centre to ensure managers have the necessary P while using your 'group development' room/centre to facilitate Q.

Many organizations are linking the kind of facilities described above with assessment centres which have traditionally selected managers using a battery of tests and assessment exercises against defined criteria. But now there is a move towards development centres (Goodge, 1994) where participants are not just tested and told whether they have 'passed' or 'failed' but are given feedback on the outcome of the exercises undertaken and help in planning their development for the future.

F. Principles of Effective Management Education and Training

One of the key advantages for introducing the arrangements discussed in the previous sections, is that it is a sign for all to see that your organization is serious about opening up development to everyone. The move towards assessment against competences has done much to breakdown the old barriers where the elite managers attended off-the-job courses (usually in the country) and the rest managed as best they could!

To end this section on 'structured off-the-job learning', we set out the principles which the MCI published (1991) on management development under the heading 'Good Practice' together with questions which you can use to check to what extent your organization follows these principles.

Please refer to Activity ESD5.5 and then consolidate the issues by consulting Box ESD5.5.

ACTIVITY ESD5.5

GOOD PRACTICE

Activity code

✓ Self-development
✓ Teamwork
✓ Communications
☐ Numeracy/IT
✓ Decisions

Task

Assume that your or your group are involved with management development for an organization of your choice.

Below you/your group will find six issues which make for good practice. Your task is to develop a range of questions under these headings to act as an evaluative mechanism for management development.

The six issues are:

- open access
- flexibility and innovation of delivery
- corporate and individual development
- a competence approach
- credit accumulation and transfer
- employer involvement.

BOX ESD5.5

Six principles for good practice in management development

1 *Open Access* Ensure that there is no barrier to a manager receiving development based on such issues as:

- age
- pre-qualifications entry requirements
- inflexible programme structure

- programme duration, timing and location
- current role In organization
- lack of information.

Example questions on a check-list for good practice:

- Is any group/section under-represented?
- What, if any, are pre-entry qualifications?
- Can learning managers take 'part' programmes according to need?
- Is information about the programme reaching all potential candidates?

2 *Flexibility and innovation of delivery* Do not rely solely on traditional methods like lecturing but ensure a range of resources, facilities, etc. are used, e.g.

- open learning and distance learning (e.g. MBA)
- work-based assignments
- computer-based training/interactive video
- action learning groups
- group seminars/tutorials.

Example questions on check-list for good practice:

- What current methods of delivery are used?
- Do these relate to managers' different learning styles?
- What alternative resources are available and how could they be obtained?

3 *Corporate and individual development* Ensure that individual development is directly linked with the business objectives of the organization through such means as:

- learning contracts between the employer, the learner and the provider/tutor which commits all parties to a development programme
- personal development journal and learning diary.

Example question on check-list for good practice:

- What is the mission statement of the organization and what is role of development plan in achieving it?
- How will objectives of the programme be communicated and agreed with the learning manager?

4 *A competence approach* The outcome of any development programme must be assessed against national management standards which take account of:

- collection of sufficient evidence to satisfy standard
- training of workplace assessors
- evaluation and monitoring of assessment.

Example questions on check-list for good practice:

- Are all recommended sources of evidence being used for data collection?
- How much of the assessment occurs in the workplace?
- Is there a process for resolving conflicts which may arise from the assessment process?

5 *Credit accumulation and transfer* Ensure that managers can gain credit for competences they already possess.

Example questions on check-list for good practice:
- Is the programme modular, designed to encourage credit accumulation?
- Is there a requirement for an 'end of programme' exam? If so, how does this conform to the concept of credit accumulation?
- Are learning managers encouraged to produce evidence of prior learning?

6 *Employer involvement* Ensure that employers are directly involved in the design and assessment of the programme. (This is aimed primarily at educational and non-company providers but equally should be a concern for in-company providers)

Example questions on check-list for good practice:
- Are employers involved in the design of the programme?
- Are work-based assignments customized to the employer's needs?

Finally, to end this section on structured off-the-job learning, here is an example of a development programme which a company might implement in-house and which meets the six MCI principles, as well as enabling managers to get accreditation against a particular management competence (see Critten, 1994). Please refer to Box ESD5.6.

BOX ESD5.6

Sample programme to meet competence levels[1]

Notice to all staff in all departments:

Improving Effectiveness Through Team Performance

As from next month, 1500–1700 p.m. every Monday afternoon for the next five weeks, we will be holding a seminar in the training room based on the above theme. It is open to all staff to attend and will provide exercises and activities which will enable you to collect evidence which can later be assessed and accredited against MCI Level I Element 5.1 : 'Develop and improve teams through planning activities'.

Below is a summary of the kind of development inputs planned but this may well change depending on the kind of needs that emerge. You are welcome to attend any of the sessions even if you may not be able to complete the full programme. We hope to repeat the programme in the coming months.

Overall objectives

- to enable you to agree joint objectives with all your team and success criteria by which they will be measured
- to enable you to review your current success as a team and plan a development programme to meet success criteria using a wide range of company resources

Session 1: Your team experience

- Open session in which you identify criteria for success of your current working team
- How clear are you that other members of team have same objectives?
- Input on how to set objectives and kinds of measurement you might use to assess success

Inter-session exercise: You meet up with members of your team and agree objectives and success criteria to be presented at Session 2.

Session 2: What is a successful team?

- Explore how teams are formed and use Belbin model to identify what kind of a team member you are.
- Discuss the kinds of roles your team has/needs.
- Watch and comment on the video 'Successful teams at work'.

Inter-session exercise: Check out other members of team using the Belbin model. Discuss what kinds of skills you need to develop to be a more balanced team.

Session 3: What stops you from being a successful team?

- Feedback results of survey
- How to measure individual competence
- Kinds of resources you need to meet your success criteria

Inter-session exercise: Agree with the group as a whole and with individual members technical competences needed and overall resources.

Session 4: Formulating the team development plan and budget

- Feedback from exercise
- Examples of team development plans, resources needed and likely cost (time/money)

Inter-session exercise: Agree group development plan, timescale needed and budget likely to be allocated.

Session 5: Handling group conflict

- Video plus some role play
- Explore model of forming, storming, norming and performing
- Take away structured exercises to use with group

Work through plan: Complete structured exercises with group and note down how conflict has been resolved. Implement development plan recording results. Produce final report.

Feedback and assessment: These sessions will be arranged when you have worked through your plan and have evidence of how well the team have achieved the targets you set. You will be required to present the report to your boss who will also have spoken individually to team members to assess their reactions to the programme. If the evidence is sufficient to meet criteria in 'Occupational Standards for Managers Level I', you will get an accreditation certificate for this module.

Source:
[1] Critten, P., *Investing in People: Towards Corporate Capability* (Butterworth Heinemann, London, 1994).

G.   Structured Learning On-the-job

Wild, the Principal of Henley Management College, has this to say:

> I recently met 150 senior managers who were just finishing a long management course. I asked them to identify the most influential things in their development as managers. Many said that the course had totally changed the way they worked, but when answering my question, none of them referred to the course content, to books or articles that they had read or the lectures they had attended. Instead, they all described events from their working lives.
>
> The most effective and enduring executive-level management development is not simply provided by courses – it is a product of

experiences. Nor is it the result of occasional activities. It is a continuous and cumulative process, and things that happen to and around managers can help them develop.

Frequently, timely, relevant and enriching experiences are the foundations for really effective management development. Everything else is a necessary stimulus, or it is enabling.

(Wild, 1994)

He makes the point that 'experience is not simply what happens, but how one uses what happens' and that there are three components of an effective development strategy that can structure learning on-the-job:

■ the provision of 'activities' themselves, i.e. a sufficient range of opportunities/issues at work which will be the source of learning;

■ the facilitating of 'insights' and concepts which provide a framework within which the learning from the activities can be interpreted; and

■ the support for learning, i.e. information and guidance which help learning to take place.

Not surprisingly he sees the Business School of the future as having a role in helping the managers to derive the necessary 'insights' from the experiences he/she encounters at work. This is similar to what Schon calls a 'practicum' which is a 'setting designed for the task of learning a practice' where tutor and student reflect together on the 'occultness of learning' (Schon, 1987). It is essentially grounded in the work experience of the professional.

In the next decade we are likely to see more companies following Wild's advice and structuring learning based on work experience but also using professionals and facilitators to help managers to understand their experience and to derive maximum learning for it.

You can find similar arguments in Mumford (1989). In figure ESD5.2 he summarizes three models of management development.

Clearly Type 2 comes closest to meeting the needs of both the individual manager and the organization. Mumford places emphasis on a multitude of resources that are available within the organization to both boss and subordinate for the purposes of management development. These include structured exercises found on more formalized management development courses. A good source of the range of such techniques available is in Huczynski 1983.

Please refer to Box ESD5.7.

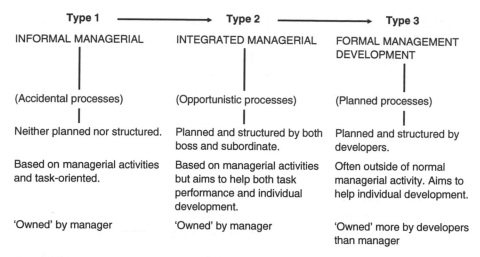

Figure ESD5.2 Types of management development

Source: Adapted from Mumford (1989).

BOX ESD5.7

The development of personal effectiveness

Burgoyne and his colleagues put forward a list of the personal qualities of an effective manager.[1] They suggested a range of methods to facilitate these qualities.

Method	Comment
Experiential groups	Group-based learning through experience.
Learning community	Not necessarily an ivory tower but an organization/section devoted to the principles of learning.
Action learning	Developed at great length in this text (see pp 172–80).
Joint developmental activity	Perhaps a project team or a mixed group coming together.
Structured exercises	As used in this series.
Outward Bound	A mountaineering course in the Welsh mountains, for example.
On-the-job	To some extent we have baptism under fire but this may not cover all of the personal qualities identified.

Source:
[1] Adapted from Burgoyne, J., Boydell, T. and Pedler, M., *Self-development: Theory and Applications for Practitioners* (Association of Teachers of Management, London, 1978).

Most importantly, management development must include the people within the organization who are crucial to any development activity. Mumford (1989) emphasizes the role of the following:

1   The boss
2   Mentors
3   Specialist advisers (e.g. trainers)
4   Peers
5   Subordinates
6   Network contacts.

What kind of feedback do you get from your boss? If you have a formalized appraisal/performance review scheme you should have evidence which you can draw on which may also indicate the kind of development you ought to plan for. But it is not just your boss who can give you such feedback. What about the staff who report to you. Have you ever asked them to appraise you – it is called 'upward appraisal' whereby a manager is rated not just by the boss and subordinates but by his/her colleagues and peers.

Margerison (1980) conducted a survey into what were the major influences on chief executives in the UK (which were closely replicated by findings in the US). These findings are reproduced in Box ESD5.8.

BOX ESD5.8

Reported major influences on chief executives

Rank Order	Statements	Score out of 100
1	Ability to work with a wide variety of people	78.4
2	Early overall responsibility for important tasks	74.8
3	A need to achieve results	74.8
4	Leadership experience early in career	73.6
5	Wide experience in many functions before 35	67.6
6	An ability to do deals and negotiate	66.4
7	Willingness to take risks	62.8

Rank Order	Statements	Score out of 100
8	Having more ideas than other colleagues	61.6
9	Being stretched by immediate bosses	60.4
10	An ability to change managerial style to suit occasion	58.8
11	A desire to seek new opportunities	56.8
12	Becoming visible to top management before 30	56.0
13	Family support (wife/parents)	55.2
14	Having a sound technical training	54.8
15	Having a manager early in your career who acted as a model (from whom you learnt a lot)	52.0
16	Overseas managerial/work experience	41.2
17	Experience of leadership in armed forces (peacetime/wartime)	40.4
18	Having special 'off-the-job' management training	32.8

Source:
Adapted from Margerison, C., 'How Chief Executives Succeed', *Journal of European Industrial Training*, **4**, 5, (1980).

If you have ambitions of becoming chief executive in the future, based on these findings, you might be forgiven for rejecting any suggestion you go on an in-company course (or external course for that matter) and start networking fast! The findings also confirm the significance of the stage of 'inclusion' in Garrett's (1991) development model that we looked at earlier. However technically effective you think you are as a manager, you will be recognized as such only if you are accepted by key colleagues and stakeholders. We now look at techniques you can use to structure your work experience and in particular to draw on the support of and obtain recognition from key colleagues.

H.   Techniques for Structuring and Recording Work-based Learning

Mapping your learning network

Please tackle Activity ESD5.6.

ACTIVITY ESD5.6

LEARNING NETWORKS

Activity code

✓ Self-development
☐ Teamwork
☐ Communications
☐ Numeracy/IT
☐ Decisions

Task

Put yourself in a circle in the middle of a blank sheet of paper and then identify significant other people at work whom you can actively use as a resource to facilitate your learning and development. For example, your 'learning network' might look something like this.

Immediate boss

Area manager   Receptionist

MANAGER

Data processing manager   Personnel manager

Secretary

Notice that your network need not and should not be restricted to other managers. You can learn as much from subordinates and support colleagues. Also, though we have restricted your network to colleagues at work, you could also include anyone in your life, at work or outside, that you could use to help you develop as a manager.

Now attempt Activity ESD5.7.

ACTIVITY ESD5.7

NEEDS AND NETWORKS

Activity code

✓ Self-development

☐ Teamwork

☐ Communications

☐ Numeracy/IT

✓ Decisions

Task

Use the headings on the form below, first to identify a particular development need you want to meet (see ESD Unit Four) and then list the key people you have identified in your learning network. Against each one describe just how they can help you. Then compare your response with examples listed in Box ESD5.9. We have added a couple of people outside of work who could help this particular manager, notably his partner!

Plan how each person in your learning network can help you achieve your objective

Objective:

Who can help?   How can they help (particular expertise, support to draw upon) and how you intend to make use of that support/expertise

Box ESD5.9 on planning and achieving your objectives should be consulted for an indicative response. Perhaps the processes of learning from networks needs some developing before we turn to a specific case of networking – mentoring.

BOX ESD5.9

Example of a plan showing how each person in your learning network can help you achieve your objective

Objective: To make more effective contributions at meetings and be more effective in following up points of action

Who can help?	How can they help (particular expertise, support to draw upon) and how you intend to make use of that support/expertise. Help given and the use made of that help.
Immediate boss	I will ask my boss to make a point of listening to the contributions I make at next three team meetings and give me feedback.
Area manager	I will ask my area manager to give me a slot at the next meeting to introduce the proposals and then give me feedback on its effectiveness.
Receptionist	I will ask the receptionist to report back on the 'mood' of managers after leaving the area managers' meeting by casually asking them whether it was a good meeting.
Partner	Moral support. Just being supportive and being prepared to notice and comment on changes my partner can detect in me.
Data processing manager	Ask for help in producing quality slides for the presentation.
Secretary	Get feedback on my attention to detail. I need to take responsibility for following action – not having to depend on being reminded! My secretary can note any difference.
Personnel manager	Ask him/her to book me on the Time Management Course.
Friend	Ask Bob if he can tell me if he notices any change when we meet for our weekly drink (it's always after a meeting at work and I'm usually complaining!).

Learning from networking: some process skills

Self-development needs the assistance of others to flourish. Some key process skills may include:

- using others as a stimulus by deriving energy/enthusiasm from a 'live spark';
- sharing views and thoughts with others – although it should not be a confessional box;
- taking advice/guidance on someone's suggestions/direction;
- building on the views/actions of others, e.g. at a meeting;
- testing out ideas by 'floating' new concepts;
- sharing experiences with others; and
- modelling behaviour on others, e.g. on a mentor.

So, by combining structure and process in learning, your colleagues and those closest to you can give you not only feedback, but also stimulate your self-development and learning.

As an additional bonus, you can create a network of evidence for which you can receive credit for management competences. We now turn to mentoring – a useful example of such network learning.

Having a mentor

Within your network of learning support you may have one or even two people who have a special role as mentor.

> Mentoring is a 'process in which one person [mentor] is responsible for overseeing the career and development of another person [protégé] outside the normal manager/subordinate relationship'. Alternatively, mentoring is a 'protected relationship in which learning and experimentation can occur, potential skills can be developed, and in which results can be measured in terms of competencies gained rather than curricular territory covered.
>
> (Clutterbuck, 1991)

The key phrase is 'outside the normal manager/subordinate relationship'; it might therefore be the boss or someone from another department. In essence, it is recreating the old apprenticeship scheme. It is interesting to speculate if, in the organization of the future, this kind of mentoring network may very well replace the hierarchy and yet still provide the manager with a role within the system. But problems can exist with mentoring. Please refer to Activity ESD5.8.

ACTIVITY ESD5.8

MENTORING – NEPOTISM OR DEVELOPMENT?

Activity code

✓ Self-development
✓ Teamwork
☐ Communications
☐ Numeracy/IT
✓ Decisions

Task

Mentoring means favouritism in the wrong hands and is merely a cloak for the old boys' network. Discuss/debate or reflect.

Critical incident diaries

In ESD Unit Four, Box ESD4.10 we touched on critical incident diaries. A useful way of focusing on your work experience so that you are better able to learn from specific activities that happen, is to keep what is called a 'critical incident diary'. As its name suggests it is a chronological record of incidents which are significant enough for you to remember. But you can also use them as a trigger for unlocking particular learning and for identifying and underpinning knowledge which would normally go unnoticed.

A further detailed example of the kind of information you should log is given below. There are two halves: one focuses on the description of the incident, who was involved and what was the outcome; the other describes the learning you have derived from the incident. Please refer to Box ESD5.10.

BOX ESD5.10

Critical incident diary

Date	What happened? (Nature of incident)	Questions raised/ decisions to be taken	Who was involved	Activities undertaken to deal with incident	Outcome
7/1/96	Wrong kind of paper supplied	Whether to accept or send back	Rep from Thompson's	1 Check on deadline for job 2 Check Thompson's past record	Refuse to accept and give ultimatum that if correct paper not sent immediately account will be closed Correct paper received within the hour
18/1/95	Unable to answer question from MD at Senior Mgt meeting	How to respond	MD Finance Director	1 I made an excuse 2 Blamed secretary for not briefing me	MD not interested in excuse Deadline given for providing info

Knowledge needed to deal with incident	Skills required to deal with incident	Reflections on outcome (e.g. Why was I able/unable to . . .)
Thompson's record (which was bad)	Assertiveness	Once I saw Thompson's record, I realized that series of errors had to stop
Lead time if there was a delay	Patience	Surprised at strength of my own feelings
MD's relationship with Thompson's	Nerve	Taught me never to accept inferior standard again
Company's policy on quality standards		Have also changed system for goods received so that problems of this kind are immediately highlighted. Also ensured everyone in department aware of new standards
New budget limits	Diplomacy	I must never again blame someone else for something that is my responsibility
MD's priorities		
Internal communication channels		Prior to every senior mgt meeting, meet with secretary to anticipate such questions. Ask her to have checked first with MD's secretary about issues likely to arise

This is just one of a number of techniques you can use to focus on your own development at work. The evidence it generates you can use to incorporate in a 'portfolio' of achievement. Another method is to keep a 'learning diary' which helps to focus on anything – whether at work or outside – which has led to some learning. Box ESD5.11 is an example of a range of sources that might trigger learning.

BOX ESD5.11

Sources

What did you do? What was trigger for learning?	What did you learn?	How might you use this now and in future?
Attended one day workshop on health and safety	New EU Directives (e.g. on lifting)	I've produced a briefing note and suggestions for action which will be discussed at next Health and Safety Committee

What did you do? What was trigger for learning?	What did you learn?	How might you use this now and in future?
Demonstration of new software pack by visiting rep	Gave me idea for how we could save time compiling monthly figures	Sent report to Sales Director recommending change of procedure
Attended meeting of Parent Teachers Association at my son's school	Discussion about how schools could better help pupils prepare for industry	Intend to recommend we invite selected teachers to spend time with us to up-date themselves on business
Article in current edition of *Management Today* on 'empowerment'	Benefits other companies have derived from introducing 'empowerment' schemes	Arrange brainstorming meeting with colleagues to discuss opportunities for our company
Presentation by Chief Accountant at last Senior Manager meeting	Change in budgetary arrangements	Good opportunity for involving my staff more (links with move towards greater empowerment of staff – see above)

You can see how you can use a learning diary like the one above to record a variety of instances both at work and outside of work as a basis for learning and development. Many professional bodies are requiring their members to demonstrate evidence of continuous professional development (CPD). You can use a diary like this to record such evidence, the detail of which you can provide in a supplementary portfolio.

So far we have focused on 'structured' learning both off-the-job and at work. But according to the Mumford–Honey model (1982), we also learn unconsciously both at work and off-the-job. It is part of the human condition to be learning all the time, even though we may not be aware of it at a particular time. Were you aware of learning anything from that documentary you were watching on TV last night? But it could happen that a colleague at work saw it too and happens to mention an incident from the programme. This brings it back immediately and, depending on its relevance, it might well be a source of learning which you might want to add to your diary. In this way what was learned unconsciously has been made explicit and structured in such a way as to find its way into your development log.

Similarly, you may be engaged on a task at work in the course of which there is 'incidental' learning (e.g. you work out for yourself how to solve a problem in the process of coming to terms with a new software package) but it does not register at the time. For a detailed account of informal and incidental learning at work see Marsick and Watkins (1990). It needs a trigger to make it explicit.

Schon (1987) has described these two processes as 'knowing-in-action' (e.g. discovering how to get round a particular problem) and 'reflection-in-action' which only happens when something happens to make us question what it is we are doing. For example a colleague might ask 'how' you managed to get a set of figures to balance. You are then forced to 'reflect' on the action you have taken and articulate what was hitherto unconscious. Schon argues that this is the way professionals learn, not through 'formal' learning but testing out their 'knowing-in-action' and 'reflection in action' in the company of fellow professionals and tutors who are able to encourage them to question continually and to reflect on their experience. You will see a direct parallel with action learning.

The moral of all this 'theory' is that any experience, whether off-job or at work can be a rich source of learning providing it can be made explicit. You can do this through structured recording of experiences so that you are constantly looking for opportunities 'out there' to use as a basis of learning. You can use colleagues and friends to remind you of experiences you have had and to help you to question and reflect on what has taken place.

Boud, *et al.* (1985) use this model to illustrate the 'reflective' process. Reflection is not a one-off process. It is an iterative process whereby you are continually coming back to the original experience and re-evaluating it. Please refer to Box ESD5.12.

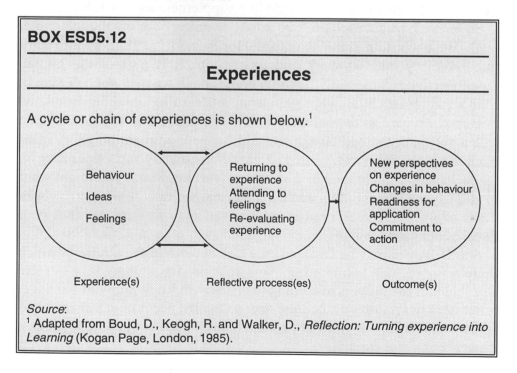

BOX ESD5.12

Experiences

A cycle or chain of experiences is shown below.[1]

Experience(s)	Reflective process(es)	Outcome(s)
Behaviour Ideas Feelings	Returning to experience Attending to feelings Re-evaluating experience	New perspectives on experience Changes in behaviour Readiness for application Commitment to action

Source:
[1] Adapted from Boud, D., Keogh, R. and Walker, D., *Reflection: Turning experience into Learning* (Kogan Page, London, 1985).

Planned or unplanned experiences

We can learn from both planned experiences which are 'safer' and unplanned experiences which involve more trial and error – and which may be quite costly before knowledge is gained. Reeves (1994), for example, encourages managers to use the experience of managing as a basis for self-development. This requires managers to develop a heightened state of awareness so that whatever they do as managers can be used as a project for the purposes of self-development.

This necessitates great self-knowledge and awareness perhaps and is seen by Reeves to be a function of the manager's stage of development. Leary *et al.* (1986) have developed such a developmental model of the manager's transitions. Please refer to Box ESD5.13. Of course every experience cannot be assumed to be of equal importance or relevance.

BOX ESD5.13

A seven stage model

■ Stage One – conformist implementer

Level 1
Static, rigid, standard – adhering to rules and procedures, obeying those in authority

Level 2
Responding by adapting, modifying or controlling rules, procedures, systems and people

Level 3
Sensitive, aware, in tune with what is happening, thus relating to norms and conventions

In these first three levels . . . the manager's behaviour is basically controlled by outsiders, at the first two levels by rules and procedures, and, at the third level, by conforming to 'correct' behaviour.

■ Stage 2 – independent experimenter

Level 4
Experiencing things and prepared to learn from this experience

---

Level 5
Experimenting and deliberately trying to find out more, to add to the stock of knowledge, to improve on the status quo, to advance 'the state of the art'

Level 6
Connecting, making large scale links, leading to much wider understanding, including the realization that most things are somehow connected. 'Sense of oneness'

These three levels are marked by the manager moving away from doing the approved things and starting to find out for her/himself what is true, right, and correct. Behaviour is now controlled from within rather than by external factors.

■ Stage 3 – autonomous agent

Level 7
Here the manager integrates with the outside world and with the task in hand. It requires taking ownership of the task and full dedication to it. Fulfilment comes from working within the constraints and from having to meet corporate purposes

This seventh and final level has considerable overlap with Level 6. A manager's sense of connectedness and a holistic view of the world is now drawn upon to integrate him/herself with the world around. 'It is about doing something important and constructive, about changing the world.'

Source: Adapted from:
Reeves, *Managing effectively – developing yourself through experience* (Butterworth Heinemann, London, 1994).
Leary *et al.*, The qualities of managing (Manpower Services Commission, 1986).

Clearly the higher the level at which you are operating as a manager, the more able you will be to derive the maximum learning from an experience.

But you also need to keep some record of the outcome as evidence of your having learned in order to consolidate your development as a manager. The very act of recording enables you to use it as a base for further development. In the last section of this unit we look at how you can keep a record of all your development activities and their outcomes in the form of a portfolio – which you can keep updated.

Using a portfolio for development to build up specific profiles

A portfolio is . . .

a private collection of evidence which demonstrates the continuing acquisition of skills, knowledge, attitudes and achievement. It is both retrospective and prospective, as well as reflecting the current state of development and activity of the individual.

(Brown, 1992)

Portfolios are more usually associated with artists or graphic designers, in which are kept a selection of the artist's works for presentation to clients. But over the last decade, with the development of a competence approach to development and the need for applicants for NVQs, for example, to demonstrate evidence of achievement, portfolios – in the form of A4 ring binders – have become the accepted way of containing all the evidence.

We have already had cause to refer to continuing professional development and the usefulness of a portfolio to contain evidence which demonstrates you are keeping up-to-date. In working with various professional groups to help them to identify what evidence they need to collect and how it is to be presented, we have found it useful to make a distinction between a portfolio and what has been called a 'profile' which is

a collection of evidence which is selected from the personal portfolio for a particular purpose and for the attention of a particular audience.

(Brown, 1992)

The portfolio is the filing cabinet while the 'profile' is a particular file selected from the cabinet for presentation for a particular purpose. That purpose might be to get accreditation against the MCI competences described in ESD Unit Three. The evidence can be collected in your personal portfolio using a range of techniques already described in this unit. But it has to be presented in a particular way to satisfy the various performance criteria of the elements for which accreditation is being sought.

Alternatively you could create a special 'profile' which helps you explore your 'personal development'. This may draw on biographical data going back to childhood; it may look at the 'highs' and 'lows' of your life and what you have learned from them; it may look at particular issues in your personal life which you want to explore and develop, such as a relationship with a partner or with your children. Redman (1994) makes the point that the uniquely 'personal' process of putting a portfolio together is an aspect of portfolio compilation which is often undervalued.

You may want to get academic credit for past learning which you can select out from all the material in your portfolio and present in a particular way to highlight your ability to reflect on learning and claim credit from an Institution of Higher Education.

Part of the development process is to be able to select out experiences and use them specifically for particular kinds of reflection which can be accredited in various ways. This is particularly useful in terms of career planning for the future. The fact that you might be a production manager now, for example, need not mean that you will be in that position in five years' time. In times of such rapid change it behoves the manager of the future to take a long look not just at his/her competence now but as we have seen in ESD Unit Three at their capability for the future.

To Stephenson (1994), a portfolio has the following characteristics:

■ the capacity to learn about the changing contexts in which skills are used and to learn from unpredictable consequences of actions taken;

■ knowledge of the context in which they (competences) are demonstrated;

■ the value systems within which judgements are made about the direction of change and the choice of skills needed to bring about change; and

■ the courage, confidence and willingness to risk and learn from failure.

The capacity to take risks is one of what Honey (1994) calls 'ten learning behaviours'. Assess yourself against each one in Activity ESD5.9. Thereafter tackle Activity ESD5.10 which is followed up by a check-list in Box ESD5.13.

ACTIVITY ESD5.9

HOW DO I RATE MY LEARNING BEHAVIOUR?

Activity code

✓ Self-development
☐ Teamwork
☐ Communications
☐ Numeracy/IT
✓ Decisions

	Frequently do this	Rarely do this	Need to do more
1 Asking questions			
2 Suggesting ideas			
3 Exploring options			

	Frequently do this	Rarely do this	Need to do more
4 Taking risks/experimenting			
5 Being open about the way it is			
6 Converting mistakes into learning			
7 Reflecting and reviewing			
8 Talking about learning			
9 Taking responsibility for own learning and development			
10 Admitting inadequacies and mistakes			

Source:
Adapted from Honey, P., 'Establishing a learning regime', *Organisations and People*, Quarterly Journal of AMED, **1**,1, (1994).

ACTIVITY ESD5.10

RESOURCES

Activity code

✓ Self-development

☐ Teamwork

✓ Communications

☐ Numeracy/IT

✓ Decisions

Task

Before we tie all the resources together, try listing the range of resources available to you both at work and outside of work under these two headings and then compare your response with ours in Box ESD5.14

Formal resources/opportunities for learning	Informal resources/opportunities for learning

---

BOX ESD5.14

Resources and opportunities for learning

Formal resources/opportunities for learning	Informal resources/opportunities for learning
Meetings	Network contacts
Study days	Social committees
External course	Parent/Teacher Association
Appraisal interview	Voluntary Work
Any interview	Feedback from partner
Reports of cuts-in-resources	Feedback from own children
Crises	Magazines
Visits to other companies/departments	Professional groups
Visitors to your department	Sporting club
Other visitors	Doing something you did not want to do
Being coached	Taking a risk
Being counselled	Seeing your local GP
Having a mentor/supervisor	Receiving counselling
Discussions with colleagues	New leisure/sports activity
Problem-solving with colleagues	Surprises
Unfamiliar tasks	Letters
Projects	
Management journals	
Books	
Reports	
Memoranda	
Being criticized at work	

Of course, the list is endless. We hope that this unit has encouraged you to take control of your own development and look upon every experience, every encounter as a learning opportunity. We also hope you are starting to document this process in the form of a portfolio from which you can select out specific evidence to present as profiles to achieve particular ends, that is, to focus on your personal development, to gain accreditation against the MCI competences, or to obtain academic credit. It may be the basis for entry into a new career or profession. For example, as part of your management role you may have carried out some training of your own and/or developed in-company the kind of learning resources we described earlier in this unit. As a consequence you may begin to consider if this is not something you might do full-time. You begin to question how you can get professional recognition for this experience.

One way is to draw out of your portfolio particular evidence that demonstrates your ability to 'develop human potential' and to present it as a profile for accreditation against a set of NVQs developed by the lead body for trainers and developers: The Training and Development Lead Body (TDLB, 1991). They define the overall purpose of trainers/developers as . . . 'to develop human potential to assist organizations and individuals to achieve objectives'. As a manager it is vital that you develop the 'potential' of your staff. As we shall see in the last unit in the book, this will be a key skill for the manager of the future. Another route is to take a formal academic qualification, such as an MBA, of course.

Finally, we list below the range of resources we have looked at in this unit. They are by no means exhaustive. As we keep on emphasizing, absolutely any experience can be used to trigger learning and development. We have also indicated some of the reasons why you might be embarking on a development programme. Your learning contract should be your route map but very often in the process of development, we see other opportunities not anticipated before. We have argued that seeing such opportunities is the very essence of a developmental approach to your life and career progression. Using this as a check-list, you might now want to go back and review your learning contract with your mentor/boss, prior to starting ESD Unit Six which helps you to review the kind of skills and knowledge that you will need to manage the kinds of changes you are likely to have to face in the future. To consolidate this unit, please carry out the self-developmental Activity ESD5.11.

ACTIVITY ESD5.11

DEVELOPMENT – FOR WHAT PURPOSE?

Activity code

✓ Self-development
Teamwork
Communications
Numeracy/IT
Decisions

What resources can you draw upon to structure your learning?	Accreditation of management competence (MCI)	Personal development	Academic credit	Career change	Other (specify)
External course					
In-house course					

What resources can you draw upon to structure your learning?	Accreditation of management competence (MCI)	Personal development	Academic credit	Career change	Other (specify)
Garratt's (1991) six stages of development					
Learning style					
Learning resource centre					
Open/distance learning					
Centre for group development					
Role play					
Action learning					
Presentations					
Appraisals					
Learning network					
Mentor					
Critical incident diaries					
Learning diary					
Other (specify)					

I.   Conclusion

We have covered a lot of ground. Certainly courses and developmental events can be useful if they meet a perceived need. The selection of the appropriate method is in part related to this perceived developmental need but other factors come into consideration, for example, learning style, etc. We examined the relative merits of structured and unstructured methods of development both on and off-the-job.

A range of approaches were put forward to facilitate some structure to work-based learning and these were also linked to wider educational opportunities.

We now turn to ESD Unit Six which pulls together our themes to date and prepares you for future change.

Bibliography

Anderson, A.H., *Effective Personnel Management* (Blackwell, Oxford, 1994).

Boud, D., Keogh, R. and Walker, D., *Reflection: Turning Experience into Learning* (Kogan Page, London, 1985).

Boydell, T., Leary, M. and Pedler, M., 'Crossing the threshold: the challenge facing trainers, developers and line managers,' *Transition*, (January, 1993).

Brown, R.A., *Portfolio Development and Profiling for Nurses* (Central Health Studies, Lancaster, 1992).

Clutterbuck, D., *Everyone needs a Mentor: fostering talent at work* (IPM, London, 1991).

Critten, P., *Investing in People: Towards Corporate Capability* (Butterworth & Heinemann, London, 1994).

Garratt, B., *Learning to Lead: Developing your organisation and yourself* (Fontana, London, 1991).

Goodge, P., 'Developing Centres for the 1990's – Third generation design,' *Organisations and People*, (July, 1994).

Honey, P., 'Establishing a Learning Regime', *Organisations and People*, Quarterly Journal of AMED, **1**, 1, (1994).

Honey, P. and Mumford, A., *A Manual of Learning Styles* (Honey, Maidenhead, 1982).

Huczynski, A., *Encyclopedia of management development methods* (Gower, Aldershot, 1983).

Leary, M., Boydell, T., van Boeschoten, M. and Carlisle, J., *The qualities of managing*. Report on a project carried out by TRANSFORM (Consultants) and Sheffield City Polytechnic. (Manpower Services Commission, 1986).

Management Charter Initiative, *Good Practice Guide* (MCI, London, 1991).

Margerison, C., 'How chief executives succeed', *Journal of European Industrial Training*, **4**, 5, (1980).

Marsick, V. and Watkins, K., *Informal and incidental learning in the workplace* (Routledge, London, 1990).

Mumford, A., *Management Development: Strategies for action* (IPM, London, 1989).

Pedler, M., Burgoyne, J. and Boydell, T., *A Manager's Guide to Self Development* (McGraw-Hill, Maidenhead, 1993).

Redman, W., *Portfolios for development: A guide for trainers and managers* (Kogan Page, London, 1994).

Reeves, T., *Managing Effectively – Developing yourself through experience* (Butterworth & Heinemann, London, 1994).

Revans, R., *The origins and growth of action learning* (Chartwell Bratt, London, 1982).

Schon, D.A., *Educating the Reflective Practioner* (Jossey Bass, San Francisco, 1987).

Stephenson, J., 'Capability and competence: are they the same and does it matter? *Capability* **1**, (1994).

Training and Development Lead Body (TDLB), 'How do you spot good trainers.' Consultation document, (TDLB, London, 1991).

Wild, R., 'The management of development', *Management Today*, (October, 1994).

ESD Unit Six

Managing Change: the Challenge of the Future

Learning Objectives

After completing this unit you should be able to:

- consolidate your views on self-development
- recognize the need for change and the process and implications of change for you, your organization, colleagues and staff
- examine the concept of the 'transformational leader'
- recognize the power implications of change for staff
- develop creative and facilitative skills
- 'read' environmental changes in a range of scenarios
- examine the implications of these changing scenarios for management competencies and competence
- link a culture of learning to self-development
- link self-development to the effective management development of the series and
- apply the generic skills of the series.

CONTENTS

A. Overview

B. Past and Present

C. The Future – a Wider Perspective

▶ The concept of change

▶ The dynamics of change

▶ Changing managerial roles?

▶ Changing the alignment process

▶ Implications for competencies and competence

D. The Future – Specific Perspectives

▶ Scenarios of change and business policy

▶ Organizational implications
  – Steady-state
  – Decline/recovery
  – Growth

▶ Implications for self-development

E. The Future – Self-development

▶ A culture of learning and power sharing

▶ Effective management

ESD Unit Six

" . . . Effective leadership or change management may not have to be based on a detailed strategic plan. It may not be something that has to be imposed. It may be something that can emerge and take form in a self-organizing, evolutionary way. "

(Morgan, 1993.)

A. Overview

This unit aims to consolidate our perspectives on self-development, to integrate these views with the wider series and to develop an awareness of change with its ramifications for self-development.

In the words of Peters (1987), 'We must simply learn to love change as much as we have hated it in the past'. The way a manager is able to understand, embrace and exploit change for the benefit of him/herself and his/her organization will be a key test of effectiveness in the future.

Before we go on to look at change we consolidate where we are at the moment.

The future is considered in general terms and the dynamics of change are examined. Changes in the role of management and the interface with leadership are touched upon. New competencies and competences are extrapolated.

From a macro picture of change we move to scenarios based on the dominant business policies of the organization. In line with *Effective General Management* (Anderson, 1995) and *Effective Enterprise and Change Management* (Anderson and Barker, 1996) we consider a range of 'snapshots' of organizational change. Next we examine their implications for self-development. We consolidate the unit and the book by advocating a culture of learning to facilitate self-development. Change and enterprise are then fused into our vision of effective management in which self-development acts as one of its key anchor points.

B. Past and Present

Clearly we believe that self-development – for everyone and not just management – is a key feature of effectiveness. As this series relates to management, we have consciously addressed this audience but the concepts and pressures of self-development are transferable to non-managers as well – although the scope available in the design of jobs through some Taylorite hangover may be another matter.

Personal effectiveness and task effectiveness are mirrored through competencies and competence. Perhaps these latter ideas are a little static – not taking sufficient account of change, and so we develop a non-static position later in this unit.

Without resources, self-development can remain a very poor relation indeed. To enrich the concept, it needs support and resources. Again changing scenarios may impact on the levels of commitment, funding and resourcing open to self-development. Learning was seen as the 'oil of the machinery'. We return to this idea in the later sections as individual learning needs a fusion with some form of organizational support system, if not some vision and practice of a culture of learning within the organization. Let us now turn to change and its implications for self-development. First we take a broad view and then we move to scenarios.

C.   The Future – A Wider Perspective

The concept of change

All societies change, or like animals, they fail to adapt and they perish. History is strewn with great civilizations such as that of the classical Greeks and that of the Romans – as well as that of the British Empire – which are buoyant for many years and then go into a decline – usually through an incapacity to cope with changed environments. Work organizations are the same. Elsewhere (Anderson and Barker, 1994), we trace the rise and fall of key business organizations over an historical period noting that few pacesetters of yesteryear have kept up with the leaders of the race today.

Our society seems to be changing even more rapidly than in the past – even allowing for past agrarian and industrial revolutions. The pace of change seems to quicken almost annually with political, economic, social and technological factors impacting on organizations. Change is not all led from the external environment though. Work organizations, collections of people coming together for the goal achievement of the institution – if not of the group, also stimulate change and impact on the external environment. For example, demands for social responsibility, attempts to have an 'edge' on the competition, new products/services, new technologies and new competencies and competences may all impact on the organization.

Morgan (1993) argues that organizations need to concentrate on their 'fracture lines', that is, 'those points of change and transformation that have the potential to alter the nature of whole industries, services and their constituent organizations'. At this point, attempt Activity ESD6.1.

ACTIVITY ESD6.1

FRACTURES

Activity code

✓ Self-development
✓ Teamwork
✓ Communications
☐ Numeracy/IT
✓ Decisions

Task (Suitable for group brainstorming)

What type of 'fractures' might occur in the next ten years which would impact on your work organization/college?

Another approach to change management is to attempt to chart themes of the present that can be extrapolated to the future. The idea of 'futurism' may sound a little like crystal ball gazing but elsewhere (Anderson and Woodcock, 1996), it is argued that it may facilitate an opportunity for scanning for entrepreneurship. If it can be used for an opportunity analysis which may signify a possible change of direction, it can also be used to illustrate constraints or indeed pending 'fractures' (see Box ESD6.1).

BOX ESD6.1

Futurism

Unless we have mystical powers, few of us can predict the future.

Futurism attempts to extrapolate existing themes and trends into the future. A form of projection or crude forecasting is attempted. It tends to be at macro level, e.g. looking at the possibility of another oil crisis, etc.

We develop this idea elsewhere for idea generation for entrepreneurs.[1] Such a tactic can also work for senior managers involved in scenario planning for their organizations.

Source:
1. Anderson, A.H. and Woodcock, P., *Effective Entrepreneurship* (Blackwell Publishers, Oxford, 1996).

Under Morgan's (1993) direction, three groups of leading Canadian executives debated possible changes that their organizations might face.

Some of the 'fractures' Morgan's executives discussed were:

- a dramatic rise in the price of oil;
- key breakthroughs in some aspect of research/technology;
- radical demographic shifts;
- free trade legislation or some industry-specific decision on regulation or deregulation; and
- 'just-in-time' management.

It may be that some of these potential 'fractures' which cause changes might seem rather remote from where you sit in a particular department where potential change may not seem so dramatic. But the chances are that, over the last few years, you will have directly experienced some of these kinds of change:

- reduced workforce;
- removal of one or more levels of management;
- reduced budget; and/or
- different attitudes towards work (and authority) from a new generation of staff.

Clearly change is endemic. In the 1960s and 1970s in particular, a movement sprang up to manage this change through a planned basis utilizing insights from the behavioural sciences. This was organization development (OD). To Bennis (1989) it is:

a response to change, a complex educational strategy intended to change the beliefs, attitudes, values and structure of organizations so that they can better adapt to new technologies, markets and challenges, and the dizzying rate of change itself.

Please refer to Box ESD6.2.

BOX ESD6.2

The aims of organizational development

OD seeks to:
- increase an organization's awareness of change;
- create a climate where organizations are more adaptable to change;
- stimulate the collaborative features within the organization (as opposed to elements making for conflict);
- facilitate key decision-making within firms;
- allow employees to contribute to the goals of the organization; and
- improve ways of working within the workplace.

This attempt at planned change perhaps suffers from a too introspective approach which tries to adapt and adopt when perhaps it needs to be more anticipative, proactive and more aware of the influence of the external environment and of business strategy on the organization.

Increasing external environmental turbulence, a more cavalier style of management and a 'Balkanization' of the labour markets have led to more change – often unplanned, usually without any inputs from the behavioural sciences and often by diktat rather than by agreement.

Elsewhere in the series it is advocated that such change may be resented by the labour force and short-lived as the participating forces have not been involved in the concept or indeed the process. Again we believe that the behavioural sciences allied to planned internal change must be attained to external changes and to business policy (Anderson and Barker, 1996). Behavioural Science must merge with Economics for such change to be long standing.

The dynamics of change

To Marguilis and Raia (1978), an organization is a system – a complex mechanism of interrelated elements. It is clearly an open system, of course, interacting with its external environment. Anyway, within the institution itself, a change to any of the sub-systems will have ramifications on the other parts. This is clearly important to understanding the process of change: touch one domino and many will fall over.

Lewin (1951) presents the classical analysis of the dynamics of change – although the perspective does assume the existence of an equilibrium rather than an ever changing scenario. Please refer to Box ESD6.3.

BOX ESD6.3

Lewin's three-stage approach to change

1 Unfreezing   This stage attempts to unfreeze staff's attachment with the past, for example. This might be done by giving information and pointing out inappropriateness of current beliefs and assumptions.
2 Changing/moving   This stage begins the transition to a new set of behaviours by providing new structures and support to embed the new attitudes and beliefs.
3 Refreezing   Finally, the new behaviour becomes the norm and is enshrined in new policies and rituals.

Source:
Adapted from Lewin, K., *Field Theory in Social Science* (Harper, New York, 1951)

Lewin's (1951) forces are of course perceived forces. Validity apart, it is going to be difficult to predict behaviour in this process of change owing to a variety of perceptions. The problem of equilibrium does not go away either in spite of a 'quasi-stationary equilibrium' being used to understand the changes in the balance of forces. However it is a useful tool in understanding the dynamics of change. Please tackle Activity ESD6.2.

ACTIVITY ESD6.2

CHANGE DYNAMICS

Activity code

✓ Self-development
✓ Teamwork
☐ Communications
☐ Numeracy/IT
✓ Decisions

Task

Using an organization of your choice highlight the key driving forces and the key restraining forces in any change or possible change within that institution. An example is given below.

Driving forces
New boss
Changing work methods

Restraining forces
Existing culture
Trade union pressure
Lack of co-operation from staff, etc.

One thing that we can say for sure is that a thesis causes an antithesis and although Hegel's logic of a synthesis may not necessarily occur, change will cause a reaction.

For the purpose of self-development this reaction can be seen in how we can go about the physical process of change with its philosophy and techniques to be mastered and in the coping mechanisms that people invoke in handling change. The techniques are covered in a range of books noted in the series and so we shall focus here on the physical process of change – as it reflects on a philosophy of management and on coping mechanisms.

How do we go about changing things and overcoming resistance in particular?

Kotter and Schlesinger (1979) provide some guidance.

The methods include:

■ coercion

■ manipulation

■ education and communication

■ support

■ participation

■ negotiation.

Coercion is a threatening stance. 'You do – or else'. It may work in the short-term or longer-term in, for example, prison of war camps but it will provoke opposition which may kill off change.

Manipulation is a form of influence – perhaps with malevolent undertones. Distortion of realities catch up with people and once labelled a 'manipulator', change may be inhibited. Related to this manipulation is the buying off of opposition through placing key opponents at the head of task groups for change, etc. Here we touch upon Machiavellianism.

Education gets over the message of change. Although it can be costly and time consuming, it seems to work. Support can reduce resistance. Again, success is not guaranteed but it can blunt the opposition edge. Participation means involving people in the decision. If they are party to the decision they may accept 'ownership' of the outcome. Negotiation involves some trading but the stakes can become high once people realize that 'principles' have a price.

In spite of the shortcomings of negotiation, it is a useful method of securing change, as is participation backed up by education and support. Coercion and manipulation – apart from the ethics – can backfire.

Carnall (1990) suggests a number of practical ways in which managers can help staff to accelerate the process of accepting change.

■ Help staff to know themselves and recognize and confront their doubts, concerns and work on them constructively.

■ Know the situation in which change is to take place and provide staff with as much information as is necessary for them to understand and take ownership of the information themselves.

■ Identify others who can help; involve them and create support networks.

■ Work on and rebuild staff's self-esteem.

Another dimension of the dynamics of change which impacts on self-development is coping mechanisms. Please tackle Activity ESD6.3 and thereafter consult Box ESD6.4.

ACTIVITY ESD6.3

COPING WITH CHANGE

Activity code

✓ Self-development

☐ Teamwork

☐ Communications

☐ Numeracy/IT

☐ Decisions

Task

Think back to a change that affected your life either at work or outside. It might have had a large or small impact; its effect may have been temporary or long-term.

Describe how you first reacted to news of the change and how you learned to cope with the consequences.

BOX ESD6.4

The coping cycle[1]

- Stage 1 – *denial* The first reaction is very often disbelief as we try and reassure ourselves that 'this is unlikely to happen to us'.

- Stage 2 – *defence* But once we know it is for real, our first reaction is often a combination of resistance and rationalization: 'A new computer wouldn't help us at all'. Very often it is a kind of ritual to help us to buy time.

- Stage 3 – *discarding* This is a turning point in the cycle when we start coming to terms with the change in a kind of stoical way – 'well, if it's going to happen we should give it a try'. Self-esteem improves as we begin to discard the past and 'grow' into the new situation.

- Stage 4 – *adaptation* This is also a key stage when staff try out the system, adapt to new procedures, to a new regime. Carnall offers some useful advice for managers at this stage:

> While managers should ensure that the right training and support are available, we argue that they should, generally remain in the background, allowing the people who are directly involved to make it work. By doing so, these people will develop the skills, understanding and attachments needed for the system to be run effectively in the longer term.
>
> ■ Stage 5 – *internalization*   Having tried out the changes and made them work now is the time for the new behaviours to become the 'norm'; for guidelines to be laid down which others can follow.
>
> *Source*:
> [1] Carnall, C.A., *Managing Change in Organizations* (Prentice Hall, Hemel Hempstead, 1990).

Understanding the concept and dynamics of change involves some of the key aspects that the manager of the future will have to address. Does this mean a new vision of management, a change in emphasis or merely an extension of the status quo?

Changing managerial roles?

Lessem (1993) considers that the kind of management competences we have explored account for less than 50 per cent of the total skills a manager will need. The other 50 per cent are what he calls 'the emerging skills of influencing, learning, facilitating and creating' – these are probably more akin to leadership skills. In particular, it seems to us, it is the 'facilitating and creating' skills of Lessem's taxonomy, that the manager of tomorrow will need.

Under these headings Lessem identifies the following sub skills:
■ facilitating skills
  ● listening
  ● recognizing potential
  ● team building
  ● building alliances
■ creative skills
  ● envisioning
  ● inspiring
  ● empowering
  ● aligning (aligning people behind the vision).

Lessem develops a model of what he calls 'Total Quality Learning' which revolves around a developmental cycle of 'learning' (inward reflection) and 'innovation' (outward action). It takes an individual manager from at the lowest level 'reacting physically' to an event, to a point where he/she 'imagines creatively' and translates this level of thinking into action which has an effect on the organization.

These are the 'soft-skills' of managing which go beyond an analytical description of the external world to one involving feeling and intuition. These are the qualities which, it is understood, comes from the right hemisphere of the brain rather than the left side in which the 'intellective' and analytical skills are centred, that is, the skills which have long been the basis of most management education and training. But, as we have tried to demonstrate, this may be changing.

Let us look at the 'creative skills' first. There seems general agreement that central to leadership is the need to 'have a vision'. By definition this focuses on the future – whereas management is often more concerned with the present in translating the vision into action.

> Leadership . . . essentially exists in the domain of the future; leaders are concerned with making something possible for themselves and others. They must determine and communicate a vision of how they want things to be, through an examination of what they stand for, what they value and what they are committed to doing.
>
> (Keeys, 1994)

Opportunities for sharing this vision can come at any time:

> An integral part of that vision is the 'how' as well as the 'what'. Once we start engaging people in a conversation about how we work together or how we relate to others as a means of delivering a vision, we are engaging in a real, live opportunity for leadership development. There is a whole range of opportunities for individual interventions. Every breakdown between two people, every new appointment to a job, every new systems introduction is a possible opportunity for us to consider what it means in terms of our leadership style.
>
> (Keeys, 1994)

What is key is that the vision you have must be an integral part of you and the way you see the world. Unless you are totally committed to and convinced by your vision there is no way you will be able to convince others.

An essential condition for enthusing others, and carrying them with you, is your own conviction that the activity you are leading is something you want to happen, one that you believe in fully. It is curious how advice to managers on how to generate the commitment of their staff always seems to take for granted that the managers themselves are committed. A crucial part of self management is being able, first to generate, and then to keep renewed, your own motivation and enthusiasm.

(Reeves, 1994)

The debate between what constitutes leadership and what makes for management (see Box ESD6.5) may have some relevance to the discussion.

BOX ESD6.5

Management or leadership?[1]

Manager	**Leader**
Administers	Innovates
A copy	An original
Maintains	Develops
Focuses on systems and structures	Focuses on people
Relies on control	Inspires trust
Has a short-range view	Has a long-range perspective
Asks how and when	Asks what and why
Has an eye on the bottom line	Has an eye on the horizon
Accepts the status quo	Challenges the status quo
Is the good, classic deliverer	Is his or her own person
Does things right	Does the right things

Source:
[1] Adapted from Bennis, W., *Why Leaders Can't Lead – the unconscious conspiracy continues* (Jossey Bass, San Francisco, 1989).

Perhaps more important than the pure management-leader debate is the 'orientations' approach of Fritz (1989). Two 'orientations' are contrasted: responsive/reactive and creative/proactive.

In the reactive/responsive orientation 'you take actions based on the circumstances in which you find yourself or might find yourself in the future' (Fritz, 1989). But the creative response is very difficult which, as Fritz admits, is hard to explain to someone in a 'reactive/responsive' orientation.

A creator creates in order to bring the creation into being. People in the reactive–responsive mode often have trouble understanding this sensibility: to create for the sake of the creation itself. Not for the praise, not for the 'return on investment' not for what it may say about you, but for its own sake.

(Fritz, 1989)

Fritz has a background in the arts and so it is not surprising he describes the creative approach in the way he does. Legge (1994) describes how what Fritz calls the 'creating process' has been used by Legge both in his role as a publisher and as a management development facilitator. This description is contained in Box ESD6.6

BOX ESD6.6

Extract from 'Fighting fires or filling buckets'

Drawing on his work as a composer and artist, Fritz describes the creating process as something that begins with a general sketch of the desired end-result, a 'dream' or very rough notion. You then frame a specific, concrete picture of the end result. For example, in my work as a publisher I do this for the whole book, visualising lay-out, typography, cover image, page length, paper type and general feel. Similarly, a manager when preparing for a discussion with a member of staff might ask himself, 'What do I want to happen as a result of this meeting?' Fritz observes that people are good at saying what they don't want (negative vision) but not good at specifying what they do want.

The next important step is to get an accurate picture of current reality, i.e. what you have now, what in the current state is relevant to the desired state? In the case of a specific book, what paper is there in the warehouse, what state is the manuscript in, what length is it? These questions create a 'structural tension' between what you want and what exists. The creating process occurs through resolving this tension, as you work from the present to a desired state . . .

In the creating process, once you are clear about what you want, and what you have, you can then take actions designed to produce what you want: action which can be evaluated and modified as you work.

Source:
Legge, M., 'Fighting fires or filling buckets', *Organisations and People*, **1** (4), (1994).

By adopting the work of Fritz (1989) we can take an individual manager from the lowest level 'reacting physically' to an event, to a point where he/she 'imagines creatively' and translates this level of thinking into action which has an effect on the organization. It also has parallels with Morgan's (1993) concept of 'imaginization', whereby he encourages managers to use images and metaphors to create a new world which at the same time frees them from the constraints and assumptions of the world they are currently in:

> Images and metaphors can be used as 'mirrors' through which people and groups can see themselves and their situations in fresh light, creating an opportunity for reflection and change.

> (Morgan, 1993)

By literally envisaging the future you can create a picture which in turn is easier to communicate to others. Clearly, having a vision is only half the story. We need to be able to convey that vision to others. Lessem (1993) calls this 'aligning people behind the vision'.

To Adams and Spencer (1986) the key to this whole approach is through 'transformational leadership'. Rosener's (1990) research indicated that women lead more towards a 'transformational' style of leadership whereas men are more likely to adopt a 'transactional' style of leadership. The latter is based on the premise that each individual should be treated separately with their separate agendas compared to 'aligning' people behind your views under 'transformational' leadership.

The effective management of change means understanding the concept, the techniques and the dynamics of change. It also requires managers to have the following:

- an action orientation and an anticipative mode rather than just merely reacting to events;

- a vision of where they are going; and

- the ability to get others to share this vision and to align themselves behind the approach.

Before we turn to these competencies and competences, we need to develop the 'alignment' process.

Changing the alignment process

Securing support for the vision can be by diktat or by consent. We favour the latter – not only from a humanistic perspective, but the commitment engendered by consensus is far longer lasting and is not based on fear but mutual respect.

One route to this alignment process – which is also relevant to individual self-development – is the concept of 'empowerment'. Elsewhere in the series (Anderson 1994) the idea of power and power sharing are discussed in length. The idea of 'empowerment' may be more akin to influence rather than to power *per se* – for the real sharing of power in organizations tends not to occur.

'Empowerment' means that individuals take far greater responsibility for their actions and that they are given the tools and the authority to take 'power' over their jobs. Organizational realities may circumscribe such an influence as 'empowerment' but it is a great ideal to which we should aspire in order to give working people more say in their working lives and to maximize their contribution to the organizational vision. Unfortunately it has become a buzz word and we need to guard against this important concept being regarded as yet another managerial fad.

Carlzon (1987) popularized the concept in the 1980s. He had become head of Scandinavian Air System (SAS) at a time when it was losing millions. Within a few years, he had turned it around so that it became 'Airline of the Year'. He did this by giving 'power' to the first-line service providers. Hitherto, check-in clerks, for example, may have been unable to meet a particular customer's needs without going through two or more levels of authority. Carlzon gave an undertaking that all staff were 'empowered' to do whatever was necessary to meet customer needs.

When managers 'empower' staff they give them the freedom to take whatever action is necessary to meet an agreed objective. But this does imply staff are very clear about what the objective of the vision is. The move towards greater 'empowerment' also reflects a trend towards more autonomy amongst the subsidiary business units of large national and multi-national companies.

Ciba UK, the British arm of the Swiss-based chemicals multi-national, Ciba Geigy, has been encouraged by the parent company to 'empower' its workforce. But as Gilliver, Ciba UK's head of Management Development and Training, says 'Empowerment is not a verb. "You" cannot empower "me". It's more a state of mind and a way of working' (Pickard, 1993).

Nevertheless as a result of company-wide seminars, there have been examples of success (see Box ESD6.7).

BOX ESD6.7

An example of 'empowerment' at work[1]

A group of three warehousemen at Ciba's Clayton Aniline factory were faced with a greatly increased workload as a result of a new automated warehouse. One hundred metres long, it could only accommodate pallets of a certain size and weight. Instead of merely unloading and loading pallets from trucks, they now had to 'repalletise' much of the material.

They complained about this. In the ensuing discussion, one suggestion was to abandon the new warehouse. Requested to think again, they came up with the idea of persuading all suppliers to send in materials on pallets made to Clayton Aniline's requirements.

This was 18 months ago. Most suppliers have now complied. The team has a log on their wall showing the number of successes and how many are still holding out. They are not giving up until everyone has come around.

Source:
[1] Adapted from Pickard, J., 'The real meaning of empowerment', *Personnel Management*, November, (1993).

Management writers such as Peters (1992), have been advocating this 'power' principle for some time. Though you find the term in the index the theme underlining much of the work is 'empowerment'. One of his favourite companies is Johnsonville Foods.

Please refer to Box ESD6.8.

BOX ESD6.8

Workgroup 'empowerment'

Workgroup 'empowerment' is the ability for workers to:
- recruit, hire, evaluate, and fire (if necessary) on their own
- acquire regularly new skills as they see fit and then train one another as necessary
- formulate, and then track and amend, their own budget
- make capital investment proposals as needed (after doing the supporting analyses, making appropriate visits to equipment vendors, etc.)
- handle quality control, inspection, subsequent troubleshooting and problem solving

- take on the task of constantly improving every process and product
- develop quantitative standards for productivity and quality – then monitor them
- suggest and then develop prototypes of possible new products, packaging, etc.
- work routinely on teams fully integrated with counterparts from sales, marketing and product development
- participate in 'corporate level' strategic projects.

Source:
Adapted from Peters, T., *Liberation Management – Necessary Disorganization for the Nanosecond Nineties* (Macmillan, London, 1992).

In addition, you should read Semler's (1994) best seller to learn how a Brazilian company, Semco, has become the Mecca for all companies wanting to find out about 'empowerment'. Not only do staff do the same as at Johnsonville Foods, but they also decide on how much they should be paid!

Before we bring all these threads together, try out the two activities to check out the capacity to 'empower' your staff – ESD6.4 and ESD6.5.

ACTIVITY ESD6.4

'EMPOWERMENT' I

Activity code

✓ Self-development

☐ Teamwork

✓ Communications

☐ Numeracy/IT

✓ Decisions

Task

- Identify a particular task/target your department has to achieve (e.g. meet deadline of x per cent of sales by y date).
- Identify what responsibilities your staff have for meeting this criteria. Are there 'tasks' that they have to achieve which then provide information which you process?

■ Consider which aspects of the tasks you can give over to them completely. [NB They will also require information and facilitation which we will look at in next section.]

ACTIVITY ESD6.5

'EMPOWERMENT' II

Activity code

✓ Self-development
☐ Teamwork
✓ Communications
☐ Numeracy/IT
✓ Decisions

Task

Rate yourself on the scale 1–5 on each of the following dimensions and then get your staff to rate you on the same dimensions.[1]

Factor	Scale	
■ ensure openness	1	5
■ promotes co-operation		
■ delegates authority		
■ manages performance		
■ develops people		
■ provides rewards and recognition		
■ communicate effectively		
■ resolves issues		
■ encourages innovation		

Source:
[1] These were the criteria Ciba UK used to survey how well they were developing managers to support empowerment. They averaged out the manager's own perception of his skills with those of his/her subordinates (which were less flattering!), but over the years the average score is getting better.

At the end of *Maverick*, Semler (1994) concludes with this simple advice:

> At the heart of our bold experiment is a truth so simple it would be silly if it wasn't so rarely recognised: *A company should trust its destiny to its employees.*
>
> I hope our story will cause other companies to reconsider themselves and their employees, to forget socialism, capitalism, just-in-time deliveries, salary surveys, and the rest of it, and to concentrate on building organisations that accomplish that most difficult of all challenges: to make people look forward to coming to work in the morning.

The sentiments expressed here remind us where we started – looking at the characteristics of leadership, or visionary management. Bennis (1989) identifies four characteristics:

- guiding vision

- passion

- integrity

- curiosity and daring.

Semler (1994) clearly has all four. But he also eschews much vaunted management techniques like just-in-time deliveries, etc. The implication is that leaders or visionary managers do not need such props; they build their own world. So far we have concentrated on what Lessem (1993) calls the creative skills. Let us now take a look at the other side of the coin – the facilitating skills. These are the support skills which the leader needs to demonstrate in order to ensure that the creative vision is achieved.

Lessem's facilitating skills involve listening, recognizing potential, team-building, and building alliances.

Facilitation is very different to just 'telling' people what to do or even to give them instruction and training. It involves a much more holistic approach, the starting point of which is the individual and/or team and their capacity to develop themselves. The facilitator is an 'enabler'. There is no fixed time or place when facilitation of development takes place.

> . . . . We can only help if we happen along at the right time and are prepared to listen, question, support, pose problems, offer resources, reflect back, counsel.

> (Boydell, Leary and Pedler, 1993).

Boydell *et al.* have carried out a survey into the changing roles of trainers and developers over the next few years in which they identify a need for a change of orientation away from training to development. They conclude with a set of guidelines which apply equally to the visionary manager and to leader seeking to facilitate the development of his/her team. These include the following:

■ an underpinning concept or archetype of the process of development;

■ an ability to make, and help others make, significant choices as they step into the unknown which involves feelings, uncertainty, risk and working in socio-political systems;

■ being clear and able to work with values, ideology and philosophy;

■ an awareness and an ability to struggle with moral and ethical issues;

■ working towards an uncertain future;

■ working with holistic, integrated processes, requiring methods and approaches that reflect this; and

■ remembering above all that the whole is greater than the sum of the parts.

Please tackle Activity ESD6.6.

ACTIVITY ESD6.6

DIMENSIONS OF FACILITATION

Activity code

✓ Self-development

☐ Teamwork

☐ Communications

☐ Numeracy/IT

☐ Decisions

Heron[1] identifies six dimensions of facilitation:

■ planning

■ meaning

■ confronting

■ feeling

■ structuring

■ valuing.

Task

Assess yourself against the following dimensions in relation to the vision/objectives you want realized.

- *The planning dimension* This requires the facilitator to be clear about aims and objectives and how they are to be achieved.

  How clear are the objectives to the group and has a plan been agreed with them to achieve them?

- *The meaning dimension* This is to do with the group's understanding of what has to be done and how they make sense of it all.

  How do you help the group to understand the 'meaning' underpinning their separate actions and how can you check their understanding on an ongoing basis?

- *The confronting dimension* This is to do with the extent to which the group openly confronts issues – including incompatible, interpersonal relationships – and is encouraged to do so.

  How do you encourage the group to confront issues openly?

  (For a good summary of how groups can be helped to be more open and, indeed, confrontational see Pascale.[2])

- *The feeling dimension* This is to do with the extent to which individual and group feelings are allowed and encouraged to surface.

  How do you encourage individuals and the group as a whole to articulate their feelings and share them with each other?

- *The structuring dimension* This is the 'formal' aspect of group facilitation, to do with the way learning and sharing within the group are organized and how experiences are recorded.

  What are the procedures in place for structuring group meetings and their outcomes?

- *The valuing dimension* This is to do with the 'ground rules' set for the group, how individuals' integrity is respected, confidences preserved and success celebrated.

  Have ground rules been agreed with the group? Would they recognize if these have been infringed in any way?

Source:
[1] Adapted from Heron, J., *The Facilitator's Handbook* (Kogan Page, London, 1989).
[2] Pascale, R., 'The Benefit of a Clash of Opinions', *Personnel Management*, (October, 1993).

This visionary management and leadership ties into the earlier discussion in ESD Unit One on the potential for a changed philosophy of management which can underpin not only the democratization process, but the wholesale shift to individuals taking control of their own destiny – inside and outside of work. The extent to which this remains an ideal remains a debating point. What is less debateable are the implications for competence and competencies deriving from a move towards a visionary approach to management and leadership. We now turn to those issues.

Implications for competencies and competence

To a great extent we have covered the competencies or personal qualities akin to our wider perspective in the last section. We shall link this up to a competence activity at the end of this section. We should focus on the implications of the wider perspective on competence, or the task orientation.

In the first section of this unit we utilized Morgan's (1993) useful idea of 'fractures'. Let us develop this idea as it impacts on competence.

It is interesting that both Morgan's 'managerial competencies for a turbulent world' and the new set of MCI competences for senior managers focus on 'Reading the environment' (MCI, 1994).

> Managers of the future will have to develop their ability to 'read' and anticipate environmental trends. They will need to develop antennae that help them to sense the critical issues and identify the emerging 'fractures' that will transform their organisations.

Please refer to Box ESD6.9 and compare this to Box ESD6.10.

BOX ESD6.9

Wider competences

Reading the environment

- Scanning and intelligence functions
- Forecasting and futurism
- Scenario planning
- Identifying 'fracture lines'

Developing contextual competences

- Building bridges and alliances
- Reframing problems to create new solutions

- Acting nationally and locally
- A new approach to social responsibility

Morgan gives the following rationale to support what he calls 'contextual competencies'.

> To build bridges, to reframe difficult problems, and to blend action at national and local levels, managers must be sensitive to how the well-being of the individual organization depends on the well-being of the whole system. It requires a special sense of responsibility, whereby managers recognize that if their organizations are to succeed, especially in the long term, they must cultivate the context that will impact their organizations positively.

Source:
Adapted from Morgan, G., *Riding the Waves of Changes – Developing managerial competencies for a turbulent world* (Jossey Bass, San Francisco, 1989).

BOX ESD6.10

MCI and external trends and stakeholders – an extract

A1 External trends

A1.1 Market review
Develop systems to review markets, identify customer needs and spot opportunities for product and service development.
A1.2 Climate
Evaluate and respond to political, regulatory and trading climates.
A1.3 Competition and Collaboration
Identify and evaluate competitors and potential collaborators.

A3 Stakeholders

A3.1 Stakeholders' interests
Identify the current and likely future interests of stakeholders.
A3.2 Stakeholders' impact
Evaluate and influence stakeholders' capabilities to help or hinder the achievement of the organisation's objectives.
NB Stakeholders are those individuals, groups and organisations who have an interest in the organisation. They may see the organisation as potentially beneficial or harmful. They include:

- shareholders
- customers

- clients
- public
- electorate
- suppliers
- employees/voluntary workers
- members
- financial institutions
- pressure groups
- media

Their interest may derive from:

- ownership
- geographical location
- social concern
- environmental concern.

Source:
MCI, *Senior Management Standards* (London, 1994).

Just as managers of the future will need to keep their antennae attuned to the external world they will also need to be sensitive to the changing culture and power base inside the organization. Pettigrew (1985) draws attention to the role of senior managers as change agents. In such a role they have to take account not just of the 'content' of change (which influences and shapes the how and why of change) but also the 'context' within which changes take place. Contrary to some views of how strategic change is brought about, Pettigrew is sceptical of the 'linear-rational' way in which managers have been trained to plan for and implement strategic change in the past.

Boddy and Buchanan (1992) suggest the way forward is through a 'content' and 'control' agenda.

The 'content' agenda requires the manager to be sufficiently familiar with the technical and procedural aspects surrounding change. Thus, if you are responsible for handling the introduction of a new computerized information system you would need to understand the new system and the resources required to maintain it in order to answer staff questions and reassure them of its benefits. You would also need to have in place a network of key 'stakeholders' and experts whose help you could call upon in the future.

The 'control' agenda has to take account of three types of information. It includes 'the tangible, visible aspects of the project'. This would take the form of the kind of plan most managers are familiar with which specifies the target to be achieved, by a given date with defined resources. It would also have built in to it procedures for monitoring progress and for taking any remedial action to bring the 'project back on track. This is what Pettigrew referred to as the 'linear-rational' approach to change. This is fine in a stable world where the odd deviation or two could be easily accommodated. But the argument of Pettigrew (1985) and of Boddy and Buchanan (1992) is that in such a rapidly changing world the manager/change agent must develop other skills.

Under the 'control' agenda, Boddy and Buchanan identify two other kinds of information which are not necessarily covered in the kind of contingency plan described above. These are:

impending changes in policy, changes around the organisation which would have a bearing on their project and changes in the external environment; and

the attitudes and commitment of other managers, their staff and of key stakeholders – a range of 'soft' information, critical to the project's progress and acceptance.

Please tackle Activity ESD6.7 and thereafter consult Box ESD6.11.

ACTIVITY ESD6.7

CONTENT AND CONTROL

Activity code

✓ Self-development
✓ Teamwork
  Communications
✓ Numeracy/IT
✓ Decisions

Task

What kind of procedures/controls might you set up to monitor the last two kinds of information Boddy and Buchanan (1992) describe, i.e. relating to 'impending policy changes' and changing attitudes of colleagues and other stakeholders critical to a project's success?

BOX ESD6.11

Control and content

It is all a question of 'reading the environment'. Here are some suggestions for anticipating policy changes:

- regular reviewing of newspapers, trade, professional journals and media reports;
- registering with Marketing/Market Research/Intelligence Agency;
- attending trade/professional conferences;
- customer/consumer surveys; and
- regular meetings of senior managers/colleagues/suppliers to brainstorm what Morgan calls likely 'fractures' which could completely transform your organization.

Here are some suggestions for keeping in touch with changing attitudes of colleagues/stakeholders:

- Listen/keep your ears and eyes open everywhere – in the staff restaurant, in the pub, at every meeting.
- Have regular meetings with all key stakeholders – colleagues, staff, outside professionals, suppliers and invite comment, questions, expression of concerns, worries. (But having done so be careful not to marginalize or put down anyone who dares to give you bad news! Welcome it. This will encourage others to open up as well.)
- Have regular meetings where you keep everyone up-to-date. Without this information they will not be in a position or feel confident enough to raise questions when they are needed.
- Provide the facility for suggestions/concerns to be raised anonymously (e.g. project comment box). Again, you must be seen to respond to such suggestions.

These are only examples of what you can do. You have probably identified other ways of keeping in touch.

Your content and control agenda constitute the visible part of your role as a change agent. They are what Boddy and Buchanan (1992) call 'public performance'. But there is a third agenda, which they call the 'process' agenda.

For Pettigrew (1985) there are two key 'processual' skills that a change agent needs: one is to get 'legitimacy' for the change that is planned – this is a concept 'linking political and cultural analysis' – and the second is the 'management of meaning' which refers to a process of symbol construction and value use designed to create legitimacy for one's ideas, actions and demands, and to delegitimize the demands of one's opponents. Here we move into the land of manipulation if not Machiavellianism. Reeves (1994) is very good in these areas – particularly on personal power while Boddy and Buchanan (1992) give us a host of 'backstage activities' to manipulate structures and relationships. Management should not have to degenerate into a process of overt or covert Machiavellianism. To manipulate change or any aspects of management may give a short-term fillip but it does court disaster and cuts across ethical dimensions of management which we have recommended throughout the whole series, political realism – certainly: Machiavellianism – no. We shall now widen our discussion to take more of an international perspective as this globalization theme may impact on competencies and competence. (See Anderson, Dobson and Patterson, forthcoming, for a debate on this globalization issue.)

Another key trend for the future is the possible emergence of the 'global' manager and the need to manage teams comprising a range of national cultures. Authors like Trompenaars (1993) and Hofstede (1980) have drawn attention to the danger of assuming that Western principles of good management have universal application. Thus while Western companies might accept the principle of 'achievement' as being a key motivator this would not be the case in 'collectivist' cultures in the East where individual achievement is far less significant than the well-being and protection of the group. If your company is a Japanese company you will be very familiar with the national characteristic that values rewards for a team performance above individual recognition.

But even within Europe, if the EU ideals of encouraging members to work more in each other's countries are to be realized, there will need to be greater awareness of our cultural differences before we can manage them in a positive way. For example, imagine you are the manager of a group that includes French, German, Swedish and Spanish personnel. Your 'consensus' leadership style is likely to be welcomed by the Swede but seen as ineffectual by the German and 'wimpish' by the Spanish. If you give feedback on staff performance which implies a need for improvement, while likely to be accepted by the Swede as helpful advice, the German would see it as an admission of failure. If you had Japanese members of staff and appeared to criticize them openly this would mean a very dramatic lack of 'face'. Trompenaars (1993) recounts the tale of a Chinese subordinate of a Dutch manager who knifed his manager to death after a 'frank discussion'.

While this may seem extreme, as a manager of the future you should be aware of the different national cultural characteristics which shape individual behaviour. In Box ESD6.12 we have summarized the various characteristics which Trompenaars (1993) and Hofstede (1980) have identified in their separate research of different cultures. After reading the information, try Activity ESD6.8.

BOX ESD6.12

Globalization and managerial dimensions

Trompenaar[1] identified seven dimensions on which research in 47 countries showed differing characteristics:

- universalism v. particularism (rules v. relationships)
- collectivism v. individualism (the group v. the individual)
- neutral v. emotional (the range of feelings expressed)
- diffuse v. specific (the range of involvement)
- achievement v. ascription (how status is accorded)
- sequential v. synchronic (how we manage time)
- controlling v. letting it take its course (how we manage nature)

Hofstede[2] identified the following dimensions after 15 years of research in 72 countries

- *Power distance* (PD)   This is the extent to which power is hierarchical and employees at the bottom end accept that power is distributed 'unequally'. Dictatorships (and Belgium and France) are high PD countries.

- *Uncertainty avoidance* (UA)   How tolerant is a country of uncertainty? To what extent does it seek to control the future or let it take its course? The new democracies (Austria, Italy, Japan) are high UA countries whereas the old democracies (Great Britain, Netherlands, USA) are low UA countries

- *Individualism v. collectivism* (IC)   To what extent is the concept of 'I' stronger than 'we'? The Anglo-Saxon bloc and the USA tend to be individualist while the East and countries like Venezuela, Colombia and Pakistan tend to be collectivist.

- *Masculinity v. femininity* (MF)   To what extent are male values like achievement and success dominant as opposed to the more feminine characteristics of caring and valuing quality of life? Japan is a high MF society whereas the Scandinavian countries tend to be low.

Sources: Adapted from:
[1] Trompenaar, F., *Riding the Waves of Culture: understanding cultural diversity in business* (Nicholas Brearley Publishing, London, 1993).
[2] Hofstede, G., *Culture's Consequences: International Differences in Work Related Values* (Sage Publications, 1980).

ACTIVITY ESD6.8

CULTURES

Activity code

✓ Self-development

☐ Teamwork

☐ Communications

☐ Numeracy/IT

✓ Decisions

Task

Regardless of whether you have any foreign nationals working for you or whether indeed you are or will be working for them, consider the extent to which your own organization matches the various characteristics in Box ESD6.12.

If you do have to put together a multicultural team you should take time out to use these dimensions to bring cultural differences into the open. When they had to set up a multicultural team, BP found that 'many team members had not realised the depth of cultural conditioning and were delighted and fascinated to talk to others about their own culture'. (Neale and Mindel, 1992)

Recognizing that you are part of a national culture is the first step. If you cannot recognize the characteristics in your own culture, you will not be in a position to recognize the key characteristics of another culture.

Increasingly, management writers are identifying characteristics of management success that need to embrace 'global' and 'international management' skills. Conger (1993) identifies the following characteristics of future leaders:

- strategically opportunistic
- globally aware
- capable of managing highly decentralized organizations
- interpersonally competent
- sensitive to issues of diversity
- community builders.

Stewart (1992) investigated competences/competencies in different countries (over eight years) in the face of changing competitive situations. She identified what she calls 'leading edge' competences/competencies – which differentiate the average from the excellent performers:

- Strategic long-term breadth of vision
- Diagnostic ability
- Identifying and implementing change
- Understanding the market (customer-driven)
- Entrepreneurial flair
- Empowerness (action-oriented)
- Team membership and laterality
- Vision and values
- Principles and rules
- Enabling style
- Charisma
- Emotional stability and openness.

In this case it seems that there are some common competences/ competencies across cultural boundaries as well as characteristics peculiar to different cultures.

Please tackle Activity ESD6.9 which pulls this section together. Next we look briefly at a micro-perspective on the future and then conclude by relating our views on self-development to the concept of effective management development of the series.

ACTIVITY ESD6.9

FUTURE COMPETENCES/COMPETENCIES

Activity code

- ✓ Self-development
- Teamwork
- Communications
- Numeracy/IT
- Decisions

Competence	Notes on how you might develop this competence further*
■ How well can you cope with change?	
■ How well developed is your personal power?	
■ Is your positional power likely to be more and more eroded?	
■ How can you help facilitate intellective skills?	

Competence	Notes on how you might develop this competence further*
■ What can you do to create conditions for a learning organization?	
■ How creative a leader are you?	
■ What are the differences between being a manager and being a leader?	
■ Are you a transactional or transformational leader?	
■ How well do you empower staff?	
■ How well developed are your facilitator skills?	
■ How able are you to read the environment?	
■ How do you rate as a change agent?	
■ What kind of content and control agenda do you have for managing change?	
■ What kind of process agenda do you have for managing change?	
■ How capable are you for establishing legitimacy for the process of change?	
■ How good are you at managing meaning?	
■ How aware are you of differences in national cultures?	
■ How do you rate yourself as a global manager?	

* Look back at resources covered in ESD Unit Five.

D. The Future – Specific Perspectives

To date our discussion has centred on a wider perspective on change and its implications for self-development. Now we turn to more 'micro' scenarios and the ramifications on self-development. The change scenarios are derived from *Effective Enterprise and Change Management* (Anderson and Barker, 1996) and some of the techniques of analysis come from *Effective General Management* (Anderson, 1995). As these ideas are treated fully in these books, we shall be brief.

Scenarios of change and business policy

The three broad strategies behind strategic development (excluding 'combination' policies) are:

- steady-state
- decline/recovery
- growth.

A steady-state is a maintenance strategy. It does not imply a 'do nothing approach'. Fine tuning of the competence effort is necessary to stay afloat. This policy of 'holding on to what we have' can be seen in mature industries or in firms with products/services coming to the end of their natural lifespan. Smaller businesses – perhaps obsessed with holding on to control – may also enter this category. Other businesses often use stability policies to consolidate their positions after a series of upheavals or change.

Decline, with the subsequent onus on recovery strategies, can occur through an ageing of the organization, a reduction in products/services or markets, or by some withdrawal of customer or supplier support. Intense competition may also stimulate the process.

Growth strategies can emanate from adding new products/services, adopting existing products or services or through some policy of integration. Increases in market share, profitability, sales turnover or higher investment and higher risk taking may also occur.

Organizational implications

Steady-state

This policy may have a role culture and tends to have the following 'S's. (See the 7S approach in Peters and Waterman, 1982.)

- A ticking over *strategy* predominates.
- A functional *structure* or link to bureaucratic principles exists.
- A fetish for information *systems* occurs.
- A proceduralized *style* of management dominates.
- Perhaps a 'fat cat' mentality amongst the *staff* will exist.
- There is a *skill* mix with a lot of training going on but not necessarily linked to organizational needs.
- A *value system* based on a pluralistic vision occurs throughout the organization (Anderson, 1995).

Decline/recovery

Rather than focus on the slippery road of decline we shall look at the recovery implications from this scenario which is often more akin to a power culture.

- Radical cuts and divestment epitomize this *strategy*.
- A 'slimming down' of the layers occurs in the *structure*.
- Information *systems* and intelligence are important but the predictable approach of management is often akin to panic and these systems may be put to one side in the real decision making of the organization.
- The managerial *style* is harder with a crisis orientation.
- The *skill* and *staff* inputs are seen increasingly as a cost, not a resource, and are slimmed down through savage cost cutting exercises.
- The *value system* allows for little debate and a unitarist approach predominates.

Growth

A forced pace of growth occurs here and a task orientation (more than a people orientation) may dominate.

- A *strategy* of reinvestment and higher risk projects tends to occur.
- On *structure*, experimentation is possible with project teams and decentralized business units.
- The *information systems* engender more business data but these systems are tools of management rather than having a creation of their own (see earlier – steady-state).
- The *style* of management tends to be task oriented (rather than people).
- New flexible work patterns, new competences and skills and new participative processes reflect the *skills* and *staff* components.
- The *value systems* emphasize the common weal (i.e. the management vision) but there is some scope for diversity in the value systems.

This is a very cryptic summary of a whole text but the three scenarios and their implications can be gleaned from this précis.

Implications for self-development

The first implication is to know your own scenario. You need to develop the flexibility of being able to cope in each of the situations – although you will certainly have a preferred scenario.

The *steady-state scenario* can be seen as a great constraint on self-development. The organization tends to be bureaucratic with too many rules and regulations and endless pieces of paper and procedures.

However there are opportunities and the scope for harnessing individual development to organizational support systems for training and development, while the value systems can almost allow development for its own sake.

The competencies and competences required in this scenario tend to be akin to an official within a bureaucracy. This may ensure survival but the self-developer needs to look more to an organic structure and to a flexible approach to management as scenarios change. The steady-state will not last for ever.

The *recovery scenario* from decline tends to involve a form of crisis management – if you survive. Perhaps a 'head down – low profile' approach is recommended in this situation but if you have too low a profile you may be doomed to be an 'unnecessary cost'.

This scenario may mean changing gear and maximizing your existing competencies and competences. There will be little or any organizational support for self-development so the onus is placed squarely on the individual.

Again, developed competencies and competences may see you through this troubled scenario. If not, past self-development experiences may increase your skill transferability elsewhere.

The *growth scenario* may call upon other aspects of self-development. A more radical innovative approach predominates. The organization is less structured and more organic – relating to its changing external environments. Flexibility, experimentation and innovation are the key themes under this scenario.

Organizational support systems will tend to encourage self-developmental possibilities. Hence business scenarios change and they have implications for the organization, management and for self-development. We have deliberately not gone down the route of looking at the implications on specific competencies and competences as these are covered in *Effective General Management* (Anderson, 1995). The keynote seems to be flexibility and the ability to read not only the external but the internal environment of the organization and adapt or adopt accordingly.

We now turn to the last section of the book that puts forward the need for a climate of learning – almost irrespective of the scenarios – and for the concept of effective management which exists across the whole series in which self-development needs to be placed.

E. The Future – Self-development

Self-development is not just about the individual taking responsibility for his/her learning. This does go along the route of meeting some of the aims of self-development but we firmly believe in a supportive climate of learning and of a developmental scheme for management – if not for all staff – to give a wider context to the whole concept of self-development. We shall touch upon these ideas before we conclude.

A culture of learning and power sharing

Earlier we discussed the need for individuals to take control – so far as is practical – of their working lives, their careers and their overall development. As we have seen earlier in this unit, this idea of being 'empowered' is an important facet of taking responsibility for self-development. The individual needs assistance. The organization must provide a support system and hopefully some resources. If there is a climate of learning in the organization, this can underpin self-development. We now turn to the idea of a 'learning organization'. Again this may be an ideal situation in many institutions – particularly given the policy options which we touched upon in the last section. An ideal or not – it does give us something to aspire to and sophisticated 'learning organizations' may stimulate self- and organization development. We shall develop this ideal situation.

Much has been written about 'the learning organization' over the last 7–8 years. Garratt (1990) has been one of the key proponents of the concept in this country as have been Pedler, Burgoyne and Boydell (1991). Senge (1990) has been a key advocate in the US.

A definition that has stuck is:

A learning organisation is one that facilitates the learning of all its members and continuously transforms itself.

(Pedler, Burgoyne and Boydell, 1991)

Unfortunately many companies regard the provision of training and development opportunities as the sole criterion for calling themselves 'learning organizations' whereas the key lies in the second half of the above definition – an organization has to show evidence that the consequences of individual learning have led to the organization transforming itself. In other words we are back to change and the facilitation and management of change which is where we started at the beginning of this unit.

For this 'transformation' to take place the learning that managers require will need to be what Argyris and Schon (1978) call 'double-loop' learning. This is in contrast to what they call 'single-loop learning'. This single-loop learning is the normal type of learning that goes on all the time. For example, walking past Accounts on your way into work, you notice that Betty is using an outdated form even though you had a meeting with her last week to introduce the new form. You therefore draw the matter to her attention. Betty realizes her error and conforms to the norm that has been agreed.

It is single-loop because it works like a closed system: a deviation from a norm is identified, corrective action is taken and everything returns to normal. An analogy that is often used to explain single-loop learning is that of a central heating system that is regulated by a thermostat. When the temperature falls below the desired level, the thermostat reacts to start up the boiler until the temperature reaches the correct temperature at which point it cuts out the boiler.

Such learning goes on all the time in most organizations. But by definition it can only serve to reinforce existing norms and systems. What if the norms were inappropriate, what if Betty did know about the new form but drawing on her experience questioned its design?

This 'questioning of established norms' was what Argyris and Schon called 'double-loop learning'. But it is not enough for Betty simply to change procedures herself – that would simply be single-loop learning. For double-loop learning to occur, Betty would have to draw her questioning of the procedure to the attention of 'the boss'. If, as a result of this process, the procedure was changed in some way, that would be true double-loop learning, that is, a questioning of the norm had led to corrective action being taken. (In the case of the central heating system analogy, double-loop learning would occur if we began to question whether the set temperature was appropriate and then changed it.)

This second kind of learning, Argyris and Schon (1978) argued, was the most useful for organizations to acquire; the process would enable them to question procedures continually and, as a result, they would be more able to respond to change.

Please tackle the Activity ESD6.10.

ACTIVITY ESD6.10

LEARNING LOOPS

Activity code

✓ Self-development

☐ Teamwork

☐ Communications

☐ Numeracy/IT

☐ Decisions

Task

Think back over the last week and try to identify whether at any time you were in a position to encourage double-loop as opposed to single-loop learning – for example, when you criticized the temp who was standing in for your secretary for not following the agreed procedure on filing invoices (which you had painstakingly gone through with her on Monday).

In this instance you certainly facilitated single-loop learning but in doing so you failed to listen to her defence of her own system which certainly was different to the standard procedure but might just have improved upon it. In other words this was an opportunity for you to encourage her to challenge the system which might have led to a new system of filing (i.e. double-loop learning would have taken place and 'transformation' of a system would have been the consequence).

Make a commitment to look for an opportunity in the coming week not just to 'correct' a procedure/activity that in some way deviates from the norm but also to consider if the practice (albeit abnormal) might not be an improvement.

Make a commitment to encourage staff to challenge existing practice if they can demonstrate that it can be improved upon.

Effective management

Self-development is a key linkpin of effective management across this whole series.

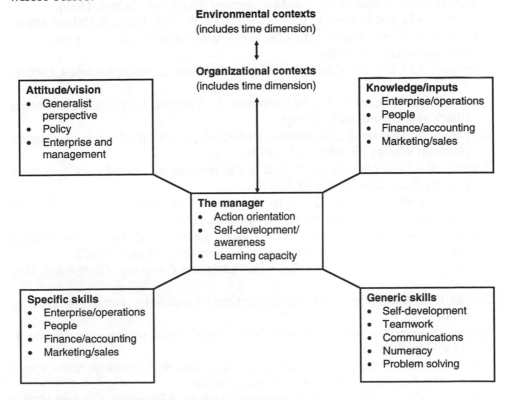

Figure ESD6.1   Effective management development

© Anderson Associates, Personnel and Management Advisors, Melbourn, S. Cambridge, SG8 6AY, England

Effectiveness is ultimately results-centred but the process of getting there can be as important for effective management. Ends and means must fuse to give us a vision of effectiveness.

We see the development of management involving knowledge, activities, vision, specific and generic skills as well as the operational real politik of the organisation and of the wider environment.

The flowchart in figure ESD6.1 illustrates the relationship between the series view of self-development and of wider effective management development. It is worth noting that self-development is placed at the fulcrum of the whole approach to effective management. This is a suitable place to close this unit.

Bibliography

Adams, J. and Spencer, S. (eds), *Transforming Leadership* (Miles River Press, New York, 1986).

Anderson, A.H., *Effective Labour Relations* (Blackwell, Oxford, 1994).

Anderson, A.H., *Effective General Management* (Blackwell, Oxford, 1995).

Anderson, A.H. and Barker, D., *Effective Business Policy* (Blackwell, Oxford, 1994).

Anderson, A.H. and Barker, D., *Effective Enterprise and Change Management* (Blackwell, Oxford, 1996).

Anderson, A.H. and Woodcock, P., *Effective Entrepreneurship* (Blackwell, Oxford, 1996).

Anderson, A.H., Dobson, T. and Patterson, J., *Effective International Marketing* (Blackwell, Oxford, forthcoming).

Argyris, C. and Schon, D., *Organisational Learning: A theory of action perspective* (Addison Wesley, Reading, MA, 1978).

Bennis, W., *Why Leaders can't lead – the unconscious conspiracy continues* (Jossey Bass, San Francisco, 1989).

Boddy, D. and Buchanan, D., *Take the lead – interpersonal skills for project managers* (Prentice Hall, Hemel Hempstead, 1992).

Boydell, T., Leary, M., and Pedler, M., 'Crossing the threshold: the challenge facing trainers, developers and line managers', *Transition*, (January 1993).

Carlzon, J., *Moments of Truth* (Ballinger Publishing Company, Cambridge, MA, 1987).

Carnall, C.A., *Managing change in organisations* (Prentice Hall, Hemel Hempstead, 1990).

Conger, 'Training leaders for the twentyfirst century', *Human Resources Review*, **3**, (1993), pp. 203–18.

Fritz, R., *The path of least resistance: Learning to become the creative force in your own life* (Fawcett, Columbine, New York, 1989).

Garratt, B., *Creating a learning organisation* (Institute of Directors, London, 1990).

Hofstede, G., *Culture's Consequences: International Differences in Work Related Values* (Sage Publications, Newbury Park, CA, 1980).

Keeys, G., 'Effective leaders need to be good coaches', *Personnel Management*, (November, 1994), pp. 52–4.

Kotter, J. and Schlesinger, L., 'Choosing Strategies for Change', *Harvard Business Review* (March–April 1979).

Legge, M., 'Fighting fires or filling buckets,' *Organisations and People*, **1**,4, (1994).

Lessem, R., *Total Quality Learning – Building a Learning Organisation* (Blackwell, Oxford, 1993).

Lewin, K., *Field Theory in Social Science* (Harper, New York, 1951).

MCI 6, *Senior Management Standards* (MCI, London, 1994).

Marguiles, N. and Raia, A.P., *Conceptual Foundations of Organisational Development* (McGraw-Hill, New York, 1978).

Morgan, C., *Riding the waves of change – Developing managerial competences for a turbulent world* (Jossey Bass, San Francisco, 1989).

Morgan, C., *Imaginization – the art of creative management* (Sage, Newbury Park, CA, 1993).

Neale, R. and Mindel, R., 'Rigging up multicultural teamworking', *Personnel Management*, (January, 1992).

Pedler, M., Burgoyne, J. and Boydell, T., *The Learning Company* (McGraw-Hill, New York, 1991).

Peters, T., *Liberation Management – Necessary disorganisation for the Nanosecond Nineties* (Macmillan, London, 1992).

Peters, T., *Thriving on Chaos – handbook for a management revolution* (Macmillan, London, 1987).

Peters, T.J. and Waterman, R.H., *In Search of Excellence* (Harper & Row, New York, 1982).

Pettigrew, A., *The Awakening Giant: continuity and change in ICI* (Blackwell, Oxford, 1985).

Pickard, J., 'The real meaning of empowerment,' *Personnel Management*, November, (1993).

Reeves, T., *Managing Effectively – Developing yourself through experience* (Butterworth & Heinemann, London, 1994).

Rosener, J.B., 'Ways Women Lead.' *Harvard Business Review*, November, (1990).

Semler, R., *Maverick* (Arrow, London, 1994).

Senge, P., *The Fifth Discipline – The Art and Practice of the Learning Organisation* (Doubleday, New York, 1990).

Stewart, V., 'Human Capital Issues in Organisational Change', selected papers from the IPMA National Conference, Asia Pacific Journal of Human Resources, (Australian Human Resource Institute, 1992).

Trompenaars, F., *Riding the waves of culture: understanding cultural diversity in business* (Nicholas Brearley Publishing, London, 1993).

Conclusion

We shall be brief.

Taking control of our own life – so far as is practicable – goes to the heart of self-development. A cynic once remarked that the world does not owe us a living. Organizations do not owe us development either. Hopefully, more progressive organizations see the development of their people as being an integral part of their overall business strategy. Self-development fits into this strategy. Where no such business and people strategy exists, the onus falls more upon the individual to develop him/herself.

Either way, self-development is critical for all members of staff within a work organization.

In this work, we have linked the idea of self-development to effectiveness – at various levels. We then moved to two views of personal and task effectiveness and examined competencies and competences respectively. Learning must pervade the concept and the process of self-development and we devoted one unit to this idea. Organizational assistance from resources to a concept of organizational learning can only be supportive of self-development. Finally we looked at changing scenarios and their implications for self-development. Self-development runs as a core generic skill in each volume throughout the series, as well as being the linkpin for individuals taking responsibility for their own working life – from reading a book such as this on self-development, to putting some of the ideas into effect; from learning logs to undertaking a study at an MBA level.

We started this book with a quotation from McGregor (1960).

The truism exists that mature learners must take a considerable responsibility for their learning. Organizational support is useful of course but real development must come from within the individual. The onus must lie with the individual.

Self-development

We have tried to demonstrate here that self-development can provide the tools and techniques for this flowering of the inner self. Structured development emanating from the organization may be a thing of the past

275

for many of us – even in sophisticated organizations – and so again the emphasis is placed back on self-help.

Self-development can enhance this self-help not only as a philosophy and mechanism for helping ourselves but it can stimulate others as well. Finally, owing to the nature of the series, we focused on self-development for managers, but the concept can be applied to everyone at the place of work for the amount of unfulfilled talent and wasted opportunity at the place of work is quite staggering. Self-development can certainly reduce this waste and move us to a higher level of humanistic capability.

Bibliography

Adams, J.S., 'Towards an understanding of inequity', *Journal of Abnormal Social Psychology*, **67** (1963).

Adams, J. and Spencer, S. (eds), *Transforming Leadership* (Miles River Press, New York, 1986).

Adlam, R. and Plumridge, M., 'Organisational effectiveness and self development: the essential dimension' in Pedler, M., Burgoyne, J., Boydell, T. and Welshman, G. (eds), *Self Development in Organisations* (McGraw-Hill, London, 1990).

Alderfer, C.P., *Existence, Relatedness and Growth: human needs in organisational settings* (Free Press, New York, 1972).

Allport, G.W., *Personality* (Holt, New York, 1937).

Anderson, A.H., 'Learning Characteristics and Learning Theories', *Training Officer – The Independent Journal for the Professional Trainer*, **29**, November 1993.

Anderson, A.H., *Successful Training Practice* (Blackwell, Oxford, 1993).

Anderson, A.H., *Effective Personnel Management* (Blackwell, Oxford, 1994).

Anderson, A.H., *Effective Labour Relations* (Blackwell, Oxford, 1994).

Anderson, A.H., *Effective General Management* (Blackwell, Oxford, 1996).

Anderson, A.H. and Barker, D., *Effective Business Policy* (Blackwell, Oxford, 1994).

Anderson, A.H. and Barker, D., *Effective Enterprise and Change Management* (Blackwell, Oxford, 1996).

Anderson, A.H. and Ciechan, R., *Effective Financial Management* (Blackwell, Oxford, forthcoming).

Anderson, A.H. and Chansarkar, B., *Effective Market Research* (Blackwell, Oxford, forthcoming).

Anderson, A.H. and Dobson, T., *Effective Marketing* (Blackwell, Oxford, 1994).

Anderson, A.H., Dobson, T. and Patterson, J., *Effective International Marketing* (Blackwell, Oxford, forthcoming).

Anderson, A.H. and Kleiner, D., *Effective Marketing Communications* (Blackwell, Oxford, 1995).

Anderson, A.H. and Kyprianou, A., *Effective Organizational Behaviour* (Blackwell, Oxford, 1994).

Anderson, A. H. and Nix, E., *Effective Accounting Management* (Blackwell, Oxford, 1994).

Anderson, A. H. and Thompson, M., *Effective Information Management* (Blackwell, Oxford, forthcoming).

Anderson, A. H. and Woodcock, P., *Effective Entrepreneurship* (Blackwell, Oxford, 1996).

Ansoff, I.H. and McDonnel, E.J., *Implanting Strategic Management* (Prentice Hall, Englewood Cliffs, NJ, 1990).

Argyris, C., *Reasoning, Learning and Action: Individual and Organisational* (Jossey Bass, San Francisco, 1982).

Argyris, C., *On Organisational Learning* (Blackwell, Oxford, 1992).

Argyris, C. and Schon, D., *Organisational Learning: A theory of action perspective* (Addison Wesley, Reading, MA, 1978).

Atkinson, J. and Meager, J., 'Is flexibility just a flash in the pan?', *Personnel Management*, September 1986.

Baker, N., 'National Targets', *Employment News*, May 1993.

Bandura, A., *Principles of Behavior Modification* (Holt, Rinehart and Winston, New York, 1969).

Bandura, A., *Social Foundations of Thought and Action* (Prentice Hall, Englewood Cliffs, NJ, 1988).

Barker, D., 'The Management Charter Initiative: an interim assessment', *Assessment and Evaluation in Higher Education*, **18**:125–134, 1993.

Barling, J. and Beatty, R., 'Self Efficacy and Sales Performance', *Journal of Organisational Behaviour Management*, **5**, 1983.

Barrow, M.J. and Loughton, H.M., 'Towards a Learning Organisation', *Industrial and Commercial Training*, **24**:9–13, 1992.

Bartol, K.M. and Martin, D.C., *Management* (McGraw-Hill, New York, 1994).

Bass, B.M. and Vaughan, J.A., *Training in Industry – The Management of Learning* (Tavistock Publications, London, 1966).

Bawtree, S. and Hogg, C., 'Assessment Centres', *Personnel Management*, October 1989.

Bayne, R., 'Four Approaches to Increasing Self Awareness', in Herriot, P. (ed), *Assessment and Selection in Organisations*, (Wiley, London, 1989).

Beattie, G., 'Ferguson explains the making of champions', *The Guardian*, 6 December 1994.

Belbin, R.M., *Management Teams: why they succeed or fail* (Heinemann, London, 1981).

Benne K.D. and Sheats, P., 'Functional roles of group members', *Journal of Social Issues*, 4: 41–49, 1948.

Bennis, W., *Why leaders can't lead - the unconscious conspiracy continues* (Jossey Bass, San Francisco, 1989).

Blanchard, K. and Johnson, S., *The One Minute Manager* (Fontana, London, 1983).

Blanchard, K. and Zigarmi, D., *Leadership and the One Minute Manager* (Fontana, London, 1987).

Bloom, B.S., *Taxonomy of Educational Objectives: The Classification of Educational Goals* (Longman, London, 1956).

Boak, G. and Joy, P., 'Management Learning Contracts: The Training Triangle' in Pedler *et al.* (eds), *Self Development in Organisations* (McGraw-Hill, Maidenhead, 1990).

Boam, R. and Sparrow, P., *Designing and Achieving Competency* (McGraw-Hill, New York, 1992).

Boddy, D. and Buchanan, D., *Take the lead – interpersonal skills for project managers* (Prentice Hall, Hemel Hempstead, 1992).

Boehm, V. and Hogg, C., 'Assessment and Management Development', in Moses, J.L. and Byham, W.C. (eds), *Applying the Assessment Centre Method* (Pergamon Press, NY, 1989).

Boud, D., Keogh, R. and Walker, D., *Reflection: Turning Experience into Learning* (Kogan Page, London, 1985).

Bourdrew P. and De Sant Maridin, M., 'Scholastic Excellence and the values of the Educational System', in Eggleston, J. (ed), *Contemporary Research in the Sociology of Education* (Methuen, London, 1974).

Boyatzis, R.C., *The Competent Manager: A Model for Effective Performance* (Wiley, New York, 1982).

Boydell, T., Leary, M. and Pedler, M., 'Crossing the threshold: the challenge facing trainers, developers and line managers', *Transition*, January 1993.

Braverman, H., *Labor and Monopoly Capital* (Monthly Review Press, New York, 1974).

Briggs-Myers, I., *Introduction to Type*, (Oxford Psychologist's Press, Oxford, 1987).

Brown, R.A., *Portfolio Development and Profiling for Nurses* (Central Health Studies, Lancaster, 1992).

Buchanan, D. and Boddy, D., *The expertise of the change agent – public performance and backstage activity* (Prentice Hall, Hemel Hempstead, 1992).

Burgoyne, J., 'Management Development for the Individual and the Organisation', *Personnel Management*, June 1988.

Burgoyne, J., Boydell, T. and Pedler, M., *Self Development: Theory and application for practitioners* (Association of Teachers of Management, London, 1978).

Burgoyne, J. and Stuart, R., 'The nature, use and acquisition of managerial skills and other attributes' *Personnel Review*, 5:19–29, 1976.

Cameron, K., 'Critical questions in assessing organisational effectiveness', *Organisational Dynamics*, Autumn, 66–80, 1980.

Campbell, J., 'The development and evolution of behaviourally based rating scales', *Journal of Applied Psychology* 57:15–23, 1973.

Carlzon, J., *Moments of Truth* (Ballinger Publishing Company, Cambridge, MA, 1987).

Carnall, C.A., *Managing change in organisations* (Prentice Hall, Hemel Hempstead, 1990).

Carroll, A.B., 'A three dimensional model of corporate performance', *Academy of Management Review*, 4:497–505, 1979.

Carrol, S.J. and Gillen, D.J., 'Are the classical management functions useful in describing managerial work?', *Academy of Management Review*, 12:38–51, 1987.

Casey, D., *Managing Learning in Organisations* (Open University Press, Milton Keynes, 1993).

Cattell, R.B., *The Scientific Analysis of Personality* (Penguin, Baltimore, 1965).

Cavanagh, G.F., Moberg, D.J. and Velasquez, M., 'The ethics of organisational politics', *Academy of Management Review*, 6:363–374, 1981.

Chapman, T., 'A Practical Approach to Self Development', *Training and Development*, October 1992.

Child, J. and Macmillan, B., 'Managers and their leisure' in Smith, M., Parker, S. and Smith, C. (eds), *Leisure and Society in Britain* (Allen Lane, London, 1973).

Clutterbuck, D., *Everyone needs a Mentor: fostering talent at work* (Institute of Personnel Management, London, 1991).

Conger, J.A., 'Training leaders for the twentyfirst century', *Human Resources Review* 3:203–218, 1993.

Coopers & Lybrand Associates, *A Challenge of Complacency* (NEDO/MSC, London, 1984).

Constable, J. and McCormick, R., *The Making of British Managers* (BIM/CBI, London, 1983).

Covey, S.R., *The Seven Habits of Highly Effective People* (Simon & Schuster, New York, 1989).

Critten, P., *Investing in People: Towards Corporate Capability* (Butterworth Heinemann, London, 1994).

Davies, J. and Easterby-Smith, M., 'Learning and developing from work experiences', *Journal of Management Studies*, 21:167–183, 1984.

Deloitte, Haskins & Sells, *Management Challenge for the 1990s* (Sheffield: Training Agency, 1989).

Department of Employment, 'Fly the kite for training', *Employment News*, London, November/December 1990.

Department of Employment, 'This is your life', *Employment News*, London, March 1991.

Dixon, M., *The Organisational Learning Cycle* (McGraw-Hill, New York, 1994).

Dreyfus, H.L., *Mind over Machine* (Blackwell, Oxford, 1986).

Drucker, P.F., *The Practice of Management* (Harper & Row, New York, 1954).

Drucker, P.F., *The Age of Discontinuity* (Heinemann, London, 1969).

Dulewicz, S.V., 'Assessment Centres as the route to competence', *Personnel Management*, November, 1989.

Dunnette, M.D., *Handbook of Industrial and Organizational Psychology* (Rand McNally, Chicago, 1976).

Easterby-Smith, M., *Evaluating Management Development, Training and Education* (Gower, Aldershot, 1993).

Easterby-Smith, M. and Bourgoyne, J., 'Action Learning: An Evaluation', in Pedler, M. (ed), *Action Learning in Practice* (Gower Press, London, 1983).

Eysenck, H.J., *Structure of Human Personality*, (Methuen, London, 1960).

Fox, S. & Dinar, Y., 'Validity of Self Assessors: a field study', *Personnel Psychology*, 4:581–592, 1988.

Foy, N., 'Action Learning comes to industry', *Harvard Business Review*, 5:158–168, 1977.

Freud, S. *The Ego and the Id* (Norton, New York, 1960).

Fritz, R., *The path of least resistance: Learning to become the creative force in your own life* (Fawcett, Columbine, New York, 1989).

Fulmer, R., 'Nine Management Development Challenges for the Nineties' *Journal of Management Development*, 11(1), 1992.

Furnham, A., 'Competences fit for the future', *Personnel Management*, June 1990.

Gabriel C., 'Psychology as a Science' in Radford, J. and Govier, E. (eds), *A textbook of Psychology* (Sheldon Press, London, 1986).

Gahagen, D., 'Attitudes' in Radford, J. and Govier, E. (eds), *A Textbook of Psychology* (Sheldon Press, London, 1986).

Garder, H., *The Theory of Multiple Intelligence* (Paladin, London, 1985).

Garratt, B., *Creating a learning organisation* (Institute of Directors, London, 1990).

Garratt, B., *Learning to Lead: Developing your organisation and yourself* (Fontana, London, 1991).

German, C., 'Self Development and Career Planning: An Exercise in Mutual Benefit', *Personnel Management*, April 1994.

Goldthorpe, J.H., Bechhofer, F. and Platt, J., *The Affluent Worker in the Class Structure* (Cambridge University Press, Cambridge, 1969).

Goodge, P., 'Development Centres for the 1990s – Third generation design', *Organisations and People*, July 1994.

Gross, R.D., *Psychology, the Science of Mind and Behaviour* (Arnold, London, 1987).

Hamner, W.C., 'Reinforcement Theory and Contingency Management in Organisational Settings' in Tosi, H.L. and Hamner, W.C. (Eds), *Organisational Behavior and Management: A Contingency Approach* (Wiley, New York, 1977).

Handy, C., *Understanding Organisations* (Penguin, Harmondsworth, 1983).

Handy, C., *The Making of Managers* (MSC/NEDO/BIM, London, 1987).

Handy, C., *The Age of Unreason* (Hutchinson, London, 1989).

Handy, C., 'Pitfalls of Management Development', *Personnel Management*, February 1992.

Harrison, R., *Training and Development* (IPM, London, 1992).

Harvey, J.H. and Weary, E., 'Current Issues in Attribution Theory and Research', *Annual Review of Psychology*, 35:431–432, 1984.

Hastings, C., *Superteams* (Fontana, London, 1986).

Heider, F., *The Psychology of Interpersonal Relations*, (Wiley, New York, 1958).

Herold, D.M., 'The effectiveness of work groups' in Kerr, S. (ed), *Organisational Behavior* (Grid Publishing, Columbus, Ohio, 1979).

Heron, J., *Catharsis in Human Development* (Human Potential Research Group, University of Surrey, 1977).

Heron, J., *The Facilitator's Handbook* (Kogan Page, London, 1989).

Herzberg, F., *Work and the nature of man* (World, Cleveland, 1966).

Hirsch, S.K. and Kummerow, J., *Introduction to Type in Organisations* (Oxford Psychologist's Press, Oxford, 1990).

Hofstede, G., *Culture's Consequences: International Differences in Work Related Values* (Sage Publications, Newbury Park, CA, 1980).

Honey, P., 'Establishing a Learning Regime', *Organisations and People, Quarterly Journal of AMED*, **1**(1), 1994.

Honey, P. and Mumford, A., *A Manual of Learning Styles* (Honey, Maidenhead, 1982).

Huczynski, A., *Encyclopedia of management development methods* (Gower, Aldershot, 1983).

Huczynski, A. and Buchanan, D., *Organisational Behaviour* (Prentice Hall, Hemel Hempstead, 1991).

Huntley, S., 'Management Development Considerations and Implementation', *Industrial and Commercial Training*, **23**(2), 1991.

Hutton, C., 'The Learning Organisation: a Blueprint for Mobilising Organisational Talent', *Topics*, **2**:13–31, 1992.

Huxley, A., *Brave New World* (Penguin, Harmondsworth, 1976 edn).

Income Data Services, 'Implementing NVQs', *IDS study No. 505*, London, May 1992.

ILO, *Teaching and Training Methods for Management Development* (International Labour Organisation, Geneva, 1972).

Institute of Manpower Studies, *Competence and Competition* (NEDO/MSC, London, 1984).

Jacobs, R., *Assessing Management Competences* (Ashridge Management Research Group, Berkhamstead, 1989).

Jones, M., *Management Development: A Participative Approach* (Manchester Training Handbooks, Department of Administrative Studies, Manchester University, 1981).

Jung, C.G., *Analytical Psychology: its theory and practice* (Routledge and Kegan Paul, London, 1968).

Kanter, R.M., *The Change Masters: Corporate Entrepreneurs at Work* (Allen & Unwin, London, 1985).

Kanter, R.M., *When Giants Learn to Dance* (Unwin Hyman, London, 1989).

Katz, R.L., 'Skills of an effective administrator', *Harvard Business review*, **52**:94, 1974.

Keeys, G., 'Effective leaders need to be good coaches', *Personnel Management*, November 1994, 52–54.

Kelly, G.A., *The Psychology of Personal Constructs* (Norton, New York, 1955).

Knowles, M., *The Modern Practice of Education* (Follett, London, 1970).

Kolb, D.A., *Experiential Learning* (Prentice Hall, New York, 1982).

Kolb, D.A. and Fry, R., 'Towards an applied theory of experiential learning', in Cooper, C.L. (ed), *Theories of group processes* (Wiley, London, 1975).

Kolb, D.A., Rubin, J.M. and McIntyre, J.M., *Organisational Psychology*, 4th edn (Prentice Hall, Englewood Cliffs, NJ, 1984).

Korn Ferry International and Colombia University Graduate School of Business, 'Reinventing the C.E.O.', *21st Century Report* (Columbia University, 1989).

Kotter, J.P., *The General Managers* (The Free Press, New York, 1982).

Kotter, J. and Schlesinger, L., 'Choosing Strategies for Change', *Harvard Business Review*, March–April 1979.

Krech, D., Crutchfield, R.S. and Livson, N., *Elements of Psychology*, 3rd edn (Knopf, New York, 1974).

Lane, J., 'Methods of Assessment', *Health Manpower Management*, **18**(2), 1992.

Leary, M., Boydell, T., Van Boeschoten, M. and Carlisle, J., *The qualities of managing*, Report on a project carried out by TRANSFORM (Consultants) and Sheffield City Polytechnic (Manpower Services Commission, Sheffield, 1986).

Legge, M., 'Fighting fires or filling buckets', *Organisations and People*, **1**(4), 1994.

Leigh, A., *Effective change – twenty ways to make it happen* (IPM, London, 1988).

Lessem, R., *Total Quality Learning – Building a Learning Organisation* (Blackwell, Oxford, 1993).

Lewin, K., *Field Theory in Social Science* (Harper, New York, 1951).

Likert, R., *New Patterns of Management* (McGraw-Hill, New York, 1961).

Livy, B., *Corporate Personnel Management* (Pitman, London, 1988).

Locke, E.A., 'Nature and causes of job satisfaction', in Long, M. (ed), *Handbook of Industrial and Organisational Psychology*

Long, C.G.L., 'A theoretical model for method selection'. *Industrial Training International*, **4**(11), 475–8, 1969.

Lowman, R.L. and Williams, R.E., 'Validity of Self Ratings of Abilities and Competencies', *Journal of Vocational Behaviour*, **31**:1–13, 1987.

Lupton, T. and Wilson, S., 'The Social Background and Connections of Top Decision Makers' in Urry, J. and Wakefield, J. (eds), *Power in Britain* (Heinemann, London, 1973).

Luthans, F. and Kreitner, R., *Organisational Behavior Modification and Beyond* (Scott, Foresman, Glenview, IL. 1985).

Mabe, I. and West, S.G., 'Validity of Self Evaluation of Ability: a review and meta analysis', *Journal of Applied Psychology*, (3)280–296, 1982.

McCall, M.W., 'Executive Development as a Business Strategy', *The Journal of Business Strategy*, January/February 1992, 25–31.

McClelland D.C., *The Achieving Society* (New York, The Free Press, 1961).

McGregor, D., *The Human Side of Enterprise* (McGraw-Hill, New York, 1960).

McNulty, N.G., 'Action Learning around the world.' in Pedler, M. (ed), *Action Learning in Practice* (Gower Press, Aldershot, 1983).

Management Charter Initiative (MCI), CMED brochure, London, 1988.

Management Charter Initiative, *Good Practice Guide* (MCI, London, 1991).

Management Charter Initiative 1, *Certificate Level Guidelines* (MCI, London, n.d.).

Management Charter Initiative 2, *Diploma Level Guidelines* (MCI, London, n.d.).

Management Charter Initiative 3, *Assessment Guidelines* (MCI, London, n.d.).

Management Charter Initiative 4, *MCI Conference Report* (MCI, London, 1991).

Management Charter Initiative 5, *Middle Management Dynamics* (MCI, London, 1991).

Management Charter Initiative 6, *Senior Management Standards* (MCI, London, 1994).

Management Charter Initiative 7, *MCI Review of Management Standards: Phase 1 Consultative Document* (Lancaster University Management School, October 1994).

Mangham, I.L., 'In search of competence', *Journal of General Management*, 5–12, 1986.

Margerison, C., 'How chief executives succeed', *Journal of European Industrial Training*, 4(5), 1980.

Marguiles, N. and Raia, A.P., *Conceptual Foundations of Organisational Development* (McGraw-Hill, New York, 1978).

Marsick, V. and Watkins, K., *Informal and incidental learning in the workplace* (Routledge, London, 1990).

Maslow, A., *Motivation and Personality* (Harper, New York, 1954).

Miller, N.E. and Dollard, J.C., *Personality and Psychotherapy* (McGraw-Hill, New York, 1950).

Mintzberg, H., *The Nature of Managerial Work* (Harper & Row, New York, 1973).

Mintzberg, H., 'The manager's job: folklore and fact', *Harvard Business Review*, July/August, 1975. Reprinted in Mintzberg, H., *Mintzberg on Management* (The Free Press, New York, 1989).

Mitchell, T.R., *People in Organisations* (McGraw-Hill, Tokyo, 1982).

Morgan, G., *Riding the waves of change – Developing managerial competencies for a turbulent world* (Jossey Bass, San Francisco, 1989).

Morgan, G., *Imaginization – the art of creative management* (Sage, Newbury Park, CA. 1993).

Mullins, L.J., *Management and Organisations* (Pitman, London, 1993).

Mumford, A., *Management Development: Strategies for action* (IPM, London, 1989).

Mumford, A., 'Individual and Organisational Learning – The Pursuit of Change', *Industrial and Commercial Training*, **23**(5), 1991.

Mumford, A., *Management Development – Strategy for Action (IPM, London, 1993)*.

Munro Fraser, J., *Handbook of Employment Interviewing*, 5th edn (McDonald and Evans, London, 1978).

Naisbitt, J. and Aburdene, P., *Reinventing the Corporation* (Macdonald, New York, 1986).

National Council for Vocational Qualifications (NCVQ), *Guide to National Vocational Qualifications* (NCVQ, London, 1991).

Neale, R. and Mindel, R., 'Rigging up multicultural teamworking', *Personnel Management*, January 1992.

O'Toole, J., *Vanguard Management* (Berkeley Books, New York, 1987).

Parker, M., 'Post modern organisations or post modern organisation theory', *Organisation Studies*, **13**(1), 1992.

Parsons, T., 'The Social Structure of the Family' in R. N. Grishen (ed), *The Family: Its Functions and Destiny* (Harper & Row, New York, 1959).

Pascale, R., 'The benefit of a clash of opinions', *Personnel Management*, October 1993.

Pearce, I., 'The Development of First Line Managers at ICL', *Management Development Review*, 5(1), 1992.

Pedler, M., *Action Learning in Practice* (Gower Press, London, 1983).

Pedler, M. and Boydell, T., *Managing Yourself* (Fontana, London, 1985).

Pedler, M., Burgoyne, J. and Boydell, T., *The Learning Company* (McGraw-Hill, New York, 1991).

Pedler, M., Burgoyne, J. and Boydell, T., *A Manager's Guide to Self Development* (McGraw-Hill, Maidenhead, 1993).

Pedler, M., Burgoyne, J., Boydell, T. and Welshman, G., *Self Development in Organisations* (McGraw-Hill, London, 1990).

Personnel Management, 'Qualification confusion', *Personnel Management*, January 1993.

Personnel Management, 'Consortium to provide NVQ programme', *Personnel Management*, March 1993.

Personnel Management, 'New line in management at London Underground', *Personnel Management*, March 1993.

Peters, T., *Thriving on Chaos – handbook for a management revolution* (Macmillan, London, 1987).

Peters, T., *Liberation Management – Necessary disorganisation for the nanosecond nineties* (Macmillan, London, 1992).

Peters, T.J. and Waterman, R.H., *In Search of Excellence* (Harper & Row, New York, 1982).

Pettigrew, A., *The Awakening Giant: continuity and change in ICI* (Blackwell, Oxford, 1985).

Pettigrew, A.M. and Reason, P.W., *Alternative Interpretations of the Training Officer Role: a research study in the chemical industry* (Chemical and Allied Product Training Board, Staines, March 1979).

Philpott, M., 'Catering NVQ targets criticised', *Personnel Management*, June 1994.

Pickard, J., 'Assessment on the sales floor', *Personnel Management*, March 1993.

Pickard, J., 'Exporting NVQs to the continent', *Personnel Management*, April 1993.

Pickard, J., 'The real meaning of empowerment', *Personnel Management*, November 1993.

Plant, R., *Managing Change and Making it Stick* (Fontana, London, 1987).

Pollert, A., *Farewell to Flexibility* (Blackwell, Oxford, 1991).

Polsky, H.W., 'Notes on personal feedback in sensitivity training', *Sociological Inquiry*, 41:175–82, 1971.

Porter, L.W. and Lawler, E.E., *Managerial Attitudes and Performance* (Dorsey Press, Holmewood, IL, 1968).

Prais, S.J., 'How Europe would see the new British Initiative for Standardising Vocational Qualifications', *National Institute of Economics Review*, August 1989.

Redman, W., *Portfolios for development: A guide for trainers and managers* (Kogan Page, London, 1994).

Reeves, T., *Managing Effectively – Developing yourself through experience* (Butterworth & Heinemann, London, 1994).

Reddin, W., *Managerial Effectiveness* (McGraw-Hill, London, 1970).

Revans, R., *Developing Effective Managers* (Longmans, London, 1971).

Revans, R., *The origins and growth of action learning* (Chartwell Bratt, London, 1982).

Revans, R., *The Sequence of Managerial Achievement* (MCB University Press, Bradford, 1984).

Roberts, M., 'The Manager's Responsibility for Self Development', *Training and Development*, August 1994, 15–16.

Robbins, S.P., *Organisation Theory, Structure Design and Applications* (Prentice Hall, Englewood Cliffs, NJ, 1987).

Rodger, A., *The Seven Point Plan* (NIIP, London, 1952).

Rogers, C., *Freedom to Learn* (Merrill, Columbus, Ohio, 1969).

Rogers, C., *Freedom to Learn for the 80s* (Merrill, Columbus, Ohio, 1983).

Rosener, J.B., 'Ways Women Lead', *Harvard Business Review*, November–December 1990.

Ross, K., 'The Learning Company', *Training and Development* **10**:19–22, 1992.

Rowe, P., 'National Vocational Qualifications and the business of Banking, Part 1 – The Skills Revolution', *Banking World*, **10**(6), 1992.

Rowe, P., 'National Vocational Qualifications and the business of Banking, Part 2 – Managing Skills as a key resource', *Banking World*, **10**(7), 1992.

Schein, E.H., *Career Dynamics: matching individual and organisational needs* (Addison Wesley, Reading, MA, 1978).

Schermerhorn, J.R., *Management for Productivity* (New York, Wiley, 1993).

Schon, D.A., *The Reflective Practitioner* (Basic Books, New York, 1983).

Schon, D.A., *Educating the Reflective Practitioner* (Jossey Bass, San Francisco, 1987).

Schroder, H.M., *Managerial Competence: The Key to Excellence* (Collins, London, 1989).

Scot, W.G. and Mitchell, T.R., *Organisation Theory* (Irwin, Holmewood, IL, 1979).

Semler, R., *Maverick* (Arrow, London, 1994).

Senge, P., *The Fifth Discipline – The Art and Practice of the Learning Organisation* (Doubleday, New York, 1990).

Smith, A., 'Management Development, Evaluation and Effectiveness', *Journal of Management Development*, **12**:20–32, 1993.

Smithers, A., 'All our Futures – Britain's Education Revolution' Channel 4 TV Programme, Dispatches, 1993.

Smythe Dorward Lambvert, *The power of the open company* (Smythe Dorward Lambvert, London, 1991).

Spranger, E., *Types of Men* (Nicmeyer, Halle, Germany, 1928).

Steedman, H. and Hawkins, J., 'NVQs are too narrowly focused to be useful for young people, says report', *Personnel Management*, September 1994.

Stephenson, J., 'Capability and competence: are they the same and does it matter?', *Capability*, 1, 1994.

Sternberg, R.J., *Beyond IQ: A Triarchic Theory of Human Intelligence* (Cambridge, Cambridge University Press, 1985).

Stevens, C., 'Assessment Centres: the British experience', *Personnel Management* (IPM, London, July 1995).

Stewart, V., 'Human Capital Issues in Organisational Change', selected papers from the IPMA National Conference, *Asia Pacific Journal of Human Resources* (Australian Human Resource Institute, 1992).

Stogdill, R.M., 'Personal factors associated with leadership: a survey of the literature', *Journal of Psychology*, 25, 1948.

Taubman, D., 'Training for our Future' *NATFHE Journal*, Spring, 1994.

Taylor, F.W., *Principles of Scientific Management* (Harper & Row, New York, 1911).

Terry, F., Masters, R. and Smith, T., 'National Vocational Qualifications', *Public Money and Management*, April/June 1992.

Thompson, P.J., 'Providing a Qualified Society to Meet the Challenge', *National Westminster Bank Quarterly Review*, February 1989.

Thorndike, E.L., *Animal Intelligence* (Macmillan, New York, 1911).

Townend, A., *Developing Assertiveness* (Routledge, London, 1991).

Training Agency, *Training in Britain – A Study of Funding, Activities and Attitudes* (HMSO Books, Class No. 658.3124 TRA, 1989).

Training Commission, *Classifying the components of Management Competence* (Training Commission, Sheffield, 1988).

Training and Development Lead Body, 'How do you spot good trainers?', consultation document circulated 1991 (TDLB, London, 1991).

Trompenaars, F., *Riding the waves of culture: understanding cultural diversity in business* (Nicholas Brearley Publishing, London, 1993).

Vroom, V.H., *Work and Motivation* (Wiley, New York, 1964).

Waterman, R.H., *The Renewal Factor: How the best get and keep the competitive edge* (Bantam, New York, 1987).

Watson, G., 'The flexible workforce and patterns of working hours in the UK', *Employment Gazette*, July 1994.

Weaver, T., 'Knowledge gets you nowhere', *Capability*, 1:6–12, 1994.

Whittaker, J., 'Making a policy of keeping up to date', *Personnel Management*, March 1992.

Wild, R., 'The management of development', *Management Today*, October 1994.

Willie, E., 'Should management development be just for managers?', *Personnel Management*, August 1990.

Wisher, V., 'Competencies: The Precious Seeds of Growth?', *Personnel Management*, July 1994.

Wood, L., 'The end of bossy bosses forseen', *Financial Times*, 18 July 1994.

Woodruffe, C., 'Competent by any other name', *Personnel Management*, September 1991.

Zaleznik, A., *The managerial mystique* (Harper & Row, New York, 1989).

Zuboff, S., *In the age of the smart machine: The future of work and power* (Heinemann, Oxford, London, 1988).

Index